THE SIMPLE ABUNDANCE PRESS
SCRIBNER

A SIMPLE ABUNDANCE PRESS BOOK

Also by SARAH BAN BREATHNACH

Simple Abundance
A Daybook of Comfort and Joy

The Simple Abundance Journal of Gratitude

Something More
Excavating Your Authentic Self

The Illustrated Discovery Journal
Creating a Visual Autobiography of
Your Authentic Self

The Simple Abundance Companion
Following Your Authentic Path to Something More

A Man's Journey to Simple Abundance

Hold That Thought

Mrs. Sharp's Traditions
Nostalgic Suggestions for Re-creating the Family
Celebrations and Seasonal Pastimes of the
Victorian Home *(published in paperback as*
Victorian Nursery Celebrations)

The Victorian Nursery Companion

SARAH BAN BREATHNACH'S

Mrs. Sharp's
TRADITIONS

Reviving Victorian
Family Celebrations
of Comfort & Joy

From the author of
SIMPLE ABUNDANCE

Scribner/Simple Abundance Press
New York London Toronto Sydney Singapore

THE SIMPLE ABUNDANCE PRESS
SCRIBNER

1230 Avenue of the Americas
New York, NY 10020

I would like to gratefully acknowledge all the writers I have quoted from for their wisdom, comfort, and inspiration. An exhaustive search was undertaken to determine whether previously published material included in this book required permission to reprint. If there has been an error, I apologize and a correction will be made in subsequent editions.

—Sarah Ban Breathnach

Designed by Angela Skouras & Björn Ramberg/Skouras Design
Text set in Bembo

Manufactured in the United States of America

1 3 5 7 9 10 8 6 4 2

Library of Congress Cataloging-in-Publication Data
Ban Breathnach, Sarah.
[Mrs. Sharp's traditions]
Sarah Ban Breathnach's Mrs. Sharp's traditions: reviving Victorian family celebrations of comfort & joy/Sarah Ban Breathnach.
p. cm.
Includes bibliographical references and index.
1. Months—Folklore. 2. Seasons—Folklore. 3. Great Britain—Social life and customs—19th century. 4. Family festivals.
I. Title: Mrs. Sharp's traditions. II. Title.
GR930 .B74 2001   646.7'8'09034—dc21   00—053799

ISBN 0-7432-1076-X

For
Katherine Éireann Crean Sharp
My inspiration

CONTENTS

SARAH BAN BREATHNACH'S

Mrs. Sharp's

TRADITIONS

MRS. VICTORIANNA SHARP

FOREWORD
The Past Asks Only to Be Remembered

> . . . in a time lacking in truth and certainty
> and filled with anguish and despair, no woman
> should be shamefaced in attempting to give back
> to the world, through her work, a portion of its
> lost heart.
> —*Louise Bogan*

Dear Reader,

One of my literary delights is delving between the lines of a favorite book to discover how the author brought it into being. Like a child, each book has a tale to tell about its conception, confinement, and birth. Since I'm fortunate to know that this sweet volume is adored by thousands of women (many of whom have written me over the past ten years with heartfelt entreaties to "bring back Mrs. Sharp"), it gives me great pleasure to introduce my first book to the admirers of *Simple Abundance.* You see, the seeds of my simply abundant life (and yours!) were lovingly sown in *Mrs. Sharp's Traditions,* which was originally published in 1990.

The tale begins once upon a beautiful Indian summer afternoon in September 1984, when, while browsing in an antiques shop, I happened across a trunkload of pristine Victorian women's and children's magazines. The owner of the shop told me that one of the area's eldest residents had died recently, and when her family had cleared out her attic, they'd found what was virtually a catalog of nineteenth-century domestic life.

I remember that moment with a clarity that is stunning, much the way Lewis Carroll's Alice might recall falling through the rabbit hole that landed her in Wonderland. For over an hour I was rooted to the floor devouring the pleasures of "Rainy Day Occupations" and wonderful family pastimes for "Cozy Home Circle Evenings." The writing was so quaint, yet very moving. The sentiments it stirred within me were reassuringly familiar, yet fresh. I was transported back to the Victorian era, when life seemed so ordered, so serene, so blissful, and so completely unlike my own. Like fifty million other women who juggled the demands of work and raising a family, all I knew about home life was that when push came to shove, what got shoved out of my life was the very thing I valued most: quality family time.

Only an hour before I had left my husband and nearly two-year-old daughter happily ensconced on the large wraparound porch of a Maine fishing lodge that we had rented for a family reunion. It was a gorgeous day—sunny and warm but with just enough of a refreshing breeze for a sweater. I sensed it was one of those delicious, fateful days when the trajectory of your life is about to shift, but you don't know how, where, or why. There's a tingling feeling that something wonderful is waiting around the corner or down the lane. And it was.

How I cherish that memory: the sunlight streaming through Katie's hair as she sat on the porch playing with her doll, her father's smile as he looked at her from the wicker chair where he was reading and caught my eye. The luxurious sense that what we had at that moment was all we would ever need.

Later there would be a trek to the wharf to wait for the lobster boats bringing in our dinner, and baking pies with the wild blueberries that had been collected that morning. But first there was exploring to do.

Antiquing is a passion of mine, a therapeutic, meditative, spiritual practice. Some people experience reverence by going to church or synagogue; Emily Dickinson did it by staying home to write poetry; I find it whenever I go antiquing. Somehow sifting through the domestic shards of those who no longer can bear witness to life's glorious mystery helps me ransom, reclaim, and redeem what is truly precious in my own life.

"Nearly every antiques and curio shop in America has fragments of the everyday domestic life of the people who lived before us. If they are old enough, these trivets, mixing bowls, cups, saucers, and other household goods are endowed with the qualities of relics, to be purchased and lovingly displayed on mantels, shelves, or bookcases," social historian Harvey Green explains in his wonderful book *The Light of the Home: An Intimate View of the Lives of Women in Victorian America*. "What was once used to feed a family, nurse a child, clean and polish a teapot, or carry on the social graces and customs of another era has a different function in the present. These objects from the past suggest some sort of life that seems like ours but is foreign. Yet the common wares of the middle class in the late nineteenth century are more than decoration . . . they are evidence of the customs and ideals of life in the domestic setting."

I left the shop with the entire lot of magazines. Little did I realize then that these passports to the past were to become the vehicle for more than adventures in time travel. They would ultimately grow into an old-fashioned resource for modern families known as *Mrs. Sharp's Traditions*.

I share this recollection because, like you, I have also stood in bookstores, flipping through books, searching for a spark of inspiration, a glimmer of hope, a hint of comfort, and a bit of uncommon sense. What I have been looking for—and I suspect you have, too—are the answers to questions as relevant today as they were a decade, or even a century, ago.

- *Why is it that some families seem so happy together? What is their secret?*
- *How can I create a beautiful, nurturing, secure home environment?*
- *Are there ways I can bring my family closer together so that every day, not just the holidays, is happy and memorable?*
- *Are there rituals I can incorporate into our family life that will sustain us during the hard times?*
- *Are there pastimes that can help us develop more of a sense of family?*
- *Are there traditions I can pass on to my child that can*

strengthen her spiritually and equip her emotionally to handle life's surprises?

- *How can I enrich my own spiritual path as a parent?*
- *Is there a way for us to learn now—before it's too late—how to realize fully the happiness of each moment?*
- *What can I do to cultivate the virtues of a simpler way of life, insulated from the commercialism, trends, and fads that bombard us at every turn?*
- *And finally, can one truly create a lifestyle that nourishes, sustains, and brings joy to all the members of our family, as it knits us closer together in love?*

Over the past sixteen years, I have joyously discovered that the answers to my questions could be found in those homemaking books and magazines from another time, when the nurturing of a family and the pursuit of the domestic arts—cooking, decorating, handicrafts, and creating family recreational pursuits—were not considered second-rate burdens but a woman's most rewarding achievements. Of course, today men are equally interested in matters close to home, which is why I believe that they, too, will appreciate these suggestions of how to create a rich and rewarding family life through home-centered traditions and daily ritual.

After we returned from our vacation, I kept my magazines in a pretty basket near my bed and, before going to sleep each night, savored the nuggets of warmth, wit, and wisdom of long-forgotten Victorian women writers who dispensed doses of good humor and practical advice. With the appreciation and awareness that only hindsight affords, I know now that my authentic self was preparing me for a long winter's nap away from the world, a psychic and physical detour that would steer me far away from five-year goals, calendars, deadlines, and the inconsequential masquerading as the essential.

A month later, my life took that detour.

Like almost everyone, I had been bruised by life, but I had never experienced a "before and after" event, the kind that years later makes your legs wobble when you think about it. That particular day I had finished an article, so I decided to take the afternoon off and treat Katie to lunch at her favorite fast-food restaurant. We both had just started to eat—the last thing I remember was smiling at her catsup-smeared grin—when suddenly the sky fell: A large ceiling panel landed on my head, knocking me onto the table. Suddenly I discovered that Chicken Little knew what he was talking about. Thank God I took the brunt of the blow. Although the panel grazed Katie's eye, she was unhurt; if it had fallen a fraction of an inch closer to her, the inconceivable could have become the unendurable. Although I never lost complete consciousness, I sustained a concussion severe enough to keep me bedridden for weeks, confused and disoriented for months, and partially disabled for a year and a half. For a long time I couldn't comprehend what I read or speak articulately. And I couldn't write because I couldn't connect two thoughts. This dark plunge into the unknown was devastating. Books, which had always been my keenest companions, became strangers, as I groped for words—both mine and others'. The accident swept away, along with the illusion of safety, my livelihood.

Over the next nine months, I eventually found my way back to the world and words by reading my daughter's picture books, and back to life by my love and reverence for traditions.

Two weeks before the accident, we had visited a nearby farm to pick pumpkins, which now sat on the front stoop, forlorn and forgotten. That morning, my husband poked his head into the bedroom before leaving for work and said he'd be home in plenty of time to take Katie on her first trick-or-treat outing. But I knew we couldn't celebrate Halloween without a proper jack-o'-lantern. How I did it, I'll never know, but that night a very weird-looking Mr. Pumpkin delighted my daughter and welcomed the little ghouls knocking on our door. (Looking back on it, the fact that I didn't sever an artery with a very shaky carving knife gives new meaning to the word *gratitude*.)

A month later I again found a profound reason to get out of bed: Katie's second birthday. Soon, the gentle rhythms of the succeeding holidays—Thanksgiving, Christmas, Valentine's Day, and Easter—and their celebrations became sustenance for the soul and just the restorative prescription my family and I needed. Encouraged, I began to adapt some of the pastimes I found in my cache of Victorian magazines to our family life. My establishing these old-fashioned rituals and amusements signified the first step toward my true physical recovery. Because my family was so delighted by these old-fashioned activities, once I felt up to it, I began offering a series of tradition-building work-shops for families. These workshops developed a devoted following among both working mothers and women who had chosen to stay at home with their children. I was thrilled to learn that I had many kindred spirits who appreciated suggestions on how to bring back a bygone era. My audiences were equally charmed to discover that the workshops were led by the "perfect Victorian mother," Mrs. E. F. Sharp, a larger-than-life figment of my imagination. Mrs. Sharp was fashioned after the popular "literary domestics," Victorian magazine columnists who specialized in writing articles, appearing in such periodicals as *Demorest's Family Magazine* and *The Mother's Magazine,* on how to make home life happier by perfecting "the art of domestic bliss." I gave the workshops dressed in a corset, petticoats, high-topped boots, and Gibson girl pouf, and discovered that my long-thwarted desire to be an actress was unexpectedly fulfilled. I must have played the part well, first in person, and later on the page (with a nationally syndicated column called "Mrs. Sharp's Traditions," written for The Washington Post Writers Group), for I received countless letters from readers who were convinced that Mrs. Sharp actually existed. Her persona and all she cherished resonated on the deepest level with her admirers. Fictional though she might have been, Mrs. Sharp is the storybook mother we all long to have, and, if we have children of our own, the mother we all so desperately try to be.

However, the idea that anyone could actually believe Mrs. Sharp was "real" tickled me: After all, I had made her 125 years old with a dozen children who ranged in age from seven to ninety-seven. But to be fair, these readers weren't alone. While I didn't acknowledge it at the time, Sarah Ban Breathnach was also secretly convinced that the dear lady existed. It was frequently pointed out to me that Mrs. Sharp was my alter ego, but I passionately denied it. I could claim to be only her amanuensis, someone through whom she dictated. In fact, in my original preface to *Mrs. Sharp's Traditions* I wrote:

"You should understand from the outset that Mrs. Sharp and I do not share the same domestic sphere. In fact, there were times during the writing of this book when our home lives were so completely opposite that I frequently thought I was penning science fiction."

To my way of thinking, Victorianna Sharp was then everything I clearly was not: serene, incurably optimistic, and deeply spiritual. The perfect role model for Victorian women was the "wife of noble character" found in the Bible's Book of Proverbs. Mrs. Sharp was the embodiment of this high calling. Her life was harmonious because she successfully managed the delicate balance of living in the world yet remaining apart from it, and she was sustained by her abiding faith in God's goodness and the generosity of Providence. She lived each day to the fullest with a deep appreciation of the past, an enriched sense of the present, and a joyous anticipation of the future.

As you can imagine, Mrs. Sharp's home was a haven of hospitality, her good taste and authentic style reflected in its simplicity, order, and comfort. Mrs. Sharp believed that details—small personal touches—

were the essence of gracious living. She loved to surround herself with beauty, and always managed to endow the mundane with a personal flair that transformed housekeeping into the soul craft of home caring—wearing a pretty apron to putter in while she tidied her house as she listened to opera, using freshly laundered Irish-linen dish towels to make her glasses sparkle, or writing down her voluminous "To Do" lists in enchanting floral notebooks tied with a ribbon. And, by focusing on only one task at a time, Mrs. Sharp always accomplished more in a week than I could have done in a hundred years.

She was also a compassionate confidante who empathized, encouraged, and inspired others with her words in ways that I never before had been able to do with my writing. Although I could only dream of the domestic bliss that enveloped her, Mrs. Sharp never made me or other women feel guilty or embarrassed because we hadn't achieved her gracious lifestyle. Instead, she wrapped her figurative arms around us and made us believe that love made all things possible.

Perhaps, dear Reader, if you come to these pages familiar with *Simple Abundance,* you might see in them the blossoming of another woman we both know as Victorianna Sharp. Still, it would take me a decade to make the connection. I had distanced myself from the creation of *Mrs. Sharp's Traditions* and denied myself the accomplishment of bringing it into the world, although it represented five years of energy, emotion, hard work, struggle, and persistence. I accepted compliments, praise, even gratitude for having written it as graciously as a bewildered go-between could. And then I wondered why I felt so empty.

A couple of years later, when I was writing *Simple Abundance,* I was having a heart-to-heart with my sister. Throughout our conversation, I still referred to Mrs. Sharp.

"Stop this," Maureen said gently but firmly. "Stop referring to Mrs. Sharp as if she's a separate person. *You're* Mrs. Sharp, even if you don't believe it. *She is who you are within.* You have got to start owning your talent, or you'll lose it."

By the time *Simple Abundance* became a bestseller, *Mrs. Sharp's Traditions* was long out of print and I had little interest or intention of resurrecting her. Why? Because now all that she represented for me was loss, and it was much too painful even to contemplate. My marriage had ended, and there was no longer a "Mrs. Sharp." The boxes containing the galleys of the book, along with my Victorian art collection, costumes, and memorabilia, were relegated to a dark corner of the attic in the new home I shared with my daughter. Just as Katie had outgrown her pinafores and bonnets so lovingly packed away nearby, I believed I had to outgrow my dreams of domestic bliss.

But our past asks only to be remembered. The memories we mourn should be no less beloved than those that make us smile. We wrong ourselves terribly when we deny the marvels these memories try to bring us. I was reminded of this last year when I received a wonderful letter from a reader who, as Heaven would have it, discovered *Simple Abundance* only because she could no longer get a copy of *Mrs. Sharp's Traditions* to give as a gift. She made such an impassioned plea for me to republish my past that, for the first time in many years, I picked up the book and reread it. It made me laugh, it made me cry, it made me feel so grateful for the mystical meandering of my life. Like a mother hugging her child once again after a long, distressing estrangement, the pain of the past fell away until what was left were only the good times, the moments of love and laughter that begged to be shared.

But I must be frank. I don't think you'd be holding this book now had I not gone in search of "something more" after the writing of *Simple Abundance.* By excavating my authentic self, I learned to transform self-loathing into self-worth, which enables me not just to own the creativity that brought *Mrs. Sharp's Traditions* into being, but to honor it. The writer Alice DeVille reminds us that "each relationship you have with another person reflects the relationship you have with yourself." My relationship with Mrs. Sharp is a perfect example of how you betray yourself when you refuse not only to call forth your authentic gifts, but also to revel in them with thanksgiving. But if we do this, the Book of Proverbs reassures us, life will to each woman "give her the fruit of her hands and let her own works praise her . . ."

This past summer Katie and I vacationed with friends on the same Maine island we had visited sixteen years ago. Once again we enjoyed antiquing, lobster rolls, and wild-blueberry pie. But the turn-of-the-century fishing lodge where my story began had been torn down to make room for a modern house. Life changes, but memories live on forever. The writer Tove Ditlevsen believed that memory was the "library of the soul," from which we "will draw knowledge and experience" all our lives. The library of my soul overflows with so many happy memories, I refuse to deny them any longer, or the truth of what came before or after their creation.

Alas, my dearly beloved Mrs. Sharp is no longer with us. But she passed on with a smile on her face, peace in her heart, and no regrets. Her last words to me were "I hope you can, too, dear."

With the republication of this book, I'm trying to do just that. While aficionados of the original volume begged me not to make any changes, I couldn't help but indulge in revising and redesigning it. Aren't second chances the golden opportunities you thought "too good to be true" the first time around? You have no idea how thrilling it is to offer the world a portion of your lost heart, long after you thought it was gone forever.

Life holds no more guarantees for me, or you, than it did for Mrs. Sharp over a century ago, yet she faced each day determined to create a work of art: a serene haven of comfort and joy for her family and herself. May we all be so blessed.

It is my fondest wish that you and yours will be as cheered by *Mrs. Sharp's Traditions* as I continue to be. I have now come to think of this book as a *Simple Abundance* for families. If these pages provide you with an entertaining and nostalgic glimpse of Victorian joyful simplicities, I'm abundantly satisfied. If I have done more and my revival of Victorian family celebrations brings you and yours contentment, encouragement, and inspiration, then, at long last, I have achieved authentic success.

—Sarah Ban Breathnach
May 2001

AT HOME WITH MRS. SHARP

Are you pleased with your family life? Forgive Mrs. Sharp for being too personal, but if your answer is no or even "I don't know," then, dear Reader, welcome home to *Mrs. Sharp's Traditions,* an old-fashioned resource created especially for you.

The Pursuit of Happiness

In modern life, the days, weeks, months, and seasons hurtle past us at breakneck speed. Do we even pause to acknowledge autumn's arrival in crimson and gold, winter's first snowflake, the sprouting of spring daffodils, or the return of lemonade leisure with the first hot summer afternoon? These simple pleasures should be savored and celebrated, but we have so little time! A century ago the four seasons of our lives were linked with traditions, and the cycle of the year held cherished pastimes for families to enjoy together. Gone forever, it seems, are those halcyon days when the pursuit of happiness at home was considered worthy of devoted attention.

The Mortar of Loving Memories

You say that you wish to step off the dreary treadmill of today's accelerated pace to enjoy happier moments with your family, but at the end of a long week you don't know how or where to begin?

May Mrs. Sharp be of assistance?

It has been both her lot in life, as well as her great joy, to have spent the majority of the past century as a preserver of home-centered customs. Family traditions played a major role in Victorian lives and were reassuring points of comfort and security. They can be for your family, as well. Throughout her long life, Mrs. Sharp has always looked upon these homegrown celebrations as opportunities to cement her family together with the mortar of loving memories.

Mrs. Sharp is pleased to show you how traditions are not simply family fossils to be hauled out once a year along with the turkey platter, but rather year-round celebrations that can be integrated readily into even the busiest lives. What joy and contentment come from seeing your children create May baskets, just as you did when you were young, or serving tea to your family using your grandmother's special teapot and knowing that you are joined together in love through ritual. What a sense of continuity comes from passing on a personalized cookbook of favorite family recipes to a child who has just married. Eventually these beloved family customs stretch like a golden ribbon over long years to bind generations together tenderly in memory. Simply stated, what more in life could any of us ask?

For the Skeptics Among Us

For the skeptics among us, Mrs. Sharp assures them that they will be pleasantly surprised to discover that the simple pleasures that amused children and brought families together a hundred years ago still have the power to charm. Trust that Mrs. Sharp knows how to adapt the pastimes and seasonal pleasures of yesteryear to family life today. And should some of the old customs not fit your modern lives, Mrs. Sharp has altered and improvised, providing her readers with Victorian traditions that have a contemporary twist.

A Pause of the Past That Inspires

So take a deep breath, be of good cheer, and come into Mrs. Sharp's parlor. The kettle is on for tea. Here, away from the distractions and demands of your daily life, may you encounter a pause of the past that inspires, so that before long you will find yourself easily incorporating good, old-fashioned memory-making traditions of love and togetherness into the lives of your very busy, modern family.

Mrs. Sharp's Story: Lessons Life Has Taught Me

Out of Necessity, a Mother Becomes Inventive

Perhaps you would like to know how I first began my career as a curator of home-centered Victorian customs? Once upon a time, it all began, simply enough, out of necessity.

Although it happened long ago, I can still vividly hear the footsteps of our family physician, Dr. Orton, as he came down the stairs to talk with me. In our bedroom my beloved husband, Edmund, lay seriously ill with tuberculosis, or consumption, as it was then known. As I went through the motions of sewing by the fire, it took all my resolve not to cry in front of the children. I was so frightened that I couldn't hold the needle steady.

Fate Deals a Cruel Blow

"Victorianna, I do believe Edmund is over the worst," the doctor said, smiling sympathetically.

"Oh, thank God," I answered, my heart leaping.

"Yes, we do indeed have much to be grateful for, but while Edmund is out of danger," he continued, "now the hardest part for you is about to begin." Dr. Orton explained that he thought Edmund could recover best at the new Trudeau Sanitarium in the Adirondacks. But he gently warned me that life would be different now. "You're going to have to"— Dr. Orton paused, clearly uncomfortable at broaching such a sensitive subject with a woman— "make a major adjustment. I don't know when Edmund will be well enough, if ever, to resume work or enjoy a full married life."

Loving Partners in This Business of Life

And with those solemn words Mrs. Sharp's happiness came to a crashing halt. It was 1890. We had been married for only five years when fate tested us.

Although Edmund and I did not go on a wedding trip, our honeymoon has lasted since our wedding day. We went directly from our wedding dinner to our little dream cottage in Takoma Park, Maryland, just outside Washington, D.C., and began our lives together as loving partners. I was not to be an inferior in my new husband's eyes but an associate. Edmund told me after he carried me over the threshold, "My darling Victorianna, I want us to be equal partners in this business of life. Let us be each other's first confidant."

So we immediately began setting up our own, separate spheres: Edmund, the practice of law, and mine, the raising of a family and the creating of a comfortable home for us to live in contentment. Being young and so much in love, we were soon blessed with adorable babies, each such a treasure that another was welcomed with open arms. At the time my husband grew ill, we had four young children, including one set of twins. We were both just twenty-five years old. It seemed as if nothing could mar our happiness. In just a few short years Edmund had built up a thriving law practice, which he maintained from an office adjacent to our home. A fair bank account grew and we enjoyed a substantial yearly income. Like most of my Victorian contemporaries, I did not hold a position of responsibility outside the home circle. With my husband indisposed, however, it would be necessary for me to come to terms with our situation and "make arrangements," a Victorian euphemism for adjusting to any change in one's circumstances.

At first I gave considerable thought to selling our house and moving to smaller quarters, but that would never do. More goes into building a house than bricks and wood. Edmund and I had poured all of our hopes, dreams, and aspirations into our cherished home, "The Vicarage" (so named in loving jest because Edmund's father had wanted him to follow in his footsteps as a clergyman). Yet we couldn't manage indefinitely on our savings. Finally, Mrs. Sharp came to the simple conclusion that she had to seek gainful employment.

Mrs. Sharp's Guilty Secret

I waited until Edmund was comfortably settled at the sanitarium before seeking work, deciding that only after I had found a job and made a success of it (as I was confident that I should) would I confide—or confess—to Edmund. As you no doubt realize, dear Reader, in every marriage there comes a difference of opinion between couples. My husband held very strong views about a woman's place, and I shared his belief that a woman's ordained role was that of mother and mistress of the home. So to speak frankly (as I always shall), if I had told Edmund my intentions, it would have been a stroke, not consumption, from which he would be recovering.

First I had to make sure of my child-care arrangements. Bridget, a young Irish girl who came in to assist me weekly with laundry, agreed to come in full-time to care for the children. With that worry eliminated, Mrs. Sharp successfully answered an advertisement for a secretarial position in the newly opened Washington, D.C., branch of the Pinkerton National Detective Agency. I was about to embark on what can only be described as a new adventure.

The World Lures Her Away

Mrs. Sharp must admit that the novelty of entering the working world was quite alluring. Taking the train into Washington each morning, enjoying pleasant adult conversation, and being able to visit the shops on my lunch break, all held an appeal. My weekly pay packet was also most welcome. Alas, my work was not particularly challenging after I had put the office in order, which was accomplished in a few weeks' time. What the male working world doesn't realize is that the same creativity and organizational skills necessary to raise a family successfully and efficiently run a home can easily be applied to workplace settings. Frequently Mrs. Sharp had assisted her husband in maintaining his files, correspondence, and bookkeeping records, and this experience was also aptly applied to the Pinkerton office. As for the handling of the temperaments of a half dozen male detectives—each of whom thought his needs the most urgent—Mrs. Sharp relied on her skills as a mother.

Dame Opportunity Comes Calling

Then one day Mr. Pinkerton asked me if I might be willing to accompany him in the surveillance of a couple suspected of being jewel thieves at one of the city's fashionable hotels. Mr. Pinkerton felt that if we posed as a married couple, this would not arouse suspicion among the criminal elements. Of course, the agency did not normally employ any "lady detectives," but as all of the operatives in our office were already engaged, my employer used this occasion to be the instrument of Dame Opportunity knocking. Mr. Pinkerton complimented me on my powers of observation, diligence, attention to detail, self-reliance, and, above all, that most necessary quality for detective work, common sense. He also admitted having a high regard for women's intuitive powers. I

jumped at the chance to use my creative intellect and embraced detective work earnestly, shortly becoming a full-fledged Pinkerton operative—or a petticoated private eye.

Her Web of Deceit Grows

Now, dear Reader, accepting a position as a clerk in an office out of necessity and embarking on a time-consuming career as a lady detective, even if both situations take place in identical locales, are not the same thing. As Edmund's stay at the sanitarium lengthened, I found it increasingly difficult to explain the nuances of my particular position. For though Edmund had accepted my going to work at Pinkerton's until he returned home, one shock to the system was enough.

She Should Have Known Better

At the agency, the remuneration at the conclusion of successful cases was very handsome. Accordingly,

during the time I worked as a lady detective I was able to accumulate a tidy sum. But the demands of my new career extracted a high price. I was extremely fatigued from both the type of work I was engaged in and with my daily trips to and from The Vicarage. Sometimes while on a case, it was even necessary for me to stay overnight in a ladies' boardinghouse. I missed my children terribly and they missed their mother, too. Our emotional estrangement began to manifest itself in eating, sleeping, and discipline problems. My beautiful home life began to unravel before my very eyes. When I was with the children, I was easily distracted because of the intricacies and intrigue of my work. Frequently, she is sorry to disclose, Mrs. Sharp became unnecessarily irritable with them. Although our worlds are separated by a century, dear Reader, Mrs. Sharp knows only too well the very real difficulties that working mothers face each day and how torn one can feel between loving duty at home and the challenge of interesting, rewarding work in the world. I began to suffer from attacks to the nervous system and was burdened with guilt because I had not been forthcoming with my husband. Despite my best intentions, my dear Edmund would be returning not to his beloved home, but to a shambles.

Coming Events Cast Their Shadows Before

Finally, one day I awoke to the realization that the making of a life was infinitely more important than the making of a living. With reluctance, Mrs. Sharp resigned from Pinkerton's and returned to her home, steadfastly determined to chart her own course but with her husband and children beside, not behind, her. I wrote to Edmund and revealed all. The next afternoon, I sat down and wrote to *Godey's Lady's Book* detailing for other women my story, "Lessons Life Has Taught Me as a Lady Detective." I wrote from my heart. I knew that many other women must be experiencing the same tension that occurs when domestic duties collide with the need for personal accomplishment. Perhaps Mrs. Sharp could offer them a glimmer of hope. I told my readers that after making my way successfully in the world, I had learned a most valuable lesson: If you want to make the world a better place, you must start with your own home. The "modern" woman had begun to embark on a journey into the realms of the intellect, business, and science (and someday even politics), Mrs. Sharp acknowledged, but she wondered, after achieving worldly success, was it possible for her to return to her home with a new realization of its value as a place for the exercise of her highest faculties? This was Mrs. Sharp's heartfelt challenge a hundred years ago.

Little did I realize, as I wrote that heartfelt essay, that I had struck a chord that would resonate with American women. The editor of *Godey's* immediately wrote back, accepted my story for publication, and enclosed a welcome check. *Godey's* also commissioned from me a series of articles entitled "At Home with Mrs. Sharp." My mission was to offer monthly advice on how to make "homemaking a high calling." Soon other periodicals began to solicit my work, and so began my career as a literary domestic.

It goes without saying, as I write this, that my story has a happy ending. Edmund eventually recovered and, returning home, began working again at the practice of law. Our married life blossomed in true felicity, including the dividend of ten more wonderful children, each a blessing. We remained at The Vicarage living a quiet, contented life. In a hundred years the only cloud to hover over our happy union was whether Mrs. Sharp should use her abilities as a lady detective to alleviate the suffering of those in need. But that, dear Reader, is, as they say, a story for another day.

MRS. SHARP'S OLD-FASHIONED PETTICOAT PHILOSOPHY OF PARENTING

May Mrs. Sharp share with you some of the principles of her old-fashioned petticoat philosophy of parenting, which for many years have guided and been a source of comfort to her?

First of all, obligations already existing in your family life can become perfect opportunities for family tradition making and togetherness.

Special family times must be scheduled into modern lives; they do not occur spontaneously. Strong, emotionally healthy, and loving families spend time together—working and playing.

Third, never forget the three *P*'s of perfect family life: setting priorities, planning, and prayer. These three elements are essential for parental peace of mind.

Fourth, by incorporating routine, rhythm, and ritual into your life, many happy moments and memories will flower.

THE VICTORIANS
AT HOME

"All happy families resemble one another," Leo Tolstoy astutely observed in *Anna Karenina*. A century later, family therapists and psychologists agree: Strong, close-knit families share traits that set them apart from troubled ones. One trait is the realization that family traditions strengthen ties within the family. Another is a continuing commitment on the part of parents to use traditions—from treasured holiday rituals to everyday customs—as a unifying thread. Our Victorian great-grandparents knew the importance of this.

An Island of Stability

For the Victorians, a happy home was viewed as an island of stability amid a sea of social change. Traditions that celebrated the joys of home and family life were the bulwark. Indeed, during the Victorian era, the pursuit of domestic bliss was promoted as an art form—from white-linen Sunday dinners to blue-gingham Fourth of July picnics—and these cherished customs were lovingly celebrated in the art painted during the latter half of the nineteenth century.

Of course, artists have always depicted scenes of everyday life: Wall paintings of domestic interiors have survived from Roman times. But the Victorian school of genre artists (painters of everyday life) were really the first to revel in portraying affectionate families at home, at work, and at play. By celebrating sentimentality and emotion, these depictions of domestic harmony elevated the home and family to beloved icons.

A century later the Victorian era is seen as a period of great tranquillity and stability largely through its powerful images of family life, which continue to color contemporary expectations and emotions.

What is ironic is that at the same time these tranquil scenes were being painted, Victorian society was undergoing the strains of tremendous technological change, which affected almost every aspect of nineteenth-century family life—from the place they called home (now suddenly the city instead of the farm), to the preparation of food, to the role of women. That a period of such profound upheaval should also, a century later, have such an image of collective stability has to be attributed in large part not to the paintings alone but to the traditions and rituals of family life they depicted. There is an important message here for today's families, living in a period of societal change far greater than the Victorians ever dreamed possible.

A Woman's Place

Women underwent the profoundest changes in nineteenth-century life. As men found work away from the home and farm, the woman's role in the family was exalted. Mother became the center of the home, responsible for making the family residence a haven of love and comfort set apart from the pressures of the world. The home itself became a "secular temple" wherein all of the heavenly virtues could be nurtured—virtues that seemed increasingly threatened by a society in turmoil. One typical domestic manifesto, profoundly influential in its time, was *The American Woman's Home,* written in 1869 by Catharine Beecher and her younger sister, Harriet Beecher Stowe (more familiar for her bestselling *Uncle Tom's Cabin*), which proclaimed the women's role "as sacred and important as any ordained to man." The role of wife and mother became the unifying thread that held together every facet of Victorian society and was subtly (and not so subtly) interwoven into the fabric of everyday life.

The temporal and spiritual joys of domestic fulfillment were popularly extolled and celebrated in everything from songs (Stephen Foster's "Home! Sweet Home" became a Victorian anthem) to magazines, religious tracts, advice manuals, advertising, theater, literature, as well as visual art. For Americans as well as the English, the perfect example of family togetherness was found in the royal role models of Queen Victoria, Prince Albert, and their nine children. The ideal home—whether it was Windsor Castle or a suburban gingerbread-trimmed villa—was viewed as a sanctuary of beauty, serenity, cleanliness, and order; anything that contributed to its embellishment or edification was considered worthy of expenditure. Above all, "Mother" was considered "the Light of the Home," as the American women's bible *Godey's Lady's Book* proclaimed in 1860. The sanctified role of women during the Victorian era solidified as social and cultural forces, from painters to poets to preachers, converged to form a cult of domesticity. "The foundation of our national character is laid by the mothers of the nation," declared Josiah Gilbert Holland in 1858, who as "Timothy Titcomb" was one of the most popular family-life writers of the latter half of the nineteenth century. It was a position no one would have dared to argue with publicly, as motherhood became as sacred and entrenched an American institution as apple pie and the flag.

The Cult of Domestic Bliss

But a large number of influential women also helped cultivate and promote the cult of domestic bliss. These were the "literary domestics," Victorian women writers who penned an astonishing range of work—domestic manuals, sentimental novels, and advice columns in nineteenth-century ladies' periodicals—extolling the woman's role as nothing less than heaven's representative on earth. From the Beecher sisters' *American Woman's Home* and Mrs. Isabella Beeton's *The Book of Household Management* to Mrs. Henry Wood's sensational novel of a woman's abandoning her child and husband in *East Lynne* and Louisa May Alcott's sublime evocation of the happy family in *Little Women*, literary domestics reigned supreme over the hearts and minds of middle-class Victorian women, reinforcing their role as self-sacrificing nurturers of husband and children who should not seek nor desire a wider world than their anointed domestic realm.

While *East Lynne*—a runaway bestseller during the 1860s and a box-office smash for four decades when it was adapted for the stage—used a melodra-matic, tear-jerking sledgehammer to hit home its message of the woman's place (with its eyebrow-raising plot involving adultery, divorce, jealousy, and revenge), most of the literary domestics preferred to be more subtle in their proselytizing. For example, in 1868, Louisa May Alcott has the mother in *Little Women*, Mrs. March, express her aspirations for her daughters this way: "I want my daughters to be beautiful, accomplished, and good; to be admired, loved, and respected; to have a happy youth, to be well and wisely married and to lead useful, pleasant lives with as little care and sorrow to try them as God sees fit to send. To be loved and chosen by a good man is the best and sweetest thing which can happen to a woman; and I sincerely hope my girls may know this beautiful experience . . ."

Whether it was *East Lynne* or *Little Women,* the end result was the same: In the perfect Victorian scenario, Father came home at twilight sullied and exhausted from toiling in the factory or marketplace to find respite, eternal order, and harmony hearthside: God was in His heaven and dinner was served promptly.

The Literary Domestics

What is interesting to note, especially with the luxury of a century separating us, is that many of the literary domestics enjoyed much more personal freedom than did their readers. This was due, no doubt, to the financial security and independence their writing provided them. In an era when women did not assume positions of responsibility outside the home, most literary domestics began their careers as a means of supplementing their incomes when the men in their lives—either husbands or fathers—were unable to provide for their families, usually because of illness or death. But a number of Victorian women writers, especially those without children, were extremely prolific, often writing two or three novels in one year as well as numerous magazine articles, all of which were eagerly awaited by both their publishers and their public. Of course, today, the florid prose, famous works, and even names—such as Mrs. E.D.E.N. Southworth, Catharine Maria Sedwick, Elizabeth Wetherell, and Mrs. M. E. Sherwood—have long been forgotten. But in their heyday, the commercial success the literary domestics enjoyed caused some of their male rivals, such as Nathaniel Hawthorne, to dismiss them enviously as "that damned mob of scribbling women."

The Home as Garden of Eden

The home as garden—nurturing family the way one would flowers—was a favorite theme with many of the literary domestics, especially those who wrote advice columns in women's periodicals. In those days many women wrote anonymously or assumed pen names, and a surprising number of women writers adopted floral pseudonyms, such as Fanny Fern, Lily Larkspur, Minni Myrtle, and Jenny June.

"Jenny June" was a particularly popular columnist for *Demorest's Family Magazine.* One of the most appealing aspects of her column, "Talks With Women," as well as the work of numerous nineteenth-century advice columnists, is her self-assured, cheerful, and always optimistic tone even when addressing sensitive subjects. Perhaps this is because Victorian women were not confused about their priorities, and society supported their efforts in the home and raising a family. This emotional equilibrium gave Victorian women the resiliency to handle whatever conundrums life might throw at them, and this confidence can still buoy a reader's spirits even a century later.

The Haven of All Hopes and Desires

In her August 1867 column, Mrs. June wonders in print about the "Influences of Home Upon Children." Her lively, astute observations are still relevant today: "There has been so much written upon home influence that it would seem as if there could be nothing left to say upon such a subject; yet so important is it, and so little is this importance felt and realized in the mass of our homes, that the old words of warning and counsel seem ever new and ever necessary to be said. . . .

"It is a high and important office, that of mother, and requires all the best and choicest qualities which belong to womanhood, trained and perfected. Much love, much patience, wisdom, knowledge, judgment,

their great work? [What would it be] were the influences of home charged, as they might be, with the electric current of active love, faith, knowledge, strength, courage, and devotion to the interests they are bound to protect?"

The Portcullis of the Past

America's late-nineteenth-century painters and writers, as well as other arbiters of culture, were well aware that a sweeping wind of change was blowing through Victorian society as the nineteenth century drew to a close, and that these forces of upheaval presented a real and present danger to American family life. By their nostalgic, affectionate, and romantic renderings of the family and stories of idealized home life, perhaps Victorian artists and writers hoped to preserve for future generations the vision of a way of life they knew was rapidly disappearing. As Ralph Waldo Emerson observed, "If a man wishes to acquaint himself with the spirit of the age, he must not go first to the courtroom. The subtle spirit of life must be sought in facts nearer. It is what is done and suffered in the house that has the profoundest interest for us all."

Today we glance at these sentimental images of Victorian family life and read the stories with more than mere nostalgia but with acknowledgment and thanksgiving. For these portrayals of domestic bliss and the messages they imparted a century ago—the importance of a loving, celebrating family and the security of the home as a retreat from the stresses of modern living—are a living legacy that continues to reach through the portcullis of the past to charm, encourage, and inspire.

self-control, with body and soul attuned to, and kept in harmony with, the laws of God and nature, compose the divinity which should hedge about a mother, but alas! too often does not. . . .

"It is no light thing, no easy task to be a mother and fulfill a mother's duties. Incessant care, incessant watchfulness, and all without fussiness, or too conscious restraint, is the price of success. . . . The making of a happy home is the first duty of a wife and mother, and the most important question to her is, How to do it? . . .

"Even under the present imperfect conditions, *home* is the central attraction of every human heart, the inspiration of nearly all effort, the haven of all our hopes and desires. What would it be were women true to themselves, to their high destiny, to

MRS. BEETON

Victoria may have sat on the throne, but during the nineteenth century, a woman named Mrs. Isabella Beeton was the undisputed queen of the literary domestics and reigned supreme over Victorian English homes. Mrs. Beeton was author of *The Book of Household Management,* a 1,112-page compendium of "tried and tested" recipes, as well as advice on matters of hygiene, etiquette, and family life. It was first published in 1861, sold more than sixty thousand copies in its first year, and for generations of homemakers served as a practical guide to achieving the art of domestic bliss. So comprehensive, authoritative, and indispensable was Mrs. Beeton's resource that when a woman married, it became a custom for her mother to give her a copy of the Bible and "Mrs. Beeton's." Nothing more, it was assumed, was needed to achieve a happy home.

While the name Mrs. Beeton conjures up an image of a dour dowager dressed in black, the real Mrs. Beeton was quite different: an attractive young woman who loved French fashions, enjoyed a passionate marriage with her husband, was an astute businesswoman and accomplished journalist. Born Isabella Mary Mayson in London in 1836, at nineteen she married Samuel Orchart Beeton, a young publisher who had made a fortune by publishing the English version of *Uncle Tom's Cabin.* Eight months after their marriage, in 1856, Isabella began editing and writing cookery and household columns—precursors to her book—for *The Englishwoman's Domestic Magazine* (the most popular English women's periodical of the Victorian era), which Sam had started in 1852. In an age when women were expected to have "accomplishments" rather than opinions and stay home tending their hearth, Isabella enjoyed a lifestyle that would have shocked her readers, commuting daily by train from the London suburbs to the Fleet Street publishing house she ran as a partner with her husband.

Three years after publishing *The Book of Household Management* and while correcting proofs for its sequel, Isabella died at age twenty-eight of puerperal fever, a week after giving birth to her fourth child. She left behind a heartbroken husband, who never really recovered from his loss, a young family, and a legacy that contributed to helping countless Victorian women achieve the domestic felicity fate denied her.

VICTORIA AND ALBERT

"When one is so happy and blessed in one's home life, as I am," England's Queen Victoria confided to her journal, "politics (provided my Country is safe) must only take a second place." But "home life" meant one thing for Queen Victoria and another thing for her English subjects and admirers in nineteenth-century America. For the Queen, "home life" meant time spent with her beloved husband, Prince Albert, but not necessarily with their nine children.

In fact, Victoria's many biographers have made clear that she did not really like children. Actually, it was Prince Albert who was closer to the children. The Queen thought babies were "nasty things," and as the children became older, their mother grew even more distant from them. Victoria believed this emotional estrangement was due to the fact that she had grown up an only child and was not used to being in the company of a brood of high-spirited youngsters.

Of course, the reality of what went on at Balmoral when not sitting for portraits of family togetherness (the children spent most of their time in a separate house on the grounds, occasionally inviting Mama and Papa "to tea") was not public knowledge during Her Majesty's lifetime. This is just as well, for it would have shocked and no doubt saddened the Queen's many admirers, who saw in her the perfect role model of loving wife and affectionate mother.

In the first role, dutiful adoring wife, however, Victoria does not wither under history's harsh scrutiny. For twenty-one years she was her German-born husband's devoted spouse. Their love for each other was deep and abiding, and while she may indeed have been his sovereign, the Queen's submissiveness to her husband set the standard for Victorian wives. When her "beloved and perfect Albert" died in 1861, leaving her a widow at forty-two, Victoria spent the remaining four decades of her life in deep mourning that bordered on the obsessive. According to Stanley Weintraub in *Victoria: An Intimate Biography*, this included such rituals as changing the Prince's towels and linens, the daily laying out of fresh clothes and shaving utensils (including hot water), and scouring his unused chamber pot.

Portrait Group of Queen Victoria with Her Children.
(Detail) by John Calcott Horsley

Weintraub notes that "the long afternoon of her post-Albert seclusion has a melodramatic quality that causes it to linger in memory tenaciously. . . ." In the end what Victoria left behind, other than the association of an age with her name—no small accomplishment—"was a yearning for continuity and tradition," including "the middle-class values that were her own and that remain beneath the fairy-tale veneer of royalty."

THE ART OF
DOMESTIC BLISS

There were four main areas in which celebrations, traditions, and ritual played a part in Victorian life. First, in the art of daily domestic living; second, through rites of passage such as birthdays, baptisms, weddings, and funerals; third, by annual customs revolving around calendar and religious holidays; and fourth, by pastimes associated with the four seasons.

But like any fine needlepoint tapestry, the vibrant colors and threads of each category blend together to create the complete fabric of our lives, so that once we have mastered the joy of celebrating, it is difficult to see where one category ends and another picks up the stitch.

Let us begin with the daily round: How to create a loving, celebrating environment for the home circle, or how do we master the Art of Domestic Bliss?

Of course, we all know how to bake a birthday cake, illustrate a Valentine, carve a pumpkin, or trim the Christmas tree. But how do we find opportunities to make every day, not just the holidays, memorable? We begin, dear Reader, once we realize that the pursuit of excellence in the domestic arts—cooking, decorating, handicrafts, and creating family recreational pursuits—can be among our most satisfying accomplishments.

"As with the Commander of An Army, or the leader of any enterprise, so is it with the mistress of a house," Mrs. Isabella Beeton instructed in *The Book of Household Management.* "Her spirit will be seen through the whole establishment." Nowhere is this more true than in the course of a family's daily life. This is why over this past century that she has been a wife and mother, Mrs. Sharp has tried to create what she likes to call "ceremonials for common days," or small moments each day that bring her and her family joy and contentment.

Ceremonials for Common Days

The most important aspect in the pursuit of domestic bliss is attitude. With a happy, serene, and positive attitude, anything can be accomplished. Ceremonials for common days are the fruits of a positive attitude, the finishing touches that add beauty, charm, and a sense of graciousness to our lives. In this frazzled age of overscheduling, eating alone, and nontraditional child care, every family needs to create its own ceremonials for common days. They can be as simple as setting the table in a certain way for breakfast, enjoying a tea party with your children after they return from school, or taking a family walk under the stars after supper.

Let us begin each common day, dear Reader, with a ceremonial all your own: Carve out private time for yourself, at least half an hour in the early morning to collect your thoughts over a cup of tea or coffee, to pray or meditate, to read a page from an inspirational book, and to plan your day. Of course, this necessitates that you rise earlier than the rest of the family.

"Early rising is one of the most essential qualities which enters into good Household Management, as it is not only the parent of health, but of innumerable other advantages," Mrs. Beeton observed. "Indeed, when a mistress is an early riser, it is almost certain that her house will be orderly and well-managed." Trust Mrs. Sharp, you need this time to yourself. It is of inestimable worth for a mother to begin her day before the rest of the family. This time alone can become a treasured retreat of serenity that can prepare you to handle whatever the day might hold in store. It is far better for Mother to create a morning retreat than for her to beat a hasty one at day's end.

Harmony at Home

Before these ceremonials, however, every home first needs to be built upon a firm foundation. The foundation for achieving harmony at home consists in restoring rhythm to modern family life through daily rituals and developing a sense of order in your household.

Restoring Rhythm with Daily Rituals

Let us begin by reflecting upon how much rhythm you have in your family life. If there is one aspect of contemporary life that has disappeared, it is the notion that there should be a regular rhythm to how we conduct our daily affairs.

When we pause to ponder why we should restore this most necessary yet neglected ingredient for ensuring harmony in the home, the natural world offers us many examples: the recurring cycle of the four seasons, the monthly phases of the moon, the ebb and flow of the tides, and the daily progression from day into night.

Prior to the Industrial Revolution, families fit work, rest, and recreation into the rhythms of the natural world. Over the past one hundred years, however, progress has made it possible for modern families to attempt to overcome the limitations of nature. Yet simply because we can eat frozen strawberries in January or blur the distinctions between night and day with electricity doesn't mean we should ignore the role that rhythm plays in our lives. If we do, eventually the tension and stress from trying to have it all and do it all will catch up with us. Just as there is a reassuring rhythm in nature, so should a comforting sense of rhythm be restored in the home through daily rituals, particularly with regard to eating and sleeping. The sense of security your youngsters will derive from so simple a concept as regular mealtimes and bedtimes can be profound.

Choices have always been a part of raising a family. Making a conscious decision about how we shall conduct the course of our daily life is one of the most important ones parents can make, for its effects will last a lifetime. Today, to help parents make these choices, an astonishing range of "experts" offers contradictory advice on every aspect of family life. But there seems to be little offered in the way of old-fashioned common sense. Mrs. Sharp's message is not revolutionary. At the end of the day, however, when you have tired, cranky children and dinner is late because you had to stop at the grocery store on your way home from work, what you need is not the latest parenting trend but a tried-and-true practical plan for homemaking so that this frenzy is not repeated.

In Praise of Order

A place for everything and everything
in its place.
—Isabella Mary Beeton

When you gaze at a picture of Victorian domestic bliss, have you ever wondered, dear Reader, why the Victorians were so happy at home? If Mrs. Sharp had to hazard a guess, it would be because Victorian homemakers realized and respected the role that order played in helping them achieve their ideal of home, sweet home. There is no ill that can befall man, woman, or child that cannot be made more tolerable in a tidy front parlor.

"Order is Heaven's first law," Alexander Pope wrote. So, too, should order be the homemaker's first aspiration. If the state of your home is continuous chaos, make it a priority to bring order into your home. After rhythm, establishing a sense of order is

perhaps the most important thing you can do to promote your own and your family's sense of well-being. Not to mention that no mother can think clearly, never mind celebrate family life, existing in clutter. Children need and thrive on order, but it must at first be imposed upon them. In fact, little ones look to their parents to bring order into their lives. Victorian mothers taught children order through imitation, housekeeping games, stories, and rhymes. A child's verse sums up life in the nursery:

I always put my things away
That I might find them another day.

Start when children are very young to teach them to tidy up after playing and put their toys away. Of course, you will need to help, to show them where everything belongs and to oversee their efforts. This requires determination, good humor, and, above all, consistency. May Mrs. Sharp speak frankly? In the beginning, it is far easier just to pick up the toys (or the clothes or the books) ourselves and be done with it. But children need and want to learn how to be organized and responsible for themselves. After toys, children should learn to put their own clothes and belongings away, make their beds and keep their bedrooms "tidy," and gradually to contribute on a regular basis to the needs of the household.

Working as a family and sharing the responsibilities of running a home lightens the load for parents and teaches children valuable, life-sustaining skills from cooperation to cooking. Each completed task builds competence, confidence, and self-esteem. Teaching our children when they are young how to grow up organized is one of the most precious gifts we can give them. They might grumble and complain while completing their chores, but they will bless you later for endowing them with a respect for, and an appreciation of, order when they establish their own homes and businesses.

If you are currently adrift, frazzled, and running about without a regular plan of affairs for your household, it will take effort to introduce old-fashioned rhythm and establish order in your family's life. But persevere, dear Reader, for you will experience a wonderful sense of contentment that happens only when there is harmony at home.

Mealtimes

It has come to Mrs. Sharp's attention that many contemporary mothers long to transform their homes from a house of nonpaying boarders into a close-knit family but don't know where to begin. To remedy this situation, Mrs. Sharp will gently suggest an old-fashioned Victorian tradition that can perform miracles.

It's called eating together.

In case it has escaped your attention, dear Reader, living under the same roof does not guarantee domestic tranquillity. However, enjoying the pleasure of one another's company at mealtimes frequently does.

Although the thought may at first be terrifying, when your children are grown, dear Reader, what they will remember best about life with you are family mealtimes. If mere contemplation of this fact makes you want to hide (or at the very least turn back the clock and start over), then take heart and take action. Decide that from now on your meals will be a special time for you and your family. A time of reassurance, comfort, and sociability. Children learn some of their most important lessons at the family table, including good manners, the art of conversation, and confidence.

"Perhaps nothing in the life of a household is of more importance than the daily meals," the Victorian compendium *Cassell's Book of the Household* instructed homemakers in 1889. "These, if properly conducted, can be made not only a season of rest and refreshment, but also a time for, and means of, useful education for young children, and of pleasant helpful intercourse when those children have grown into youths and maidens."

Of course, Mrs. Sharp is not about to fly in the face of reality and paint an unrealistic picture of what can and cannot be achieved with regard to family life. In today's hurried and busy world, with so many demands upon our time, families frequently find it necessary during the week to eat in shifts, grabbing a quick snack before rushing off to a meeting, soccer practice, or drama rehearsal. But at some point parents must draw the line and reclaim eminent domain over meals. Some practical suggestions on how to do this might include saying no to all early-evening meetings of classes, to make it a family rule not to accept phone calls during this time (or if you have a telephone answering machine, put it to good use), and, it goes without saying—but Mrs. Sharp will say it anyway—to turn the television set *off* during dinner.

The Ritual Family Feast

One old-fashioned tradition that Mrs. Sharp believes should be lovingly restored to modern family life is the ritual Sunday dinner. For Victorian families, this meal was the highlight of the week, to which all members of the extended family were invited (including the babies) and expected (illness being the only acceptable excuse for nonattendance). Of course, everyone arrived in their best bib and tucker with hearty appetites and an abundance of amusing stories to share.

Think about choosing one day in the week—Sunday works very well for most families—to set a beautiful, inviting table using your best china, linens, and flowers for the week's most festive feast. Promote a party atmosphere, for after all, you are inviting your favorite guests to dinner. Have the family put on their party clothes and come ready to "dine" instead of just eat. This will be the day that you can try out new recipes or enjoy old family favorites. Mrs. Sharp has several cookbooks that she enjoys dipping into for inspiration for new Sunday dinners, but her family always manages to have beloved family desserts as a finale. You might want to enlist your children's help in planning the menu together. To encourage a lively discussion at the table, have everyone prepare one anecdote about the best thing that happened to him or her all week. You will be amazed at how effectively these simple suggestions will work to bring your family closer together.

Keep in mind, however, that in the beginning the children might complain when you ask them to change for Sunday dinner. You might also have to endure long silences when it's someone's turn to talk about his or her week, but after just two or three family feasts, they'll come around to realizing they don't have to wait for Thanksgiving to enjoy dining together as a family.

Certainly some of childhood's most potent memories are the meals shared at the family table. With loving dedication and diligence, your young ones may yet be blessed with an abundance of happy ones.

A VICTORIAN CHILD'S TABLE MANNERS

Teach it to take its seat quietly;
To use its napkin properly;
To wait patiently to be served;
To answer promptly;
To say thank you . . .
Never to make remarks about the food . . .
Teach the child to keep his plate in order;
Not to handle the bread or to drop food on
   the cloth or floor . . .
To fold its napkin and to put back its chair
   or push it close to the table before leaving;
And after leaving the table not to return.

—*Good Housekeeping, May 25, 1889*

The Children's Hour:
Bath and Bedtime Rituals

Eventide holds some of the most precious, intimate moments you will ever share with your children. It should be a time of winding down from the flurry of the day's bustle by drawing near to one another for warmth, comfort, and reassurance through nighttime rituals. Victorian families called this inviting interlude "The Children's Hour." In an age when children were admonished to remember their place, nighttime in the nursery was their special time to bask in their parents' undivided attention, love, and devotion.

Any home with children inevitably has a bath

and bed routine. However, if your "children's hour" resembles more of a nightly tug-of-war than a relaxing respite for both parents and children, let

Mrs. Sharp make a plea for a more gentle transition from day to night.

Begin the nighttime ritual by having the children tidy up their toys and personal belongings. Just because everyone is tired is no reason that Mother should have to pick up all of the toys. To make the job easier, have one large basket in the living room or playroom into which children can collect their toys quickly. In the morning, before play begins again, the basket can be emptied and the toys put away properly. At Mrs. Sharp's we also keep a basket on each stairway so that items that belong on another floor can conveniently be collected. At the end of the day it is someone's job to carry the basket upstairs and deposit the items where they belong.

Now, while the children are tidying up, draw a lovely bath for them using a gentle, nonirritating milk foam, bath oil, or bubble bath. Let each child have his own bath basket in which to keep a variety of soaps, a small nailbrush, and sponges. If your bathroom is not large enough to store all the baskets, they can be kept in each person's room and carried to the bath. Mrs. Sharp enjoys personalizing bath baskets to suit the ages and personalities of her children. Today in the shops you can find a wonderful assortment of bath products for babies, children, and adolescents. But after the bath, when children are dry, nothing soothes like

Johnson's Baby Powder, no matter what the age of the child. Each member of the family should have his own small container.

Let each child pick a favorite color and color-code towels and washcloths. Have towel racks scaled to your child's height so that he can reach and replace his own towels and wash- cloths. Thick, terry-cloth bathrobes are wonder- ful for children to put on after the bath and can very often finish drying a squirming child who doesn't want to stand still.

If your child has had a particularly stressful day, let her take her bath using a night- light instead of overhead lighting. Massage her legs, arms, and tired shoulders with bath oil after she gets out of the tub, then give her an extra cuddle and carry or escort her to her bedroom.

Every parent knows that children adore water play, but in Mrs. Sharp's house not every bath is designated a "play" bath, especially on school nights. But on those chosen nights, we start the bath routine a half hour earlier, and the play part of the bath comes only after each child has been thoroughly cleaned (this includes hair washing). Families with more than two children should have a plan that alternates regular bath nights with a thorough washing up at the sink (called a sailor's bath), shower, or a quick stand-up bath in the tub just to remove the day's dirt. To keep things moving, an adult should always supervise bath time (even after children are old enough to bathe themselves) because children left on their own will dawdle the night away. However, instead of the admoni- tion "Hurry up" (which chil- dren spend their entire lives hearing) Mrs. Sharp uses the phrase "It's get- ting time now . . ." While the older chil- dren are bathing, Mrs. Sharp helps tidy up their rooms (everyone always sleeps better when the room is in order).

When the children return to their rooms, they discover that Mother has drawn the curtains, turned on a soft light, and turned down the beds. Their nightclothes are neatly lying on the pillow. If it is a winter's evening, Mrs. Sharp will warm up the beds with hot-water bottles. During the winter, we use flannel sheets; in summer, cool cotton.

After dressing for bed, the children select what they will wear the next day (down to socks and loca- tion of shoes) and lay out their clothes for the morn- ing. This well-spent five minutes at night makes a considerable difference in the morning.

Now it is story time, a half hour until lights are out. Story time is sacred in Mrs. Sharp's home. As with dinner, no phone calls are accepted while we're putting the children to bed. This uninterrupted attention gives children a wonderful sense of security and, by focusing so completely on them, Mrs. Sharp eliminates much of the tension that inevitably comes when they prolong bedtime. Very often, pleas for one more cup of water are really requests for much-needed attention after a long day apart.

As for the evening's oral entertainment, when the children were smaller, we read a variety of short picture books, but children adore continuing sagas, and even tots as young as four will settle down to hear a chapter a night. This sharing of a longer story together, as it unfolds over many nights, can become a conversation topic and a wonderful bond between parent and child.

Then the storybook is closed for the night, prayers are heard, and little ones of all ages are tucked in and kissed good night. One of Mrs. Sharp's favorite nighttime traditions began when the children were very small and has continued as they have grown older. After Mrs. Sharp turns off the lights, she always lies down next to them or (depending on the child) sits on the bed and holds their hand in the dark. What an opportunity it is for heart-to-heart talks, as the children cuddle closely. Here is

where we have some of our most intimate, private moments. At this special time, happy events of the day are recalled, secrets are shared, or a sympathetic word is offered. The children and Mrs. Sharp also talk about upcoming events that we're looking forward to, but now difficult subjects are broached in the dark. Or during the day, courage might have wavered in their young hearts, and Mother can reassuringly assuage fear during these affectionate times of close confidences. The slate is also wiped clean over any transgressions that may have occurred earlier, and everyone goes to bed with a free conscience. In every house, the ledgers of love should always be balanced every twenty-four hours.

Soon the most blissful moment any parent experiences all day arrives. The children are asleep. Basking in the serenity and the stillness of the house, with everyone safe and secure, Mrs. Sharp counts her blessings.

Family Night

I love my House, I love my Nest.
In all the World,
My Nest is Best!

"Home is where we start from," the poet T. S. Eliot reminds us. "Home" is also the place where most adults long to return each night and look forward to retreating to at the end of a busy week, echoing Mr. Bird's sentiments from the children's favorite *The Best Nest*.

All of us want our children to grow up believing their nest is best. A century ago Victorian parents were urged to give much thought to creating amusing diversions that were the mainstay of our cozy home-circle evenings. "Where there are young people forming a part of the evening circle, interesting and agreeable pastimes should especially be promoted,"

Mrs. Isabella Beeton advised in *The Book of Household Management*. "It is of incalculable benefit to them that their homes should possess all the attractions of healthful amusement, comfort and happiness; for if they do not find pleasure there, they will seek it elsewhere. It ought, therefore, to enter into the domestic policy of every parent, to make her children feel that home is the happiest place in the world . . . to imbue them with this delicious home-feeling is one of the choicest gifts a parent can bestow."

One of the ways that parents can reinstate home as the place where their children's best and happiest moments are spent is to set aside some special time each week for just the family. If there is one thing Mrs. Sharp has learned over this past century, it is that special family times don't just happen, they must be planned. That is why families need to plan and then set aside one night a week for family-night fun. Schedule it on your calendar, inviolate, just as you would any other important event.

In the Mood

Setting the climate is very important to the integration of family night into your lives. Fun is the most important ingredient to ensure the entire family's enthusiastic cooperation and participation. Make the evening festive, like a party. Plan on serving favorite family refreshments. Do they adore ice-cream sundaes? Pizza? Popcorn? Then this is the evening to have it—and in future, only on family night.

Keep the mood of the evening lighthearted; no discussion of business or discipline problems is permitted. Above all, at least in the very beginning, keep

family night short. For your first family-night assembly, it should be an hour or less.

Since coming together for pure enjoyment might come as a shock for all of you, ease the family into togetherness gently. Give everybody two weeks' notice so that they can arrange their schedules. Then a week's notice. Count the days down: "Three more days until our first family night. I'm excited, aren't you? We're going to have so much fun!" Spread the enthusiasm. It's catching. Trust Mrs. Sharp—this plan works.

What Shall We Do?

"Family night sounds wonderful, Mrs. Sharp, but now that we're all gathered around the popcorn bowl, what exactly are we supposed to do?"

Endless are the diversions your family can enjoy together, dear Reader. Here are a few ideas that our family has found of unfailing interest, to spur on your imagination:

Work on the family photograph album.

Browse through gardening catalogs and plan the family garden.

Work on seasonal handicrafts, such as valentines, an Easter-egg tree, May Day baskets. (In part two of this book we'll take a walk through the year together with Mrs. Sharp's Victorian family savoring old-fashioned seasonal pastimes. Many of these suggestions can easily be adapted for family-night fun.)

For your first family night, why not hold a "Getting to Know You" party? Encourage each member to share his favorite family memory and see if there is a common thread. Next, ask everyone to contribute suggestions for the good times to come. Write these suggestions down on index cards for future family-night fun.

And Mrs. Sharp promises, you *will* have fun together.

If you have never had a family night before, introducing one into your busy lives will call for a lot of rearranging and a certain amount of inconvenience. It is worth all the effort, however, for the harvest of precious memories your loving family will reap in the future is beyond measure.

MAY MRS. SHARP BE OF ASSISTANCE?

*I*f family night is to succeed, it is important that you plan an activity for each week. Mrs. Sharp knows you would not dream of attending a staff meeting unprepared, but you might think you can "wing it" with the family. Please do not even try. Rest assured, the results will be disastrous.

Instead, take all those index-card suggestions for future activities, and for a pastime to bridge the gap between old memories and new hopes and plans, why not make a family night fun box to hold the raw materials for memory making?

Mrs. Sharp uses a sturdy cardboard letter-size storage box that the entire family helped decorate (another family-night project) using photographs, pretty scraps of wrapping and wallpaper, pictures cut from magazines and greeting cards, and the children's drawings and stickers.

Inside we keep the recipe-size card-file box that

contains seasonal suggestions for future family nights, divided by months. For example, "Try candle making first week of February for Candlemas Day, February 2," along with the name of the resource where we can obtain the candle-making supplies. Our storage box also contains a letter-size accordion folder that keeps larger newspaper and magazine clippings of ideas. This is where you will put that special article you used to stuff into the back of the kitchen junk drawer (only to find it a year later). Finally, there is a family night calendar, so that we can schedule our fun.

The first week of each month we check both the folder and the file box to integrate seasonal delights into our family repertoire of activities. Decide at the end of each family night what you will do the following week, and then each Monday check the supplies you'll need so that you'll be prepared.

Sundays with the Children

In virtually all Victorian households, Sunday or the Sabbath was set aside as a day of worship, rest, and family time. Victorian families were devoted to their Sunday rituals: morning church services followed by the week's most elaborate dinner, to which the entire extended family was invited, followed by afternoons set aside for wholesome family recreational pursuits ending with evening Bible readings and the singing of hymns. It was considered one of Mother's responsibilities to come up with spiritually uplifting and morally edifying pastimes for the entire family. In fact, so widespread was this typical observance of the Sabbath that many women's periodicals such as *Good Housekeeping* regularly included columns containing Sabbath activity ideas for mothers who were expected to set aside Sundays for character building and the religious training of children. For example, youngsters had to put their regular toys away on Sundays and play only with toys of a religious theme, such as Noah's ark or Bible games. Making scrapbooks devoted to religious themes was also a popular Sunday-afternoon pastime.

"Sunday ought to be the most cheerful, sunniest, happiest and best day of the week in every home," the 1893 Victorian book *Sundays with the Children* declared. Unfortunately, the author of this book conceded that in many homes Sunday was "the dullest and most dreary day of the week to the children and the most taxing and the most wearying to the parents, especially to the mother." However, the author felt that with the proper attitude and planning, parents could make the Lord's day a refreshing interlude of rest and renewal.

Today, Sunday is still very often the only day that families can count on being together. And while many contemporary families still attend Sunday services regularly, they are less likely than their Victorian ancestors to devote the entire day so rigorously to activities of a religious nature.

Mrs. Sharp believes, however, that there is a significant difference between reverence and religion. Furthermore, there is much to be said about setting Sundays apart from the rest of the week. Certainly modern families need whatever time they can carve out to refresh their spirit. Making Sunday a special day for nurturing family togetherness is an old-fashioned way to renew the bonds of affection. Toward this end, Mrs. Sharp suggests that families accept the challenge of trying not to do household chores on Sunday but to elevate the day by sharing some special time together. An excursion to a wonderful new art exhibition or a Sunday saunter out in the country enjoying the sunshine, fresh air, and the company of our loved ones is much more renewing to everyone's spirit than a trip

Scripture Cake

1 cup Psalms 55:21 (2 sticks butter)

1 cup Jeremiah 6:20 (sugar)

3 Jeremiah 17:11 (eggs)

1 tablespoon I Samuel 14:25 (honey)

½ cup Judges 4:19 (milk)

2¼ cups Leviticus 6:15 (flour)

1 tablespoon Amos 4:5 (baking powder)

2 teaspoons II Chronicles 9:9 (spice mixture:
   1 teaspoon cinnamon, 1 teaspoon nutmeg)

A pinch Leviticus 2:13 (salt)

1½ cups I Samuel 30:12 (raisins)

1 cup Numbers 13:23 (chopped figs)

½ cup Numbers 17:8 (chopped almonds)

Preheat oven to 350°. Butter and flour a loaf pan.

Many Victorian versions of Scripture cake end by advising cooks to blend together and follow King Solomon's advice for rearing a well-behaved child, found in Proverbs 23:14—or, to translate, "beat well."

In a large bowl, cream the butter (an electric beater works well) until light, beating in the sugar a tablespoon at a time until fluffy. Add eggs, one at a time, beating well. Stir in honey and milk. Sift together the dry ingredients: flour, salt, baking powder, and spices. Gradually add the dry ingredients to the butter mixture, blending until thoroughly mixed. Stir in the raisins, figs, and almonds.

Turn mixture in baking pan. Bake for 50 minutes.

to a crowded discount department store for this week's sale. Yes, dear Reader, we all need to do that occasionally, but do we have to do it on Sunday? Can't we make an effort to find diversions that lift our families' morale with laughter and happy memories?

At Mrs. Sharp's, we enjoy seasonal outings on Sunday, followed by a special family dinner. About once a month we also enjoy inviting family and friends to Sunday afternoon tea, a perfect time for relaxed entertaining. After a hectic workweek, Mrs. Sharp finds it particularly pleasurable to putter in the kitchen on Sunday afternoons, listening to opera and experimenting with new recipes that the family will later feast on.

When the family has friends over for Sunday afternoon tea, one Victorian teatime favorite is Scripture cake, a delicious confection made only from ingredients mentioned in the Bible. Victorian homemakers, who were expected to know their Bible as well as their cookbooks, had to decipher the mysterious ingredients, but Mrs. Sharp will help you out!

Birthdays

Most Victorian adults were hopelessly sentimental when it came to children, particularly their own. Nowhere is this largesse more evident than in how the Victorians celebrated their children's birthdays. Even parents who practiced "moderation in all things" the rest of the year were known to indulge in birthday extravaganzas: lavish juvenile tea parties, followed by special entertainment such as a magic lantern, Punch-and-Judy puppet shows, or conjuring-trick performances. Next came a series of elaborate party games or dancing until the overwhelmed birthday child erupted into torrents of "too much birthday," signaling the event's successful conclusion.

In fact, so widespread was the notion a century ago that a child's birthday party was to be an example of excelsior in excess that in 1889, *Cassell's Book of the Household* felt compelled to comment: "People who give children's parties, very often seem to forget that the object of the entertainment is to give the children pleasure in a sensible way, so that they and their parents do not suffer for it afterward. If children are kept up beyond their usual bedtime, although for a short time they enjoy the idea that they are staying up late, that enjoyment only lasts a very little while, and they soon begin to feel cross and tired. If they are given rich food, they are sure to be upset the next day, and cause worry and trouble to themselves and others . . ."

Mrs. Sharp believes that one of the reasons that the Victorians went overboard on birthdays was because of their tenuous hold on life. In the prevaccination era, when children's mortality rates were fifty percent, we were genuinely thrilled to know that our children had made it to another birthday, and this was cause for great celebration.

Today's parents often indulge at birthday time for another reason: guilt. With so many mothers working outside the home, trying to make sure that our child has a memorable birthday party is a tangible way to assuage that nagging sense that somehow we neglect her the rest of the year. We don't, of course, but this burden, coupled with a genuine lack of time and the fervent desire to "give" our children as exciting a birthday party as their little friends had, often means we go against our better judgment—with the resulting party ending in exhaustion, great expense, and great sighs of relief that the ordeal is over for another year.

Still, there should be a way for us to create memorable and meaningful birthdays for our children. Next to Christmas Eve, there isn't another day in the entire year as special. As any parent can attest, birthdays are vital reference points for a child's growing sense of self-esteem. Children have such high hopes for an upcoming birthday—how can we live up to their expectations? After a century of celebrating children's birthdays, Mrs. Sharp believes she's discovered some ways that can help you create a day your child will fondly remember all year long.

A Birthday Worth Remembering

The first suggestion is to return the focus of the birthday to your child, taking it off the birthday party for your child's friends. This can be done by giving a modest birthday party on the weekend before or after a birthday (if it occurs during the week). Then on the child's actual birthday, celebrate the happy anniversary at home from dawn to dusk. The essence of our celebration: You are an important member of our family, we love you, and our lives would not be the same without you!

For instance, at Mrs. Sharp's house, the birthday celebration traditionally starts with a visit during the night from the birthday fairy, who leaves a much-desired gift at the foot of the child's bed. This excitement is followed by a festive breakfast complete with coffee cake and candles. By draping and securing silk cloth over a chair, we create a special "throne" for the birthday child, who gets to wear a special gold crown at all family meals.

In our dining room, Mrs. Sharp's seasonal table has been completely redecorated during the night, and all the child's gifts and cards are piled there awaiting her. Since opening just one or two presents at a time also increases the pleasure for a young child, Mrs. Sharp parcels out the gifts throughout the day.

Other small celebratory touches include packing a birthday cupcake in the school lunch box and letting the birthday child choose her favorite foods for dinner. There is also a dispensation from all chores on birthdays.

Finally, after a wonderful candlelight feast, family members also present the birthday child with a gift of themselves: We all prepare recitations in the child's honor describing how the child has grown or what special accomplishments he or she has achieved during the year. This "presentation" is done while we are enjoying birthday cake.

This homegrown family celebration of birthdays, which has evolved over the years, has given our children many precious memories. Creating your own family traditions for birthdays is a gift of love your children will never outgrow.

Difficult Days:
Crisscross and Convalescence

Into the life of every child comes a broken cup. On an ordinary day the broken cup will be a piece of kitchen crockery. On a crisscross day, Mother, the cup will be from your beloved antique English-porcelain tea set.

Crisscross days are not sent to try our patience, dear Reader, but to stretch our souls. We must humbly ask for grace to get through them. They also require us to realize our limitations.

If there's one thing Mrs. Sharp has learned about child-rearing, it is that whenever we are tired, worried, distracted, or not feeling well and need the children to behave, they will be at their worst. Their little antennae pick up loud and clear the signals that we're not really there for them. They then become determined to get our attention, one way or another. Usually, it's the other way that succeeds.

Crisscross currents can strike at any hour, although often they begin first thing in the morning and continue their downward spiral until an explosion of screams, tantrums, and tears clears the air. If by ten o'clock in the morning the echo of your own voice rings in your ears, Mrs. Sharp suggests you stop whatever it is you are doing (you're not going to get it done anyway today, so you might as well give in gracefully), sequester and separate the children, and send them to

their rooms to play quietly or allow them to watch television or videos. (Even Mrs. Sharp knows when she is licked.) What you are trying to do is carve out an important half hour for mother's R and R: retreat and regrouping. Put on the kettle and have a cup of tea, turn on soothing music, sit down, and take a few deep breaths. Crisscross days can be gotten under control as soon as we realize we're having one. They escalate in intensity only if we ignore the warning signs.

After you have restored your equilibrium, take the children into your confidence. Gather your young ones in your lap or sit with the children on the sofa and look at them lovingly. Explain to them, speaking softly and slowly (a change from just a little while ago), that you are having a "crisscross" day, and no matter what the hour, tell them everyone's going to start the day all over again. Give them a kiss and say, "Good morning!" At Mrs. Sharp's house she has made a tradition of having a pancake supper on a crisscross day to symbolize that she can always start over and begin anew. Finally, in order to erase any lingering effects from a crisscross day, Mrs. Sharp always apologizes for her part and asks the children's forgiveness. She then asks them if they are sorry for anything, and, of course, they are. Remember, dear Reader, it always takes at least two to create a crisscross day. We make up with hugs and kisses all around and start over again.

Difficult days are really blessings in disguise, for they always bring us closer together with the realization that when there is love at home, we experience heaven on earth.

The Land of Counterpane

When I was sick and lay a-bed,
I had two pillows at my head,
And all my toys beside me lay
To keep me happy all the day.
—Robert Louis Stevenson

When a child is sick and confined to bed, special soothing traditions are needed—ones that comfort, amuse, and distract. First of all, there is nothing so important as a parent's presence with a sick child. A parent's loving care can create an atmosphere of peace and serenity, which fosters recovery by offering a child a sense of security.

After a child has recovered enough to be interested in amusing diversions but not well enough to resume a normal routine, having a retinue of special treats set aside that are enjoyed only when a child is "under the weather" can make the experience memorable. One of Mrs. Sharp's traditions for convalescence includes letting the girls wear Mama's pink satin bed jacket, and the boys Papa's old, soft smoking jacket. Mrs. Sharp also brings her jewelry box to the sickbed for her daughter to carefully examine and then wear Mama's jewels (Mrs. Sharp has only costume jewelry, dear Reader, but her few baubles might as well be the crown jewels since the children are forbidden to touch Mrs. Sharp's box at any other time). Sick day surprises also include a box containing favorite books, games, and puzzles that were Mama's and Papa's when they were children, and old family albums that are brought out only when someone is confined to bed. Mrs. Sharp isn't quite sure how that tradition started, but the custom was comforting and provided the children with a happy diversion, so it stuck. Part of the ritual includes Mother sitting in the room with her sewing while the child looks through the album, so that there can be a running commentary on all the relatives.

Mrs. Sharp also putters around the sick child's room keeping it tidy. Children's spirits are lifted in a clean bedroom, and frequently just the act of picking up the clutter a sick child's room collects cheers them immensely. Mother brings extra-fluffy pillows to the sickbed, smooths the bedcovers, and makes the child comfortable every couple of hours. Mrs. Sharp also places a small table beside the bed, which holds a small silver bell for the child to ring if he needs something; the table is the perfect spot for a glass of juice, a fresh box of tissues, and a small vase with flowers. Nearby there is also a small waste-paper basket for discards.

Occasionally a child is too sick to come to the dinner table, and when this occurs, Mrs. Sharp gets out her best silver serving tray. As well as trying to make the meal appetizing, serving it with flourish— on a pretty china plate with a crystal goblet and crisp, white linen napkin—creates a special ceremony that pampers our convalescent. When one is sick, it really is the small touches that count the most. Reassuring rituals that say "I love you" are frequently just the remedy sick children respond to best.

The Joy and Comfort

January cold desolate;
February all dripping wet;
March wind ranges;
April changes;
Birds sing in tune to flowers of May;
And sunny June brings the longest day;
In scorched July the storm clouds fly;
Lightning-torn August bears corn;
September fruit;
In rough October earth must disrobe her;
Stars fall and shoot in keen November;
And night is long
And cold is strong in bleak December.

—Christina Georgina Rossetti, 1830—1894

Often many parents feel at a loss as to how to bring their families closer together. May Mrs. Sharp be of assistance? One of the easiest ways to start is by letting Mother Nature assist Mother Mortal in this regard. There is a rich resource of home-centered rituals readily available to you in the recurring chronicle of the seasons and calendar holidays. Each month lends itself to creating new family customs from a rich tapestry of Victorian pastimes. All you need is a calendar, a little planning, and gentle direction. Introducing seasonal

· JAN · | · FEB · | · MAR · | · APR · | · MAY · | · JUN

# of Seasonal Pastimes

pleasures into your repertoire of home-circle activities can ease the family into the celebrating spirit, naturally, albeit in an organized manner.

So please join Mrs. Sharp as we take a walk through the year with a Victorian family. Travel with us back in time to 1899. The warm, old-fashioned celebrations and traditions of yesteryear can be revived and adapted to modern family life. You will be delighted to discover that what worked a century ago to bring a family closer together—the joy and comfort of homebred, hearthside pastimes—still works today.

I remember, I remember
How my childhood fleeted by,
The mirth of its December
And the warmth of its July . . .

—W. M. Praed

JUL • AUG • SEP • OCT • NOV • DEC

JANUARY.

Happy New Year, dear friends! As we listen to the bells ring out the old year and ring in the new while the clock strikes twelve, let's hug our loved ones tightly before beginning our walk through a Victorian family's year together. First we'll attend a Victorian New Year's Day open house and then we'll amuse ourselves with cozy Home-Circle Pastimes.

Like the two-faced Roman god, Janus, who was supposed to be the doorkeeper of heaven and for whom the first month of the year is named, most of us during January try to forecast what the future holds as well as look back on the past. Yet after a century of anticipating coming days and reflecting on those that have passed away, Mrs. Sharp has finally learned it is making the most of the present moments we spend with our families that brings us the greatest joy. Always remember, dear friends, today is the tomorrow you wished for yesterday.

January might seem bleak after the bright lights of Christmas and Chanukah. But Mrs. Sharp believes this season of King Jack Frost offers families enriching opportunities for "getting to know you" with both healthy outdoor pursuits and relaxed indoor pleasures.

century ago New Year's afternoon, rather than the night before, was the time for gala entertaining and celebration in the form of New Year's Day open houses. Tradition held that all the ladies of a family (and all boys under the age of ten) remained at home to receive callers while the gentlemen went out to pay visits.

During the 1870s in large cities, it was fashionable for bachelors to make rounds of New Year's Day calls to the homes of eligible young ladies. Newspapers even printed lists of the homes that would be open and the hours they were receiving visitors. The only requirement for admission was a calling card. The young man would be introduced to the eligible women of the household, under the watchful eyes of parents and assorted relatives, before being encouraged to partake of the lavish refreshments.

Not surprisingly, the custom quickly became sport. Young men would try to rack up as many as fifty calls a day (being more interested in becoming intoxicated than in meeting their hosts' eligible daughters), and young women would eagerly collect calling cards as if they were butterfly specimens. By the late 1880s, the hospitality of the day had so been abused that opening up one's house on New Year's Day to strangers was snuffed out by social disapproval. During the 1890s, however, the tradition of New Year's Day open houses evolved into "family calls" and receptions for invited guests only. After World War I, the custom of New Year's Day "calling" virtually disappeared and New Year's Eve parties increased in popularity.

Mrs. Sharp's earliest recollection of New Year's goes back to her own Victorian childhood.

She recalls being abruptly awakened from a sound sleep by the clamoring of bells, booming cannons, and the blowing of whistles. As she raced out of bed and ran into the hallway, she expected to hear Papa's voice bellowing "Fire!" However, that New Year's Eve all she met was Mama on the landing, gently sending her various children back to bed. As Mother tucked little Victorianna snugly underneath the covers, she explained that all the noise was the baby New Year come to call. Since Mrs. Sharp's knowledge (at that time) of babies was limited to her younger brother, who did indeed make quite a lot of noise, it made perfect sense that the New Year babe would also make such a racket upon coming into the world.

What didn't make sense, however, was the hustle and bustle throughout the house the following morning. The long dining room table was laid out with a sumptuous and tempting array of food and drink, which the children were forbidden to touch, not to mention taste. Upstairs all the girls were starched, sashed, and beribboned while the boys protested loudly (but to no avail) as they were buttoned into the requisite new salt-and-pepper Norfolk suits received as Christmas presents from Grandmama.

For Mrs. Sharp's older sisters, however, New Year's Day was a thrilling event. As they curled their hair, powdered their noses, and laced themselves into tight corsets, she was reassured that someday, when it was "her" turn, she'd understand what all the excitement was about.

Mrs. Sharp must admit that by the time she was old enough to appreciate the tradition of New Year's Day, the custom was enthralling. Perhaps the most memorable New Year's Day was in 1885, just after she had turned twenty. That year, a shy but very handsome young clerk in her father's law office, who had just moved to Washington, came to pay his compliments. She has his card still. His name was Mr. Edmund Sharp. Today, of course, there are many people who enjoy going to and hosting New Year's Day open houses. But our family now prefers to stay home, reflecting with anticipation on the days ahead. "A good beginning makes a good ending," an old adage advises, so we try to start the New Year off in a peaceful but happy frame of mind.

We also wait to receive a visit from a special guest, Dame Fortune, who might pass by if we're out and who never leaves a calling card. She always comes laden with gifts—blank calendars full of endless possibilities: 365 mornings and evenings, fifty-two fresh weeks, four new seasons with their cherished pastimes, and another twelve months full of holidays and ample opportunities for memory making. To celebrate, Mrs. Sharp's tradition is a present of brightly wrapped calendars for each family member. The calendars have been "left" on the front doorstep and are usually discovered by the children just before supper.

Then we enjoy a traditional Southern New Year's Day dinner of baked country ham, corn bread, and "Hoppin' John," a dish that has appeared on the New Year's Day tables of both rich and poor for over a century. Tradition tells us each ingredient ensures our good fortune—the black-eyed peas, luck; the rice, health; and the collard greens, prosperity.

THE CUSTOM OF VICTORIAN CALLING

Of late, it has become fashionable, for ladies in many cities and villages, to announce in newspapers the fact of their intention to receive calls upon New Year's Day, which practice enables gentlemen to know who will receive them. . . .

"Upon calling, the gentlemen are invited to remove overcoat and hat, which invitation is accepted unless it is the design to make the call very brief. . . . Gloves are sometimes retained upon the hand during the call. . . . Cards are sent up and the gentlemen are ushered into the reception room. The call should not exceed ten or fifteen minutes, unless the callers are free and it should be mutually agreeable to prolong the stay. . . .

"The two or three days succeeding the New Year's are ladies' days for calling, upon which occasion they comment upon . . . the new faces that made their appearance among the visitors. It is customary upon this occasion of ladies meeting, to offer refreshments and to enjoy the intimacy of a friendly visit. This fashion of observing New Year's Day is often the means of commencing pleasant friendships which may continue through life."

—*Hill's Manual of Social and Business Forms, 1880*

January Joys

Winter is upon us, dear Reader, and we are shut in from all the world, cozy and warm around the hearth. Outside Mrs. Sharp's window, the earth is tucked in under a blanket of white. Down the lane, the stone walls look as if they are topped with baked meringue instead of snow. Occasionally, icy branches brush against the streaked, bubbly glass windowpanes covered with frost flowers and ferns. Last night the snowfall was heavy, so this morning huge snowdrifts cover the road and crest in the fields like frozen ocean waves. It will be a while before the road is cleared enough to hear even the jingle of sleigh bells. All that we hear is the soliloquy of silence. Nature is resting today.

So are we. All living creatures need rest and renewal, especially mothers. The comforting rhythm of slow winter days affords us this rest, and the new-fallen snow provides our family with the perfect opportunity to pause and take stock of our home life.

One of the reasons Mrs. Sharp loves the month of January is that no matter what the weather is like outside—crystal clear and sunny or lead gray with sleet pelting the window—inside The Vicarage the fire at hearthside is constant—bright, crackling, and warm. I believe that our spirits are the same. Outward circumstances, the stress of hectic modern living colliding with the priorities of work and home, may batter and weary us, but if there is peace and tranquillity in the home, we, too, can find respite to weather the storms of life.

Since the family will spend so much time together in the parlor in the coming months, we gather together some of the games, books, and supplies we'll be using in the weeks to come. Now we are ready for winter's pleasures—spending our days by the fire, reading, sewing, working on handicrafts, playing games, and sipping tea and hot cocoa. Later the children will go out to play in the snow. The boys will build snow forts, and the girls, snow cottages. Later in the afternoon the children will cut out paper snowflakes or play board games. Tonight we'll have a taffy pull.

So come celebrate with our family the fun and warmth of hearth and home during the long, dark nights and crystal-cold days of winter as we explore together the old-fashioned arts of housebound amusement and the simply abundant pleasures of winter days.

January.

K.Pyle.

The shrill wind blew about the house
 And through the pines all night :
The snowflakes whirled across the fields
 And hid the fence from sight .

By dawn the drifts had blown so deep
 No horse nor sleigh could go :
The dog-house and the chicken-coops
 Were buried in the snow .

There was no thought of school that day ;
 We worked with shovels all ,
And cleared a path from house to barn ;
 The snow was like a wall .

I wished our house was covered up,
 Like that one in the book
My Grandma showed to me one day
 Beside the chimney-nook .

The story said the chimney-pot
 Just showed above the snow ,
And all day long the lamps were lit
 Down in the house below .

Home-Circle Pastimes

Probably the most frustrating aspect of our hectic modern life is that busy families rarely see their nearest and dearest, never mind spend enjoyable, memory-making time together.

The remedy: Set aside some special time for the family.

This was not a problem for families during the Victorian era, of course. Every evening after supper, we retired to the front parlor to enjoy the pleasures of home-circle evenings.

You might ask: What's so old-fashioned about this tradition, Mrs. Sharp? We also spend every evening together in the living room.

Yes, dear Reader, but with the television off? Please do not panic. Mrs. Sharp will hold your hand through the withdrawal stage. She'll even suggest what your family could be doing together instead of watching television.

It's called having fun. Victorian families had an abundance of popular parlor amusements, or "fireside pastimes," for their entertainment. For example, in her book *Home Amusements,* written in 1881, Mrs. M. E. Sherwood declared that there were a "thousand and one devices by which the modern family can amuse itself." Among the most popular: a wide assortment of board games; fortune-telling, magic, or conjuring tricks; "brain games" (riddles and word puzzles); musicales, theatricals, charades, and "the most artistic of all Home Amusements—the *Tableau vivant,"* or living pictures, a diversion in which a group would act out a famous painting or scene while onlookers would guess what it was.

Popular parlor pastimes also included visual entertainments such as the zoetrope (a spinning viewfinder that gave the appearance of animation), the handheld stereoscope (a picture-viewing device that displayed two photographs taken at different angles in order to produce a three-dimensional effect), and the magic lantern, an early projector that beamed pictures onto a wall from transparent color slides.

While it is unlikely that modern children will be as transfixed as Victorian youngsters at the thought of an evening peering through a stereoscope imagining they are on a trip through the Sahara Desert, there are a number of amusements that retain the power to charm contemporary children. A favorite Victorian family winter-evening pastime that has withstood the test of time is a taffy pull.

An Old-Fashioned Taffy Pull

One family night in January at Mrs. Sharp's is always reserved for an old-fashioned taffy pull. Care to join us? Fear not, dear Reader: It is not as bad as you imagine. Messy, yes. But the pleasure and delight we all experience make a taffy pull a wonderful winter tradition.

Here's how to do it: In a large saucepan combine 1¼ cups light brown sugar, 2 tablespoons mild white vinegar, and 2 tablespoons butter. Stir once and bring the mixture to a quick boil. Let the mixture continue to boil until it registers 270° on a candy thermometer, then add ½ teaspoon vanilla. Pour onto a large greased platter and wait five minutes or until the taffy is cool enough to handle.

Next, don aprons and smocks. Grease everyone's hands with butter. Poke a hole into the taffy with your finger; if it stays put, you're ready to begin. Roll the taffy into a ball. Form two teams of helpers and start pulling, but don't let the taffy break. Roll the taffy into a ball again and pull. Repeat this process at least five times or until the taffy is light and firm. Stretch it into a twisted rope, cut into small pieces, and enjoy!

Now, who says your family doesn't stick together?

Board Games

oys for Victorian children were viewed as tools intended to both amuse and instruct our "rising generation." Board games, in particular, were recommended as "healthful, home-circle pursuits" because they imparted gentle moral instruction and often religious training under the guise of diversion.

Toys have also always been accurate social barometers of a society's preoccupations. For example, during the Civil War, board games took on a military flavor, such as Union Games; during the 1880s, with the rise of the affluent middle class, a game of banking and commerce known as the Monopolist was extremely popular (and preceded Monopoly by more than half a century).

The first American board game was the Mansion of Happiness, which appeared in 1843. The object of this game was to teach our young ones the difference between good and naughty behavior. So in the game, young players landing on the squares representing virtues, such as "gratitude" and "honesty," moved more quickly to their goal: the Mansion of Happiness. Bad children, on the other hand, quickly learned that naughtiness never pays—or at the very least doesn't aid in winning games. It's a valuable lesson for children of all ages.

THE MANSION OF HAPPINESS.

Mrs. Sharp is particularly keen on board games as a way to draw families closer, for playing together provides some of our fondest memories. The dynamics of board games also make them fascinating windows for viewing the people who make up our family. Amid the laughter and good cheer, the oldsters can gain valuable insights into their youngsters' personalities, children gain a glimmer of their parents' limitations, and everyone creates memories of home: a mansion of happiness.

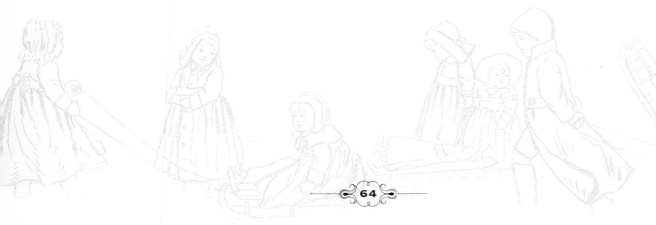

The Treasures of the Snow

Hast thou entered into the treasure
of the snow?
Or hast thou seen the treasures
of the hail?
—*Book of Job*

Outside, the snow provides opportunities for old-fashioned family entertainment. All Mrs. Sharp's children were extremely inventive with their snow creations, thanks to the help they received from two well-loved and dog-eared Victorian volumes known as the "Handy Books." Fortunately, there are now contemporary reprints of these nineteenth-century children's classics. By dipping into them your family can take a nostalgic trip back to those halcyon days when children could happily occupy themselves for hours with seasonal pastimes and diversions of their own creation.

The American Boy's Handy Book: What to Do and How to Do It was written by Daniel Beard, one of the founders of the Boy Scouts of America. Considered the quintessential guide to boyhood since 1882, this manual directs seasonal activities from unraveling the mysteries of homemade fishing tackle in the spring to the how-tos of sleigh making, snowball warfare, and Tom Thumb iceboats in winter.

Its companion volume is *The American Girl's Handy Book: How to Amuse Yourself and Others,* written by Daniel Beard's two very talented sisters, Lina and Adelia Beard. First published in 1887, its seasonal suggestions of games, decorations, projects, party ideas, and amusements have withstood the test of time.

However, one of Mrs. Sharp's children's favorite snow activities takes place before a roaring fire. It's when Mother serves a Victorian child's snow luncheon in the front parlor: tomato soup, grilled cheese sandwiches, snowman salad, cocoa with whipped cream, and snow ice cream. To make snowman salad, take tinned pear halves and cover with cottage cheese. Add raisins for eyes, nose, and mouth, carrot shavings for hair, and breadsticks for arms. For old-fashioned cocoa, gently warm milk over a low flame. For each cup of milk add 1 tablespoon "real" cocoa, and 2 tablespoons granulated sugar, stirring constantly until the cocoa mixture simmers to the desired temperature, hot but not boiling. Pour into pretty china cups and top generously with freshly whipped cream and chocolate shavings.

For snow ice cream, take 1 cup milk, 1 teaspoon vanilla, and ½ cup sugar. Beat well until frothy. Place mixture in a large bowl and add enough clean, fresh snow until the liquid is completely absorbed by the snow. This delicious concoction will have the consistency of sherbet.

After the children have had their luncheon, for an amusing afternoon's diversion, have everyone create Victorian paper snowflakes.

The Seasonal Table

Victorian families let the four seasons weave the fabric of their family life together in harmony and creativity with handicraft projects to beautify their home.

Nothing of Mother Nature's was wasted or overlooked. Walks in the woods resulted in a bounty of seed pods, moss, grasses, nuts, twigs, and leaves with which to create seasonal handicrafts. Trips to the seashore meant an abundant assortment of seashells for display, as well as the raw materials for such novelties as a set of sea-urchin candlesticks or a clever catchall for mail and newspapers made from a discarded horseshoe crab shell.

Victorian families excelled at the art of creating seasonal "tablescapes," displayed on sideboards, in wall-hung shadow boxes, or in glass-domed decorative pieces. "We have been into rooms which, by the simple disposition of articles of this kind," Catharine Beecher and Harriet Beecher Stowe observed in *The American Woman's Home,* "made the air so poetical and attractive that they seemed more like a nymph's cave than anything in the real world."

Modern families will also enjoy the Victorian custom of bringing the four seasons indoors. A wonderful way to begin is with Mrs. Sharp's tradition of a Seasonal Table. This is a small, permanent table in the dining room that reflects, through the objects we choose to display on it, our personal walk through the year together as a family.

The focal point of Mrs. Sharp's Seasonal Table is our family's Seasonal Tree, upon which we hang a wondrous assortment of seasonal ornaments. The Seasonal Table is also the place where the children display treasures they discover, such as pretty stones, a bird's feather, or a few wildflowers, perhaps waxed to preserve their beauty all year long.

The Seasonal Table is the simplest of activities. Yet because it allows the scope of your imagination and creativity free rein, it can also become a highly sophisticated and satisfying work of art. You will also be delighted as your family's enthusiasm for and contributions to their Seasonal Table grow over the months and years.

Besides being an enchanting tradition, the Seasonal Table helps the children develop a sense of the year's rhythms and an appreciation of the four seasons. We know that there will be paper snowflakes and evergreen branches in winter; pussy willows and a bird's nest in spring; seashells in summer and autumn leaves displayed in the fall. Most of all, this adapted Victorian custom gives the family a permanent focal point for ceremony and celebrating.

Come what may, our family's beloved Seasonal Table reflects what is happening at the Sharp household, and its magic will work wonders in your home as well.

MRS. SHARP'S SEASONAL TREE

A Seasonal Tree is a wonderful project for the family to work on together. First you will need to gather together (either from outdoors or a craft shop) wild grapevines; you need approximately twelve yards of grapevines for an eighteen-inch cone-shaped tree. Be sure to soak them for at least forty-eight hours so that they will be pliable and easy to work with. Next take a two-foot-by-three-foot rectangular piece of chicken wire and wrap it into a tight cone shape. Secure it in place with florist's wire.

Beginning at the base of the tree, loop a piece of the wet vine into the chicken wire and wrap it tightly around the base. Continue in this manner, tucking the ends inside the tree through the holes, until all of the chicken wire has been covered by vines. Secure the vines at the base of the tree to the chicken wire with thin florist's wire. Let your tree dry completely in a warm spot in the house; in winter this might take four or five days.

You know how much the family looks forward to trimming the Christmas tree, dear Reader. Well, with Mrs. Sharp's Seasonal Tree, the fun lasts all year long as our decorations change seasonally. Mrs. Sharp uses a basic decoration of thin silk ribbon (the colors depend upon the season), baby's breath (glycerin-preserved baby's breath works best), and tiny seasonal ornaments, which are hung on the grapevine tendrils or tucked in around the tree.

The real fun for everyone begins when we add dollhouse miniatures to create seasonal scenes. Available at hobby and craft shops, these miniatures mirror real life with an astonishing range of accessories (from birthday cakes to tiny seasonal delights such as carved jack-o'-lanterns) all made to a one-inch scale.

Starting with just a few pieces at a time, you will be amazed at how quickly your collection grows. It can even become a tradition for each family member to add one miniature per season. (For safety's sake, do not use dollhouse miniatures with children in the house under the age of three.) Your family will also enjoy making some of their ornaments. Just keep the size of the objects you select in proportion to the tree; almost anything under two inches works well.

For some suggestions to get you started, here's how Mrs. Sharp's Seasonal Tree evolves during the year:

Winter: White tissue-paper snowflakes, "winter" miniatures, ice-blue and silver silk ribbons. For Valentine's Day, assorted fabric, wooden, and paper heart ornaments; Victorian "scrap" pictures of cupids, doves, and flowers; red and pink silk ribbons.

Spring: Tiny green paper shamrocks for St. Patrick's Day, then Easter miniatures. Pussy willow stems tucked into the tree; soft pastel-colored silk ribbons. After Easter, tiny gardening tools, seed boxes, and flowers.

Summer: Striped red-white-and-blue ribbons, tiny American flags, picnic miniatures, assorted small seashells, vacation mementos, flowers, and fruit.

Autumn: Miniatures of Indian corn, jack-o'-lanterns, tiny trick-or-treat bags, and school days' mementos. Next, dried golden yarrow, tiny autumn leaves, pinecones, and wheat stalks. Finally, our tree is topped with silk ribbon streamers in rust, beige, and gold.

Christmas: Tiny clear twinkle lights, inserted through the chicken-wire holes in the frame of the tree so that the cord is disguised. Red, green, and gold silk cords wrapped around the tree in four places. Sprigs of holly, mistletoe, evergreens. At the top, a gold-painted wooden star glued onto a florist's pick. Add an assortment of miniature Christmas ornaments—one each day during Advent.

Birthdays: The night before a child's birthday, the "birthday fairy" redecorates our tree with miniatures of wrapped packages, balloons, a "Happy Birthday" banner, and birthday cake.

VICTORIAN PAPER SNOWFLAKES

efore the children begin to make their snowflakes, an adult or an older sibling should cut out a hexagon template from cardboard. The hexagon can then be used to trace all the paper snowflakes. Mrs. Sharp suggests you cut out a number of these cardboard patterns so that each child can have one.

Give each child a piece of white drawing paper and have him or her trace around the pattern with a pencil, then cut it out. Using white tissue paper will also give you a pretty effect. Next, direct the children to fold it in the following way: Place the paper hexagon so that a horizontal edge will be toward the front of the table; fold the front edge to the back one. Leave it thus and make a fold by turning the lower right-hand corner up to the upper left-hand corner. Next, make another fold by turning the lower left-hand corner up to the upper right-hand corner. If you have followed these directions carefully, your paper will be in the form of an equal-sided triangle. There will be six of these triangles lying on top of one another.

On the top triangle, draw in your design—anything you like. Just be sure the design is uniform and the "cuts" do not come to the center of the snowflake, where the triangles are joined.

Next cut out your designs. When you unfold your triangles, the children will delight in the variety of shapes of "snowflakes" they have created; mount them on colored paper. For a winter still life, suspend a dozen tissue-paper snowflakes on thread from twig branches planted in a pot of sand and place on your Seasonal Table.

Love to my Valentine

February arrives outside The Vicarage cold, wet, and gray. Some days it feels as if all the world is hibernating and that spring will never come. But the days are short and so is the month. When the sun shines, we take walks outside to look for our shadows. How many more weeks of winter?

Being an incurable optimist, Mrs. Sharp likes to think that spring is on the way soon as she spots "February's fair maids," the tiny snowdrop flowers pushing their way up through the frozen earth. With the holidays long gone, the young people in our house are alert for new amusements. What does February have in store for the family? Fireside pastimes such as candle dipping, making patriotic desserts, and crafting homemade valentines. Come join us!

February.

Sunsets red and quiet air ;
Ponds are ice and trees are bare ;
Fields are frozen far and near ;
February days are here .
Bitter cold the night draws down
On the country and the town ,
But in cheerful warmth we sit ,
And the nursery lamp is lit .

Then, when mother stops our play ,
Father puts his book away
And he makes upon the wall
Shadow pictures for us all .
There a rabbit wags its ears
Or a grinning face appears
Or a swan with feathered wings
Ships and many other things ;
Last of all a night-capped head
Then we know it's time for bed .

K. Pyle .

Candlemas Day

Pleasant wit, and harmless fun,
And a dance when day is done,
Music friends so true and tried,
Whispered love by warm fireside,
Mirth at all times together
Make sweet May of Winter weather.
—Alfred Dommett, 1811—1887

For Victorian families, the second of February, or Candlemas Day, was the traditional ending of the holiday season, calling for the removal of every last trace of Christmas decorations. This custom was centuries old.

As well on this day, midway through winter, it was also customary for the lady of the house to make an inventory of the family's supply of candles to see if there were enough to last through the remaining dark nights. It was hoped that by this time one need not still get up by candlelight in the morning. However, if a family's supply of candles had begun to run low, this, then, was the day to replenish it.

All children love candles. They also enjoy candle making once they are introduced to this old-fashioned pastime, which is a lovely activity to do together as a family on Candlemas Day.

At first the thought of dipping your own candles may seem daunting, but like most Victorian pastimes all it really requires, besides the proper supplies, is patience and enthusiasm.

First the fragrant beeswax is melted, then strips of candle wicking are carefully lowered or dipped into the wax, quickly lifted out, allowed to dry, then dipped again. Slowly and rhythmically, like a dance, the candle begins to take shape.

Besides being fun, candle making is a cooperative venture; as the family becomes a candle-making crew working together, there is harmony and unity. Finally, after time and effort—and much anticipation, which always adds to the enjoyment—the finished candle appears. Yet the end product—a beautiful lighted taper—is merely a reflection of the joy and pleasure you and your children have experienced crafting together.

An easy way to celebrate Candlemas Day is to gather as many candles as possible, then light them throughout the house for a festive and spectacular evening. For fun, and to help the children imagine what it was like to grow up long ago, try not to use any electric lights. To have candles reflect more light throughout the house, place them before mirrors. Enjoy a candlelit dinner together and be sure to read a short story before bedtime by candlelight. Another favorite Candlemas tradition in Mrs. Sharp's house: Each child selects one special candle; when the candle burns down, it's time for bed!

While candle dipping is relatively simple, it can be dangerous for small children because the process involves hot wax. Mrs. Sharp suggests that little ones make their candles by rolling a sheet of beeswax around a wick—the result is always wonderful.

Both candle-dipping and candle-rolling kits with full instructions are available in large craft supply stores.

Glancing Back

How Candlemas Got Its Name

Following Jewish tradition, on the fortieth day after a woman gave birth she would go to the Temple to present her child to the Lord. Candlemas Day was the day—February 2—that the Holy Family visited the Temple in Jerusalem with the newborn Christ Child. A prophet named Simeon saw Jesus there and declared the baby to be "the light of the world." Hence, it became traditional to bless the liturgical candles that would be used throughout the year.

The time-honoured epoch for taking down Christmas decorations from church and house is Candlemas Day, February 2nd. Terribly withered they are by that time. Candlemas in old times represented the end of the Christmas holidays, which were far longer than they are now. . . .

It is found desirable now, in many houses, to remove [Christmas greens] after Twelfth Day, January 6th (the Epiphany); and by that time they are quite dusty and dirty enough, and everybody (except the children) are tired of holiday-making, and ready to return to the sober business of life.

—*Cassell's Book of the Household, 1889*

Lincoln Logs and Cherry Pies:
Celebrating Patriotic Holidays with Children

*D*ear Reader, do you know what the twelfth of February is? At Mrs. Sharp's house, it is the day she serves Lincoln's log for dessert. Do you know what February 22 is? It is when our family enjoys luscious Washington pie together. Yours should, too.

WASHINGTON TAKING COMMAND OF THE ARMY.

In most American homes during the Victorian era, families observed the birthdays of both General Washington and Mr. Lincoln, the only two American presidents honored with a national holiday.

Today, unfortunately, with the exception of Independence Day, little attention is paid to the observance of patriotic holidays. As the origins and meanings of these very special days have slipped through the cracks, we have lost one of the most important legacies we can pass on to our children. There is no better place to begin restoration than with a homegrown observance of Washington's and Lincoln's birthdays.

Mrs. Sharp has a Victorian ditty she would like to share with you:

We cannot all be Washingtons and Lincolns
And have our birthdays celebrated
But we can love the things they loved,
And we can hate the things they hated.

They loved the truth, they hated lies.
They minded what their mothers taught them
And every day they tried to do
The simple duties that it brought them.

Perhaps the reason little folks
Are sometimes great when they grow taller
Is because, like General George and Honest Abe,
They did their best when they were smaller!

Victorian parents believed that patriotism began in the cradle. But patriotism is a difficult concept for children under six to comprehend. However, while we might not be able to "teach" our children patriotism, we can instill in them the love of American history, the knowledge of our country's need for men and women to love and serve it, as well as our admiration for those individuals who do.

This is done in a number of ways. During the nineteenth century a wide variety of patriotic toys were manufactured to amuse and instruct our young ones. There were Yankee Doodle drawing books to color, and both boys and girls played with dolls of George Washington and Abraham Lincoln. Patriotic toys and books are still available, just harder to find. However, very often museum and historical-site gift shops sell them. Mrs. Sharp will often purchase a new puzzle or game with a patriotic theme or historical biographies for the older children and coloring books for the younger ones, when visiting such shops. She then puts them away for Lincoln's and Washington's birthdays.

One toy that Mrs. Sharp always brings out every February is Lincoln Logs. Do you remember playing with Lincoln Logs when you were a child? Probably, because children have been playing with them for more than eighty years. Created in 1918 by John Lloyd Wright (the son of Frank Lloyd Wright), Lincoln Logs—as the name implies—were meant to inspire young children to build playthings from our American past, such as the log cabin in which Abraham Lincoln was born. Today Lincoln Logs are manufactured by Playskool and are still as much fun for your young ones to play and build with as they were for you.

Here's to the hatchet forever distinguished by fame.

Another way to make history come alive for children is with celebration. One of the simplest pleasures Mrs. Sharp's family enjoys is seasonal food, such as two special desserts that deserve their moment of annual glory: Washington pie and Lincoln's log. Washington pie, naturally, is a cherry one and Lincoln's log is an ice-cream-roll cake with fudge sauce. Each dessert is served on the birthday of its namesake, providing a perfect opportunity for the family to discuss the life of each great man.

(Of course, dear Reader, as the children grow in understanding, so do the biographies.)

Our distinctly American holidays embody a reflection of our best selves. The traditions of those holidays, which we choose to pass on to our children through the retelling of American folklore, history, or the serving of special food, mirror those values. Children remember best what their parents teach them to cherish. There is a reason that freedom flourishes first on front porches and in front of fireplaces.

A Brief History of the Victorian Valentine

Perhaps no memento so perfectly captures the essence of an entire era as the valentine does for the Victorians. Hidden within the undulating paper curves of these charmingly conceived, lovingly crafted tokens of affection—the more elaborate the better—lie fascinating clues to the gilded age in which the valentine was transformed from mere ephemera into art.

For behind the lavish decorations stood not just the secrets of Victorian hearts but of Victorian society as well. Valentines were among the few tokens that could freely be exchanged between men and women, and much was read between the lines, or in this instance, the hearts and flowers. Depending upon the elaborateness of the lace filigree, the number of cupids, or the cleverness of imported "trick" valentines (which opened to reveal moving parts), a hopeful young lady could measure the true emotional involvement of her suitors.

Until the early nineteenth century, valentines were primarily handwritten love letters. As printing techniques became more sophisticated, the Victorian valentine business boomed. The London stationery firm of Joseph Addenbrooke is considered one of the major contributors in the evolution of the commercial valentine. During the 1830s, Addenbrooke discovered while embossing paper borders that by filing off the raised relief, he could create paper that imitated lace. Soon lace paper or "doilies" became the rage as English stationers competed fiercely to provide elaborate doilies that rivaled real lace.

Collectors of valentines consider the period between 1840 and 1860 to be the "Golden Age of Valentines." This is because during this time the printing technology of chromolithography was perfected, allowing an astonishing assortment of beautiful, decoratively printed designs known as chromos.

Because chromos were easier and less expensive to print than woodcuts or cumbersome copperplate engravings and afforded graphic artists a wider range of colors (as well as textures and tonal quality) than previously available, these decorative pictures soon became part of nineteenth-century mass culture and were used to embellish practically everything. But the largest share of chromos was printed in large sheets blown as "scrap" to satisfy the insatiable demand of the popular nineteenth-century hobby of compiling scrapbooks (or books with scrap pictures). In fact, these inexpensive pictures could be considered the great-grandparents of the embellishment craze of today: stickers.

Now with both lace-paper and chromo cutouts of cherubs, hearts, and flowers as valentine prerequisites, the art form of both homemade and commercial valentines began to flourish. Soon the embossed and lace paper became layered, folded, honeycombed, and held together with small accordion-pleated paper hinges that permitted three-dimensional valentines. Swags of fringe, feathers, fabric, tinsel, and glitter, including powdered color glass, were added. Printed verses became hidden behind secret doors, and valentines began to have moving parts that permitted hearts or cherubs to twirl. Victorian valentines were limited only by the sender's imagination, which for our great-great-grandparents meant flights of fancy that still have the power to amuse, entertain, and awe.

In 1847, a young woman named Esther Howland of Worcester, Massachusetts—who is credited with being the "Mother of the American Valentine"—received a typical commercial English valentine from a friend. Very taken with it, she was inspired to try to make some of her own.

As the story goes, Esther persuaded her father, who was a stationer, to order a supply of large blank lace-paper sheets and other valentine materials from England. When she had finished making a small assortment of samples, she persuaded her brother, who worked as a traveling salesman for their father, to take her cards with him.

After he returned with five thousand orders, Esther set up shop in a spare room of the family's home, engaged a handful of her friends to help her, and began the first assembly-line production of American commercial valentines. Most of Miss Howland's cards were so elaborate they had to be packed in boxes to protect the delicate confections. Their elaborateness was matched in their price, with the majority of them costing between $5 and $10. Despite their cost, Miss Howland's valentines were extremely popular; in 1880 she sold her business (which netted her over $100,000 a year) to another American valentine competitor, the George C. Whitney Company.

By the end of the nineteenth century, improvements in color-printing processes soon gave elaborate commercial valentines the preference over homemade sentiments. Two companies on either side of the Atlantic competed fiercely for the valentine market: Marcus Ward in England, and in America, Louis Prang, who perfected the graphic art of lithography. Prang also began trimming his valentines with silk fringe, and soon this distinguishing feature replaced the lace-paper borders on the most elegant and highly desired Victorian valentines.

Gazing upon a Victorian valentine is to return to a more romantic era. To hold one today, as fragile as a dream, is to know, as the nineteenth-century poet Katherine Lee Bates did, "Old love is gold love, old love, the best."

Entertainments from the Past

CUPID'S TEA

Oh, the joys of Love's Own Day. Each year more than 850 million commercial valentines are exchanged. However, the cleverest store-bought valentine cannot match the splendor of a handcrafted paper confection. In today's impersonal, mass-produced age, the handcrafted card for family and friends is a rare token of affection (and perhaps unexpressed passion). Dear Reader, this St. Valentine's Day, assist your family in preserving this dying custom. What happy home-circle memories can be fashioned out of paper, glue, and imagination!

To inspire you, why not have a "Cupid's Tea" the weekend before Valentine's Day for all your family members and close friends? The purpose: to create homemade valentines.

First, assemble all your materials. Quality paper-lace doilies are a must: heart-shaped, round, and square in white, ivory, red, pink, and gilt. Of course you will need authentic late-nineteenth-century illustrations so popular on Victorian valentines: hearts, flowers, cherubs, fans, doves, little children, animals, birds, and sweet messages. Today, beautiful reproductions of these are available as stickers. If you need help with writing your loving sentiments, there are Victorian verses in poetry books to inspire you.

Now bring out embellishments—ribbons, lace trimming, silk fringe, pieces of floral fabric—as well as an assortment of craft materials—paper ribbon, cardboard, colored paper, wrapping paper, heart-shaped gift tags. Quality art paper that has been given a watercolor wash offers a dainty background. Don't forget glue, rubber cement, double-sided tape, and scissors (safety-edged for small children).

When you have completed all of your valentines, making them as lavish and sentimental as you can imagine, it's time to "post" them. Take a large square gift box with a lid and cover the sides and top with Valentine's Day wrapping paper. Decorate it with doilies, ribbons, and crepe-paper ruffles, then cut a slit in the top so that everyone can deposit their "mail."

If valentines arrive in the mail from friends and family before the big day, save them to go into the box as well.

Finally, it is time for a delicious and rewarding late-afternoon tea party. Working as Cupid's assistants has given everyone an appetite. Serve a heart-shaped cake with pink icing, heart-shaped open-face sandwiches (cream cheese and jam), and miniature heart-shaped scones with clotted cream and strawberry preserves.

Love's Own Day:
A Family Affair

In Mrs. Sharp's household the celebration of St. Valentine's Day is a family affair. Yes, dear Reader, Mrs. Sharp is dimly aware that the fourteenth of February has over the centuries evolved into a high-spirited holiday when lovers can publicly wear their hearts on their sleeves without appearing or feeling foolish.

It also seems highly likely that, once upon a time, Mrs. Sharp must have been somebody's sweetheart before she became the mother of a dozen children. However, with regard to St. Valentine's Day, it has been her personal experience (especially if married to a Victorian husband who feels surely he said it all when he uttered "I do") that if you're married, have children, and don't wish to continue being the only one remembering that romance is the elixir of life, then you must actively start transforming this lovers' holiday into an annual celebration of home, sweet home.

After all, it is so easy for us to take for granted our nearest and dearest, assuming their affection and loyalty while, all too often, we knock ourselves out for mere acquaintances. Thus, it's a tradition at Mrs. Sharp's house to let all members of the family know just how special and loved they are.

Valentine's Day Breakfast

On the morning of the big day the young folks in our family awaken in great anticipation. There will be an exchange of valentines at school, but Mother always starts the day off with her early-morning greeting: "Good morning to you, valentines. Has any sweet child been stung by Cupid's bow and arrow?"

The children tell Mama that they must have been: Cupid left a special, old-fashioned valentine underneath each child's pillow.

After everyone is dressed, we begin our celebration at breakfast with heart-shaped cinnamon toast and strawberry muffins with hot drinks served in heart-patterned mugs. The table is bright and cheery with red-and-white heart place mats and napkins.

School Surprises

After the children have finished breakfast, it is time to be off to school, but the day's merriment is just beginning. Later each child will find in his book bag a small gift he can use at school, perhaps a new heart-shaped pad, pencils, pencil sharpener, or eraser. As well, there is also a funny valentine from Mama and Papa tucked into lunch boxes along with heart-shaped sandwiches (use cookie cutters) and cookies. Festive red-and-white paper napkins complete their Valentine's Day lunches. Mrs. Sharp also makes sure that the children have valentines for all their schoolmates (not just their chums), and, of course, there is a loving missive for Teacher.

The Dolls' Tea Party

After school there's a valentine tea party for all the dolls and stuffed-toy friends who keep the children such good company throughout the year. Dolls and toys are, as you no doubt realize, very generous to those good children who take such loving care of them, so when the small folk arrive at the party, they're sure to find tiny foil-covered, heart-shaped chocolates and valentines waiting for them in the arms of their faithful companions. (Of course, earlier

Mrs. Sharp has assisted the dolls and animals in their valentine making without the children's knowledge!)

One old-fashioned family that have always enjoyed the happy company and conviviality of their dolls and toys is that of the famed children's book illustrator Tasha Tudor. For four decades, admirers of Miss Tudor's many stories and charming lifestyle have been familiar with the tales of Miss Sethany Ann, Nicey Melinda, and the Captain Crane family. These marvelous dolls come to life, celebrating the holidays with the Tudor family and holding memorable fairs; they even have their own postal service, Sparrow Post. This endearing fantasy is lovingly described in Tasha Tudor's Valentine's Day anthology, *All for Love*. When her children were little, Miss Tudor used to create tiny little magazines, catalogs, and cards for them and their dolls. Your young ones will be charmed with the custom as well.

A Wedding in the Woods

After tea, it is time for the children to offer homemade valentines to their wild feathered friends, the birds. For centuries it has been an old country superstition that on St. Valentine's the birds select their mates; our children always enjoy preparing the wedding supper. Earlier during the week we make peanut-butter balls with birdseed, raisins, and chopped nuts. We chill them in the freezer and hang them in netted produce bags adorned with red ribbons on tree branches.

The Tie That Binds

Evening falls and the dining room is illuminated by glowing candlelight for our family St. Valentine's Day party. At each person's place setting there is a gold-foil paper cornucopia filled with penny-candy motto hearts, chocolate kisses, and pink mints. During dinner the children ask again to hear the story of their parents' courtship. As the two widely divergent stories merge into one, amid great hilarity, it seems Father and Mrs. Sharp do indeed remember their first St. Valentine's Day.

The children toast us with gifts of memorized romantic verse. After dinner, the older children, their eyes twinkling with fun, bring in a "special surprise valentine," with a tag that reads "For Mama and Papa." It is the baby all wrapped up in big sheets of white paper, tied with a pink ribbon, and a little heart-shaped hole cut out for her face! As our St. Valentine's Day celebrations draw to a close, the wonderfully familiar becomes transcendent.

Family traditions, such as our homegrown celebration of Love's Own Day, require an investment of creative and emotional energy. But most of all, they require commitment. Like enduring love, they are true affairs of the heart.

For you a motto I have found.
And one I think that suits,
Almost afraid to send it round
I tremble in my boots.
I think you are a pretty miss,
So what's the harm to send a kiss?

Two of the most popular Victorian writers of handicraft articles for girls were the sisters Lina and Adelia Beard. Here are two of their suggestions for unusual, old-fashioned valentines.

The Mirror Valentine

Take two pieces of stiff red or white cardboard and a small piece of broken mirror. Cut two hearts according to the size of your glass (Fig. 1), then with strong paste fasten the mirror to one of the hearts. Cut another heart exactly like the first, and in the center leave a heart-shaped opening as large as possible, yet small enough to cover the edges of the glass.

On one side of the top of the valentine write, "Look Into This Mirror Clear," and on the other side write, "And My True Love Will Appear" (Fig. 2). At the bottom point of the valentine, paste on a cupid or small embossed paper flowers or birds. You might want to glue on some pretty bows or lace on the top part of the valentine. Using strong paste, fasten the heart-shaped frame over the glass and lay the valentine under several books until the paste holding the two pieces together is completely dry. Be sure to place a clean piece of paper on top of and underneath the valentine to keep it fresh and clean.

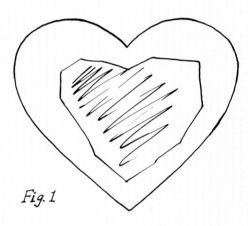

Fig. 1

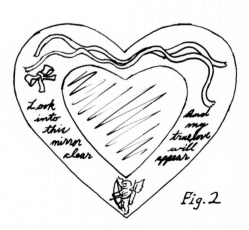

Fig. 2

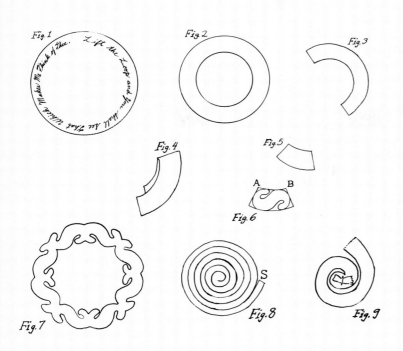

A Birdcage Valentine

Cut from white cardboard a circular disk and around its edge write, "Lift the Loop and You Shall See That Which Makes Me Think of Thee" (Fig. 1). From fancy gold-foil paper cut out a circular band smaller in circumference than the cardboard (Fig. 2); fold it through the center (Fig. 3); bring the folded ends together, and again fold (Fig. 4). Fold it once more (Fig. 5), and from this cut out an S-shaped figure (Fig. 6), being careful not to cut the folded ends marked A and B. Unfold the paper and you will have an ornamental gold band (Fig. 7), which should be placed on the white cardboard to fit just inside the handwriting. Glue it down slightly in a few spots with a little paste. Next make Figure 8 of fancy white paper. Cut out a circle the same size as your inner disk, and inserting scissors at the beginning, cut a spiral around and around in one unbroken strip until the center is reached. In the center make a short slit and push the two ends of a narrow white ribbon through the slit; then turn the spiral over and paste each end of the ribbon flat against the paper (Fig. 9). Have ready a picture of a bird and fasten it to the center of your disk that has previously been decorated with the gold-paper design. Slide the end S of the spiral under the edge of the gold band, placing the spiral so that it will lie flat and even inside the golden paper and cover the center of the valentine. Lift the cover by the loop of ribbon, and the bird and motto will appear.

MARCH.

The madcap month of March arrives—the last of winter and the first of spring. Blustery winds and soft spring breezes alternate as we take our walks together. Can't March make up her mind which it shall be? But there is no question about the fun the family will share this month—a maple-sugaring-off party, St. Patrick's Day, fairy wayside walks on the first day of spring, the planning of the children's garden, making a pussy willow wreath, and the planting of our living Easter basket.

Maple-Sugaring-Off Party

In the annals of great Victorian seasonal rituals, one of the pleasures of springs past was the gathering of sap and the making of maple syrup.

When the snow was still on the ground, the bark of the trees would start to glisten in the sunshine. "The sap's arising," the children exclaimed excitedly as moist black spots announced that the sap—which had been stored in the tree roots all winter—had begun its spring journey upward. Off to the sugar orchard went New England families, carrying drills, spouts, pails, and oilcloth. The men bored holes in each tree, then drove a small wood or iron spout into the hole. The children followed close behind to hang a pail on each spout to catch the sap. Over the pail they placed a wooden or oilcloth covering to keep out falling twigs, dirt, and insects. As the sap filled the buckets, the children took them off in relays, exchanging them for empty ones. Next the men arrived driving horse-harnessed sleds to collect the sap. Down in the sugarhouse, a temporary accommodation near the barn, the women boiled the sap all day and long into the night over a roaring fire until it thickened into golden nectar.

But, of course, the syrup had to be tested.

Maple Sugar Recipes

A grown-up poured some of the hot syrup onto cold, clean snow, where it congealed and became like taffy. After the sugar-on-snow appetizer—which tradition said had to be eaten with plain cake doughnuts and sour pickles—everyone gathered for a feast of pancakes, baked ham, and maple-syrup trimmings.

Lack of maple-sugar trees notwithstanding, Mrs. Sharp's family holds a "Maple-Sugaring-Off Party"—at least in spirit—with a dinner composed entirely of recipes using real maple syrup. Mrs. Sharp's traditional menu features:

> **Baked Ham**
> **New England Baked Beans**
> **Maple Syrup Sweet Potato Soufflé**
> **Maple Graham Bread and Butter**
> **Maple Custard**
> **Maple Syrup Mousse**
> **Maple Nut Ice Cream**

For party favors, all the children receive maple sugar candy that has been poured into little molds shaped like maple leaves and log cabins.

This simple joy of sharing a maple-sugaring-off dinner in March, or hot cross buns only at Eastertime or pumpkin pie at Thanksgiving, offers modern families a rich resource of security and stability.

March.

It was raining hard when I went to bed;
The creek was over its banks, they said,

And in the morning far and wide
The meadows were flooded on every side;

There was water over the yard below,
And it looked like a place I did not know:

The wind swept by with a rushing sound,
And the dog-house floated around and round.

When father went out to the barn that day
I thought he'd surely be swept away.

In long gum boots he stepped from the door,
And the water was up to his knees and more.

I thought, if the flood should never go down,
We'd build a boat and row to town,

For there we would buy our bread and meat
And pies and all things good to eat,

And living here for all our days
We would almost be like castaways.

K.P.

St. Patrick's Day

Follow the ways of your ancestors.
—Old Irish proverb

Did your mother come from Ireland, dear Reader? This would come as no surprise to Mrs. O'Sharp. Forty million Americans claim Irish ancestry, but on March 17 that number increases considerably when we all celebrate St. Patrick's Day.

The earliest recorded American observance of the day honoring St. Patrick—the patron saint of Ireland—was in Boston in 1737. But the Irish as an ethnic group did not begin to make their presence felt in America until their numbers began to swell during the nineteenth century.

St. Patrick's Day became the day the new immigrants remembered their strong ties to the "auld sod" with parades and banquets. By the turn of the century, the celebration of St. Patrick's Day had become a distinctly American custom, with everyone, no matter what his nationality, wearing a bit of the green.

Curiously, the celebration of St. Patrick's Day in Ireland has evolved into a high-spirited holiday only in the past twenty years. Since St. Patrick's Day was (and still is) a holy day, people attended Mass and all the pubs were closed. An authentic St. Patrick's Day observance with music, dance, food, and liquid refreshment had to take place at home.

But then, as the Irish proverb reminds us, "there is no fireside like your own fireside," which probably explains why over the years Mrs. Sharp hosts a "ceilidh" on St. Paddy's Day, to which you're all invited.

A ceilidh (Gaelic for "dance," and pronounced *kali*) is a gathering of family and friends to hear traditional Irish music, do a bit of step dancing, eat thick slices of soda bread slathered with butter, drink cups of strong tea or other liquid refreshment, and engage in the Irish indoor sport of conversation.

But the heart of any ceilidh is Irish music, of which there are two distinct types: energetic dance tunes or lamentful narrative songs, usually ballads. In Irish reels the main melody is repeated over and over again until it leads into another similar tune, forming a "set," and the listener unfamiliar with its unique circular structure frequently comes away with the impression that he has been tapping his feet to one long Irish jig for two hours.

SEARCHING FOR SHAMROCKS

The day before St. Patrick's Day, the children search for shamrocks. Earlier Mrs. Sharp had obtained little pots of them at the florist and "planted" the green clumps in the brown earth, where they'll easily be discovered. Once the children have found their bit of green, we'll make shamrock corsages for everyone with green, orange, and white bows.

On St. Paddy's Day, the children will find lucky shamrock sandwiches (cut with cookie cutters) in their lunch boxes. After school, they invite their friends over for a treasure hunt, looking for an Irish leprechaun and his pot of gold in the back-yard. Although not one leprechaun can be found, the children do discover small mesh bags of gold-foil chocolate coins!

Celebrating St. Patrick's Day can help remind everyone that when we search for the end of the rainbow, we often find the pot of gold in our own backyard.

Irish dancing works up an appetite, so at Mrs. Sharp's party there is an abundant spread. The Irish are not known for their cookery, but only because authentic Irish "receipts" have been passed down orally: "a pinch of this and a jigger of that."

The Irish are known for colcannon, their national dish. (Corned beef and cabbage is not a traditional Irish meal; it's an American-Irish invention.) An Irish children's rhyme describes it:

Did you ever eat Colcannon
That's made from thickened cream,
With greens and scallions blended
Like a picture in your dream?
Did you ever take potato cake
When you went off to school
Tucked beneath your jacket
With your book and slate and rule?

Mrs. Sharp's Colcannon

1 pound new potatoes, peeled

4 leeks (or one bunch scallions), chopped

1 small cabbage, chopped

Milk (just enough to moisten potatoes)

3 tablespoons heavy cream

2 ounces butter (½ stick), softened

1 teaspoon ground thyme

Salt and pepper (to taste)

Bring a pot of water to a boil and cook potatoes until tender. Slowly sauté the chopped leeks and chopped cabbage separately until soft and limp (but not brown).

Mash the potatoes with a hand masher, then add the leeks and milk and mash together until smooth. Next mash in the cabbage, adding the heavy cream, butter, and thyme; blend well until smooth and fluffy. Season with salt and pepper. Put this mixture into an ovenproof dish and place under broiler to brown.

If the colcannon is prepared up to the point of browning ahead of time, reheat covered with foil in a 350° oven for a half hour. Uncover and brown under broiler.

Serves six.

Mrs. Sharp's Favorite Irish Soda Bread

4 cups white flour

1 teaspoon baking soda

½ teaspoon salt

1 tablespoon sugar

1½ cups sour milk

Preheat oven to 400°. Sift dry ingredients together. Make a well in the center. Add sour milk and stir together with a wooden spoon. The dough should be thick but not too wet. Turn dough onto a floured surface and form with hands into a round loaf. Place the loaf into a cast-iron frying pan or heavy round casserole dish that has been greased with butter. Score the top in the form of a cross with a wet knife. Bake for 40 minutes. Bread should cool for an hour before serving.

Note: Soda bread is daily fare in Ireland, made fresh for breakfast and tea. If the loaf is made with whole-meal wheat flour, it is known as brown bread; if made with unbleached white flour, it's Irish soda bread. Authentic Irish soda bread is made with sour milk, not buttermilk, or milk soured by adding vinegar or lemon juice. To sour milk, simply leave it out overnight.

THE STOLEN CHILD

Where dips the rocky highland
Of Slewth Wood in the lake
There lies a leafy island
Where flapping herons wake
The drowsy water-rats;
There we've hid our faery vats,
Full of berries
And of reddest stolen cherries.
Come away, O human child!
To the waters and the wild
With a faery, hand in hand,
For the world's more full of weeping
   than you can understand.

Where the wave of moonlight glosses
The dim grey sands with light,
Far off by furthest Rosses
We foot it all the night,
Weaving olden dances,
Mingling hands and mingling glances
Till the moon has taken flight;
To and fro we leap
And chase the frothy bubbles,
While the world is full of troubles
And is anxious in its sleep.
Come away, O human child!
To the waters and the wild
With a faery, hand in hand,
For the world's more full of weeping
   than you can understand.

Where the wandering water gushes
From the hills above Glen-Car,
In pools among the rushes
That scarce could bathe a star,
We seek for slumbering trout
And whispering in their ears
Give them unquiet dreams;
Leaning softly out
From ferns that drop their tears
Over the young streams.
Come away, O human child!
To the waters and the wild
With a faery, hand in hand,
For the world's more full of weeping
   than you can understand.

Away with us he's going,
The solemn-eyed:
He'll hear no more the lowing
Of the calves on the warm hillside,
Or the kettle on the hob
Sing peace into his breast,
Or see the brown mice bob
Round and round the oatmeal-chest.
For he comes, the human child,
To the waters and the wild
With a faery, hand in hand,
From a world more full of weeping
   than he can understand.

—William Butler Yeats, 1889

Fairy Wayside Walks

*You see, Wendy, when the first baby laughed
for the first time, its laugh broke into a thousand
pieces, and they all went skipping about,
and that was the beginning of fairies. . . .*
—Sir James M. Barrie, Peter Pan and Wendy, 1911

Modern parents often ask what the main difference is in raising children today and when Mrs. Sharp was a young mother in the 1890s. The obvious answer is television, which has all but killed the art of self-amusement as Victorian children knew it. But the true main difference is that today's children and their parents are not familiar with nature lore, folktales, and the fairy tradition that was so much a part of Victorian childhood.

A century ago, every mother and child knew the magic that was to be found in the fields, woods, backyard, and nursery, for the fairies lived openly among us. We had fairies of every description: pillow fairies, birthday fairies, garden fairies, wayside fairies. Deprived modern children have only the tooth fairy, who can hardly be expected to carry the load alone.

Parents, please! This spring, do yourselves and your children a favor and invite the fairies to make their homes near yours. A marvelous way is with the books by famed English children's illustrator Cicely Mary Barker, creator of the classic *Flower Fairies* series, first published in the 1920s.

These books are enchantment themselves.

Miss Barker, an accomplished botanical artist, instructs young and old readers on how to discover fairies in their flower or plant homes through verse and full-color portraits.

Next, take a woodside spring outing. Granted, you may not "see" the fairies as Miss Barker did on her nature walks, but you'll be able to see the flowers that the fairies care for. As your children discover the magic of crocus, snowdrop, primrose, and willow catkin, you'll be charmed to discover that old-fashioned childhood friends are still the best.

SPRING'S FIRST VISITOR

Mrs. Sharp's family knows that spring is here when the season's first visitor arrives. As the family takes an outdoor excursion searching for Mistress Pussy Willow Catkin, the children recite her story. You might like to share the accompanying Victorian child's verse with your young ones.

We gather our armful of pussy willow branches to take home (you can also gather them at the florist or supermarket) to make a spring pussy willow wreath. Would you like to make one, too, dear Reader? Simply lay the branches, piece by piece, on a wire form as a base and secure them with florist's wire, curving and overlapping as you go. Next attach a festive bright bow with long streamers, which will gaily whip in the March winds if you hang your wreath on your front door as Mrs. Sharp does on the first day of spring, to welcome the new season of joy.

While Mrs. Sharp is making her wreath, the children make pussy willow pictures. Here's one: Draw a picket fence. Next line up a row of cats sitting on the top ledge of the fence by gluing on four or five catkins (the furry part of the pussy willow). Complete your "cats" by drawing their ears and long tails on the paper.

Pussy Willow wakened from her cozy winter nap.
For the frolicking spring breeze, on her door would tap.
"It is chilly weather, though the sun feels good;
I will wrap up warmly and wear my furry hood."
Mistress Pussy Willow opened wide her door;
Never had the sunshine seemed so bright before.
Never had the brooklet seemed so full of cheer;
"Good morning, Pussy Willow, Welcome to you, dear!"
Never guest was quainter, than when Pussy came to town,
In her hood of silver gray, and tiny coat of brown.
Happy little children cried with laugh and shout,
"Spring is coming, coming, Mistress Pussy Willow's out!"

The Children's Garden

Oh! the things which happened in that garden!
If you have never had a garden, you cannot
understand, and if you have had a garden, you will
know that it would take a whole book to describe
all that came to pass there.

—Frances Hodgson Burnett, The Secret Garden, 1911

In March, dear Reader, frost still blankets the ground in the early morning, but this is the best time to begin planning the children's garden.

To put everyone in the proper mood, we read aloud the children's classic *The Secret Garden*. Written by Frances Hodgson Burnett, who also wrote *Little Lord Fauntleroy* and *The Little Princess*, this enchanting tale of the redemption of two miserable children through tending an abandoned garden is sure to have your children eager for their own bit of earth. As the children bring back to life a forgotten and overgrown garden, its revival becomes a metaphor for their own restoration. As one of the children, Colin, describes it, "The sun is shining . . . the sun is shining. That is the Magic. The flowers are growing . . . the roots are stirring. That is the Magic. Being alive is the Magic, being spring is the Magic. The Magic is in me—the Magic is in me. It is in me—it is in me. It's in every one of us."

Help your children discover the Magic with a garden of their own. Let the little ones begin with the seed catalogs, scissors, paste, and paper. It matters not whether they choose flowers that cannot grow in your part of the country; what matters is that by letting them plot their garden on paper, you will get a glimpse of the type of garden they have their hearts set upon. Then you will be able to better assist them in planning a garden that will at least capture in spirit what they dream about.

Picture Mrs. Sharp's garden for the children: a square of fifteen feet, limited only by imagination. There are paths for little feet to walk and run; a place

for the trundling of carts, carriages, and wheelbarrows. Each side of the path is edged with a colorful flower border, which changes with the seasons. Behind it in rows of various heights and hues is an old-fashioned sampler of flowers.

In the opposite corner of the garden is our patch of ornamental and everlasting flowers. It is here that we will sow and then harvest the makings of future gifts and decorations: mixed gourds, Chinese lanterns, strawberry popcorn, miniature fingers of Indian corn, strawflowers, statice, and baby's breath. Next to it is a small cutting garden, for the children love to cut bouquets to keep and give away as presents.

In the center of the children's garden is an archway, covered with climbing roses. Next to it, we find Mother Nature's Toyshop. In their enchanting book for children *Mother Nature's Toyshop,* Lina and Adelia Beard described it this way:

Mother Nature is every bit as fond of the little folks in her human family as of the grown-ups, and while she prepares untold joys for lovers of the outdoors among men and women and larger boys and girls, she never forgets the little ones.

For their benefit she keeps an open toy-shop full of marvelous playthings, all free to any child who wants them, and instead of the children paying her for what they take she pays them for coming to her by giving them rosier cheeks, brighter eyes and stronger bodies. She puts more glee into

their laughter and greater happiness into their trustful little hearts.

As in the large department stores in big cities, the goods in Mother Nature's shop are changed for each season of the year; so the little shoppers have constant variety and hail every new season with fresh delight . . .

If you would like to plant a Mother Nature's Toyshop for your children's garden, here are some of the flowers and plants you might include: daffodils, lilacs, daisies, jack-in-the-pulpit, phlox, hollyhocks, sweet peas, snapdragons, nasturtium, sunflowers, honeysuckle, pansies, columbine, poppies, bluebells, and bleeding hearts.

Let us continue our walk: At one end we find a tent made of beanpoles tied teepee style. It is covered with climbing morning glories and provides a shady retreat for our little boys. At the opposite end of the garden stands a little white clapboard playhouse—the domain of Mrs. Sharp's daughters—complete with lace curtains and window boxes, which awaits guests large and small for tea. Scattered throughout the garden are miniature thatched cottages (guest accommodations for birds or fairies), a small goldfish pond, child-size benches, stone animal statuaries, and a sundial that declares "I count only the happy hours!" Indeed, many of them are spent here in our backyard child's Eden.

Perhaps you are saying to yourself, "This is all wondrous, Mrs. Sharp. But now that you've aroused our interest, we've not the slightest idea of where to begin. What's more, the whole project seems overwhelming!"

Pardon Mrs. Sharp for her reverie. She has, after all, been working on her children's garden for the past century, which is why it is just reaching perfection. You needn't wait that long, nor should you be that ambitious in your first season. A small patch of earth or even a window box is all you need to begin.

But as well as seeds, a plot of earth, water, and sun, children need proper gardening tools. Children are very earnest gardeners; if they do not have the right equipment, they will become discouraged. Do not sabotage their best efforts by giving them toy tools that will break and frustrate them. Buy your children the best small-size tools you can afford.

"Great was my pride and delight when I was first given a garden of my own to do just what I liked," reminisced Gertrude Jekyll, the famous Victorian horticulturist. May your children also know this delight, and the "Magic" that only their own garden can bring!

If the children are eager to visit Mother Nature's Toyshop this spring before their garden has bloomed, bring home a bouquet of daffodils. It will provide them with an amusing interlude playing with "Daffodil Dancers" and animals.

To make your Daffodil Dancers, cut off the blossom of the daffodil, leaving a very short stem. These little stems will become the dancer's hat when you turn the blossom over. To make the flower stand up, push three wooden toothpicks firmly up into the center of the flower. Spread the toothpicks like a tri-pod to make the flower stand alone steadily. After you have made several dancers, gather them together as the "daffy down-dilly ladies just come to town" in their fancy capes and pretty gowns. Place them on a tin tray and gently tap from underneath and watch the dancers begin to move.

For daffodil animals, gently peel away the outer petals, leaving the short green stem and the long flower cup. Hold the cup sideways so that the stem becomes the animal's head and long green nose; insert four wooden toothpicks for legs.

MAY MRS. SHARP BE OF ASSISTANCE?

Frequently Mrs. Sharp's younger friends will exclaim over her "collections" of seasonal accessories that give our family such pleasure. How they wish they could do the same!

May Mrs. Sharp share a few secrets? While our family is on intimate terms with the good and generous fairies, there is no traditional elf who arrives in the dead of night before a holiday to festoon her dining room table with gaiety. Would that there were! Nor did Mrs. Sharp lose her mind one holiday at the emporium buying decorative novelties. Instead, our collection of seasonal decorations and cooking equipment has grown steadily but slowly, perhaps one item per holiday, until we've accumulated an abundance of accessories.

Victorian mothers were also thrifty, imaginative, and organized. You can be, too. Dash rather than cash is always the better choice, for creativity needs to be nurtured before it can blossom. This way, a plain red tablecloth that is the essence of Christmas in December with evergreens becomes romantic for Valentine's Day (with white paper-lace heart doilies as place mats), or patriotic (with dark-blue-and-white-checked napkins and miniature flags) for Independence Day.

Of course, all this organization takes a little extra effort in the beginning (such as remembering not to store them with the Christmas decorations), but it is well worth the time and trouble. Why? Because wood and stone might build a house, but loving memories—such as special table settings—are the small touches that make any house or apartment your *home*.

APRIL.

April is a saucy flirt, beckoning the family outdoors with bright sunshine smiles and then, in a temper, sending us all rushing back indoors dripping wet from her mercurial showers. That's why our favorite April amusements are both indoors as well as out. Among the April pleasures awaiting Mrs. Sharp's family: a festive All Fools' Day dinner, an observance of Arbor Day, and the joys of a well-stocked Rainy Day Cupboard. Eastertide usually comes this month with a weeklong celebration of painted eggs, hot cross buns, decorating new bonnets, and putting up our beloved Easter egg tree, creating Easter nests in the backyard, and hosting an old-fashioned egg hunt for the children and their friends.

April Fools' Day

The first of April, some do say
Is set apart for All Fools' Day.
But why the people call it so,
Nor I, nor they themselves, do know.
But on this day are people sent
On purpose for pure merriment.

—*Poor Richard's Almanac, 1760*

The origins of All Fools' Day have been lost in antiquity, but surely there must have been some reason for its existence. Mrs. Sharp suspects the reason is that every family needs one day a year to let loose. Which is why, on the first of April, our entire family become April's fools.

Some historians believe the custom of All Fools' Day goes back to Roman times and the legend of Persephone, the daughter of Ceres, who was spirited away by Pluto to live in the lower world. Although Ceres could hear the cries of her daughter and spent all of spring searching for her, it alas was a "fool's errand," for she could never find her.

Another popular belief is that All Fools' Day began in France after the adoption of the Gregorian calendar by Charles IX in 1564, which changed the New Year from April 1 to January 1. News traveled slowly in those days, and since it had been common for people to give New Year's greetings and gifts, those who continued to observe the old calendar—either by choice or in ignorance—were called April's fools.

At Mrs. Sharp's house on the first of April our merriment is devoted more to the idea of playing together as a family than to playing practical jokes. We try to devise comical surprises and absurd but amusing (and unembarrassing) situations. One of the family's favorite games is switching roles—Father and Mother become babies and the children take on the role of adults. This is often a hilarious, not to mention revealing, reversal.

Other All Fools' suggestions include a spontaneous outing for fun—perhaps to the zoo, if it's a nice day, or a spur-of-the-moment treat of ice cream. The idea is to take a break from the daily routine and play together. Another favorite All Fools' Day custom is a treasure hunt, with Mrs. Sharp hiding small surprises throughout the house but in the most unlikely places.

The day ends with a festive All Fools' Supper, a menu of delicious but disguised foods: mock turtle soup, eggplant caviar, beef "birds" in fried-potato nests, the season's first fresh asparagus (dressed as wheat sheaves). Our finale is appropriately known as "April Fool," that delightful English confection of fruit and whipped cream.

As we linger around the dinner table, the family is reminded of life's true joy: "He who is of a merry heart has a continual feast."

Rainy Day Occupations

One of the hardest challenges for parents are rainy days, when energetic children must stay indoors and limit their activities.

What can be of enormous benefit to both parents and children is a plan to help them realize it is never really the weather that is disagreeable, only our attitudes toward it. Even the stormiest hours can be made bright if there are special treats and activities that are enjoyed only on rainy days. Every Victorian mother had what we called "rainy day occupations" to pass the hours pleasantly while the family was cooped up indoors.

One of Mrs. Sharp's most beloved rainy day traditions is to prepare crumpets for teatime. We then enjoy them before a cozy fire. Afterward the family writes letters to friends and family far away. The younger children draw or paint pictures using special art supplies. We do this only on rainy days, but the custom is so pleasant for both ourselves and our absent dear ones that it is looked forward to with great pleasure.

Mrs. Sharp's favorite rainy day tradition, however, is the Rainy Day Cupboard. How the children delight when Mother opens it to reveal a treasure trove of inspiration in neat, clearly marked boxes. How Mrs. Sharp delights in knowing the children can happily occupy themselves all afternoon!

Most parents have heard of Rainy Day Cupboards or boxes. But how many of you actually have them or use them? It is a pity not to, for you have all the basic elements already in your own household. All you have to do is pull them together.

As with any ritual, it is important that once you establish your Rainy Day Cupboard (or drawer or box), you limit its use to the particular time you will really need it, namely on rainy days. There can be no exceptions.

For instance, there was once an occasion when Mrs. Sharp found small Nell sobbing as if her heart would break.

"My darling, whatever can the matter be?" her loving mother asked.

"I want to finish work on my scrapbook and need some pictures of cats from the scrap collection. But that old sun just keeps on shining. I've been waiting for days to finish my picture. Oh, please, Mama, can't I *just this once* have permission to go to the Rainy Day Cupboard?"

Well, you know that Mrs. Sharp was sorely tempted. Of course, dear Reader, you would have allowed her access to the special cupboard as well. But Mrs. Sharp held firm: She knew that once there was entry into the Rainy Day Cupboard on a sunny day for even a piece of scrap-paper kittens, the linchpin to a family ritual would have been weakened.

"I'm sorry, sweetheart, but the Rainy Day Cupboard is just that—a cupboard for wonderful occupations, such as our scrapbooks, to amuse us on rainy days."

"Well, whatever shall I do until then?" Nell challenged.

"Pray for rain, dear, and when you are finished, bring Mother her workbasket and let's see if we can make some pretty clothespin people to amuse you this afternoon."

It goes without saying that parents are permitted access to the Rainy Day Cupboard anytime they wish to retrieve supplies, but it is a good idea to have duplicates, such as a special pair of scissors, just for the Rainy Day Cupboard. Otherwise, your Rainy Day Cupboard will soon become the "craft closet," and the novelty of it will not be there when you most need it. Trust Mrs. Sharp: Once you institute a Rainy Day Cupboard, you'll wonder how you ever got along without it. And, yes, she's been known to stretch the definition of inclement weather to include wintry days.

RAINY DAY CUPBOARD

April is the perfect time to rethink the lost art of creating a Victorian mother's Rainy Day Cupboard. Here are some of the basic elements to get you started:

Empty scrapbooks or blank artist's sketchbooks
 (find these at art-supply stores)
Glue, paper, paste
Cellophane tape, double-sided sticky tape
A file of old Christmas cards, postcards, fancy
 magazines, seed catalogs, and old calendars for
 cutting up
Sheets of interesting or pretty wrapping paper such
 as Victorian scrap-paper reproductions
Stickers
Tiny scraps of interesting fabrics such as lace, fur,
 velvet, and corduroy
Pieces of colored felt
Elastic
Odd buttons
Yarn and odd balls of wool
Bag of stuffing (either wool bits or used stockings)
 for soft toys or puppet heads
Feathers
Scissors
Small bells
Beads for stringing

String
Empty spools from thread
Pipe cleaners
Popsicle sticks
Stiff cardboard
Soap for carving
Bits of wood, sandpaper
Natural materials: pinecones, small twigs, large,
 flat, smooth stones and shells collected on nature
 excursions
Discarded rolls of wallpaper
Empty matchboxes
Empty Styrofoam meat trays
Empty aluminum, disposable muffin tins
Egg cartons
A variety of small paper bags
Small boxes
Envelopes
Colored index cards
Art supplies: special crayons, paints, and
 colored pencils
Modeling clay

NOTE: In Mrs. Sharp's cupboard, similar items, such as natural materials or art supplies, are kept together in small, labeled boxes.

Victorian Scrap Projects

A favorite Victorian rainy day occupation was the making of scrapbooks, scrap-picture folders, and screens. Scrap design delightfully involves a lot of time—easily several hours, or for a large project, such as a screen, several days.

The frames for the screens should be made before planning your designs and finding your scrap pictures. To make the frames, get two strips of pine, two inches wide, two inches thick, and fifty-two inches long. Sandpaper them carefully. You will also need two twenty-inch-long strips for the crossbars (see figure), and four braces, each measuring eight inches on the longest side. Assemble them together with screws. Tightly stretch three and one-half yards of heavy sky-blue or white muslin over the two twenty-inch bars. Tack together on the underside of the bar with carpet tacks. Draw a line across the screen ten inches from the top and another ten inches from the lower bar. This gives you space for two narrow pictures and one large one in the center.

Now it is time for us to cut pictures from illustrated magazines and heavy wrapping paper. They must be colored, glossy pictures only. The arrangement of your

pictures upon the background is a great delight, the result very much like a painting.

Study your design and notice that to get the proper perspective, the small and more distant features should be put on first; the other things introduced must gradually grow larger as they approach the lower part of the screen or foreground. This gives a chance to overlap the pictures as much as desired. Leave one quarter of the space for sky. Begin with pasting on distant mountains and bits of faraway woodland; next the nearer trees and distant houses; then put on the smaller and most distant people. Paste one picture

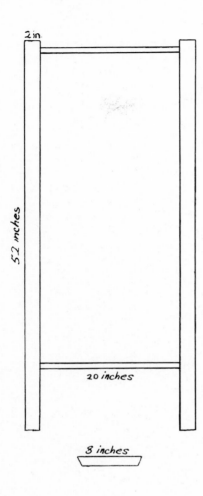

2 in.

5·2 inches

20 inches

8 inches

partly over another if necessary, working downward, and placing the largest pictures in the foreground.

The screen can be made as one scene, or divided into two or three, as in the illustration. Do not hurry about the work. Hold the cut pictures against the screen, and do not paste until you feel sure that the figure is in the correct place. You can fasten them with straight pins to get the effect, if you feel uncertain. Put paste evenly on the backs of the pictures and press to the background with a clean napkin or handkerchief. Be sure that the edges are well pasted. When your picture is completely dry, spray it with an acrylic fixative (available at art-supply stores) to achieve a glossy finish.

Eastertide:
March Hares, Painted Eggs, and Hot Cross Buns

Perhaps no season is so anticipated or yearned for as that of spring. Once again our family's spirit awakens, along with the natural world, from its long winter sleep. Mrs. Sharp is content with the first sighting of daffodils, but her youngsters prefer less subtle pleasures. For them, a trip past a large confectionery shop window displaying chocolate eggs does wonders, as chocolate and sugar eggs announce Easter is close at hand.

For more than fifteen hundred years, the feast of Easter, marking the resurrection of Jesus Christ, has been the focal point of springtime for Christians around the world. Yet the Easter season is not only a Christian story, but a promise of renewal for all.

The earliest origins of Easter come from an ancient pagan festival celebrated by the Saxons long before the birth of Christ. This festival, held just before the vernal equinox, was in honor of the old German goddess of light, Eostre, to celebrate the death of winter and rebirth of spring.

In the eighth century, the poetic name Easter, meaning "new beginning," was incorporated into Christianity's observance of Christ's resurrection, thereby blending nature's renewal with man's spiritual rebirth.

The most popular Easter symbols—colored eggs and the Easter bunny—are secular ones and can be traced back to Eostre's spring festival. On this day, the Teutonic goddess was honored with a feast of eggs, which were the symbol of new life. Farmers would gather wild-duck eggs, then give them to their wives to color red—the Saxon color of good fortune—with vegetable dyes. After the eggs were colored, they were rolled over the fields so that their contact with the soil would make the earth fertile.

According to legend, Eostre's favorite animal was a large, handsome bird, which in a fit of anger she turned into a hare. This is why each Easter a beautiful hare continues to build a nest to fill with colored eggs.

Chocolate or candy Easter eggs began to appear in the late 1800s, as did marzipan Easter symbols. In Eastern Europe the decoration of Easter eggs with intricate patterns transformed them into exquisite works of fragile art. Immigrants brought this tradition to America, and during the late 1880s it became a favorite Victorian pastime.

The celebration of Easter in America was introduced by German Protestant immigrants in the mid-1700s, but Easter was not widely celebrated here until after the Civil War, when its theme of resurrection

and renewed hope could offer the bereaved new meaning during the years of Reconstruction.

In Mrs. Sharp's home, the celebration of Eastertide begins on Palm Sunday with the children's procession of palm stick crosses. This charming custom comes from Germany, Austria, and Holland, where children parade in the street; at Mrs. Sharp's we invite friends over in the afternoon for a backyard procession.

Each palm stick cross is as unique as its little creator, but the basics begin with two dowels lashed together as a cross and secured with craft wire. Now let each child add greenery, such as boxwood, palms, spring flowers, and colored ribbon streamers. Finally, each cross is topped off with a bread-dough chick. Use your favorite bread dough (refrigerated breakfast-roll dough also works well) to form a small, round bun, then pull out a head and beak and add a raisin for each eye. To give the chick a shiny coat, brush an egg-yolk-and-water glaze on it just before baking. Don't despair if your dough creation doesn't look much like a chick to you; it will to your child, especially if she makes her own.

Hot Cross Buns

The children know Easter is almost here when Mrs. Sharp begins making hot cross buns on Good Friday. They sing:

> Hot cross buns! Hot cross buns!
> One a penny, two a penny,
> Hot cross buns!
> If you have no daughters,
> Give them to your sons.
> One a penny, two a penny,
> Hot cross buns!

Mrs. Sharp's Hot Cross Buns

Of all the English sweet rolls, hot cross buns are the most venerable, dating back to the fourteenth century. According to legend, on Good Friday the poor would visit abbey kitchens, where monks would give each person a spicy currant bun with iced crosses. Because the cross is the most important religious symbol of Easter, hot cross buns were considered blessed and believed to impart powerful protection. By the eighteenth century, whether for luck or just good eating, street vendors would sell them by the bushel. Today hot cross buns are usually available at bakeries throughout the season of Lent, but at Mrs. Sharp's house we steadfastly cling to tradition, savoring them all the more because we eat them once a year, at tea on Good Friday.

2 packages dry yeast
⅓ cup sugar
⅔ cup milk, scalded
3½ cups all-purpose flour
½ cup melted butter
¼ teaspoon salt
3 eggs, beaten
⅔ cups currants
½ teaspoon cinnamon
1 egg white

Soften yeast in warm water. Dissolve sugar in scalded milk. Let milk cool, then combine 1 cup flour, yeast, and milk-sugar mixture. Beat together. Add butter, salt, eggs, and remaining flour. Hand beat until light (about 5 minutes). Cover with damp dish towel, set in a warm spot, and let rise until doubled (about 1 hour). Beat down and then add currants and cinnamon. Roll dough ½ inch thick on a floured board. Shape into buns (or cut into circles using a small juice glass). Place on a greased baking sheet. Cover and let rise for about 30 minutes or until dough feels springy and is about double in size. Cut a deep cross into the top of each bun with a sharp knife. Brush with slightly beaten egg white. Bake at 350° for 12 to 14 minutes.

To make a glaze, dissolve 4 teaspoons granulated sugar in 6 tablespoons of milk and boil for 2 minutes. Brush warm buns twice with this syrup to glaze.

The Easter Egg Tree

While the dough for the hot cross buns is rising, your children may want to decorate an Easter egg tree. This is a Victorian custom sure to entertain the entire family. Mrs. Sharp remembers a description of an Easter egg tree in the April 1906 issue of *Mother's Magazine:*

The tree was an evergreen and, instead of a Santa Claus or fairy at the top of the tree, "Br'er Bunny" had the post of honor. This was a large toy rabbit and everywhere among the branches hung gayly colored eggs by loops of ribbon. Little baskets were made from eggshells, with fine wire for handles, and hung from the very tips of the branches. They were filled with tiny candy eggs. Rabbits and little chicks of candy and cotton batting peeped out from among the branches. Eggshells were painted and finished up to represent clowns, brownies, and gnomes. The tree was lit with candles in tin holders, and everyone, both young and old, voted the tree as pretty as any Christmas tree.

To create an Easter egg tree, use either a plain tree limb with many branches spray-painted white, or (if you prefer a natural tree) branches of flowering cherry, dogwood, or pussy willow. If you can't find suitable branches in your own backyard, they are usually available at florists or landscape nurseries.

Plant the tree branch firmly in a heavy pot full of damp sand and stones. I like to place this pot in a large Easter basket, covering the top of the sand with colored excelsior (available at craft shops) or paper grass.

Nestle wooden eggs into the grass around the branch.

The children trim the tree with blown-egg ornaments they have created, as well as such seasonal delights as miniature chicks, lambs, bunnies, and doll-size baskets. With colored excelsior we fashion tiny bird nests to rest between the branches.

To make blown-egg ornaments, have your eggs at room temperature. Take a large needle—a long carpet needle works best—and carefully pierce a hole at either end of the egg. Make one of the holes larger than the other. Hold the egg over a bowl and gently blow the contents out. Rinse the egg with water so that no egg residue remains (which would cause an unpleasant odor) and let it dry completely (overnight works best) on a paper towel. The next morning, paint your eggs. After you have decorated an egg, take a twelve-inch length of brightly colored embroidery floss; thread the carpet needle and pull it through the egg's two holes. Knot one end. If you would like to keep your egg ornaments looking fresh, spray them with acrylic fixative, available at art-supply stores.

Keep in mind that children will break a lot of eggs, so Mrs. Sharp likes to salvage some of the broken eggshells by gluing tiny chenille chicks, flowers, and ribbons to them for pretty novelties.

Egg Decoration

Egg decoration was a popular pastime for Victorian families between Palm Sunday and Easter. A century ago most of the colorings for eggs were prepared from natural materials or plant dyes. Today modern children know only of store-bought dyes for their Easter eggs. If you have always decorated Easter eggs using commercially prepared kits, then you are missing some simple, old-fashioned fun, for the effect of eggs dyed from natural materials is enchanting.

First, some general instructions: Use only white-shelled eggs for coloring. Place your eggs (up to six can be successfully dyed at a time) in the bottom of a pan. Next add approximately two cups of natural-dye materials on top of the eggs. Cover the eggs with water and add a tablespoon of household mordants—alum, cream of tartar, or white vinegar—to the dye solution. Bring the eggs to a boil. Simmer gently for fifteen minutes. Remove the eggs from the heat and let them sit in the dye bath for an hour. After you have taken your eggs out of the bath, allow them to cool completely and then brush with cooking oil to make them shine.

Green eggs: Cook with fresh spinach. The spring herb tansy will also give you a bright green.

Pink eggs: Use two cups of shredded raw beets (do not use canned); or use the juice from a package of frozen raspberries with one tablespoon of vinegar. Crushed fresh raspberries (juice and pulp) will produce a darker pink color.

Yellow eggs: The weed goldenrod will produce a warm yellow; so will the spice turmeric. Use one tablespoon of turmeric for each cup of water covering your eggs.

Blue eggs: Combine one cup crushed frozen blueberries and juice with a tablespoon of vinegar; the outer leaves of a red cabbage will also produce a pleasing tint of blue.

Old-Fashioned Egg-Stra Amusements

Other old-fashioned ideas for egg decoration include:

Taping thin strips of masking tape in pretty designs around the eggs and then dyeing them will produce pleasing patterns. For a delicate orange-brown mottled effect, before boiling, wrap the outer skins of onions around eggs (hold them on with cotton thread); red-onion skins will produce a charming cinnamon color. To make pretty natural patterns on the eggs, gather small leaves, parsley, or spring flowers such as violets, freesias, or hyacinths and wrap them around the egg, securing with thread.

Cover the egg in a piece of clean nylon stocking to keep your plant design in place and dye.

To write mottoes or make designs, Victorian children would dip a clean quill pen into melted hot lard or beeswax and then write on their eggs before dyeing them. You can use a white wax crayon. After the egg is dyed, the design written in crayon will remain white.

Commercially prepared Easter egg dyes do have their place in Mrs. Sharp's world, however, and here it is. Take plain wooden eggs, available at many craft shops, and dye them in the commercial dyes for perfect Easter decorations that will not spoil or smell. Decoupage the dyed wooden eggs by gluing on Victorian seasonal scrap pictures and then varnishing them.

An enchanting egg craft for children is decorating plain wooden eggs with thin sheets of candle-decorating beeswax. They will also enjoy painting watercolor washes on blown eggs, then using fine artist's markers to draw on designs.

Mrs. Sharp's children always delighted in this Victorian Easter surprise—a chocolate egg within a chicken egg. Carefully pierce both ends of a large uncooked egg with a sharp needle and blow out the raw egg. Rinse with water and let the eggshell dry completely. Put a piece of tape over the hole at one end, then carefully pour melted chocolate through a small funnel into one end of the eggshell. Let the chocolate cool and harden. There will be a small hole at the top of the egg where the funnel was, which is why Mrs. Sharp sticks a tiny chenille chick in the hole as a decorative disguise. On Easter morning when the children peel the eggshell, they will discover the chocolate egg waiting for them.

The Living Easter Basket

One of springtime's cherished customs in Mrs. Sharp's family is our living Easter basket, which we start two weeks before Easter. This is the manner of it:

Take a brightly colored basket and layer the bottom with gravel or small pebbles. Add a couple of inches of potting soil and sprinkle on fast-sprouting ryegrass seeds. Keep the soil moist and place the basket in a warm, sunny spot with a plate or dish under it to catch any seepage. In a week, the basket will be lined with living grass, a charming alternative to cellophane. When your grass is several inches high, tuck some old-fashioned yellow beeswax chicks, lambs, and bunnies into the basket along with dyed or painted wooden eggs.

Easter Nests, Egg Rolls, and Bonnets

The day before Easter, one of the loveliest traditions Mrs. Sharp's children enjoy is the creating of the Easter egg nest for the Easter Hare. Each child prepares his or her own nest in the backyard for the Easter Bunny to leave his treasures for the children.

To create the nests, the children gather flowers, grasses, twigs, and other natural materials, then add colored ribbons, paper grass, or shredded tissue paper. It's wondrous to see the nests they can create from such different materials. The next morning they find their Easter baskets in their nests. As for the Easter nests, days later we often discover a bit of the children's nests—a bright pink ribbon, for example—borrowed by the birds for their own nests!

In many countries, the Monday and Tuesday after Easter are celebrated as holidays, with families taking their first spring outings. In the United States, however, First Families since Dolley and James Madison have set aside Easter Monday for egg-rolling parties.

When Mrs. Madison began the Washington Easter Egg Roll in 1816, it was held on the long, sloped grounds of the U.S. Capitol. In 1880, Congress finally became fed up with broken eggs and smelly yolks, not to mention the antics of hundreds of Washington-area children—including the children of President and Mrs. Rutherford B. Hayes—and prohibited future egg rolls on Capitol grounds. Mrs. Hayes invited the

country's children to the White House the day after Easter for the first White House Easter Egg Roll, where the tradition has continued for more than a century.

For all the thousands of families who cannot roll or hunt for Easter eggs at the White House, may Mrs. Sharp suggest holding your own Easter egg hunt?

Let each child invite a couple of friends over on Easter Monday and tell them to bring an empty basket. Instead of dyeing eggs for a large group of children, Mrs. Sharp uses plastic eggs, which she fills with candy; plan on four eggs per child.

Count how many eggs you are hiding around the backyard before depositing them. This way you'll know when the hunt is officially over. To make the hunt fair, Mrs. Sharp divides the children into two age groups. We have the older children search in one part of the yard and the little ones in another.

Before the hunt begins, explain some simple rules: Each child must stop after finding four eggs, and there is no fighting over the eggs. To give the hunt extra zest, Mrs. Sharp also hides two gold-foil-wrapped eggs (one for each age group), which are usually available at confectionery shops. The finders of the golden eggs receive a small chocolate bunny as a prize.

After the hunt is over, have everyone head out to the driveway or street (which is closed off to traffic).

Now it is time for the Easter egg roll. Again divide your participants into two age groups. For the younger children, mark out with chalk a straight path about eight feet long; for the older children it is fun to curve the pathway. Make two paths for each age group. Give each of the children a long-handled spoon to push hard-boiled eggs inside the pathway. Anyone whose egg crosses out of the chalk lines is out. The child whose egg successfully crosses its path's finish line first wins the round. Keep on playing the game until you have one winner. Each winner, again, can be presented with a chocolate egg or rabbit.

Now it is time for everyone to adjourn for a picnic of egg-salad sandwiches, cookies, and lemonade!

No spring interlude would be complete without an afternoon of hat decorating, Mrs. Sharp's last Easter tradition. This is the most charming of customs, and both Mother and her daughters enjoy this annual feminine rite.

Plain straw hat bases can be found at many craft stores. From the dry-goods emporium or dimestore, Mrs. Sharp procures assorted colors of hat veiling, trim, flowers, feathers, and ribbon. Then our fun begins. At the end of the happy afternoon we have an Easter bonnet parade before a festive tea party, at which time Father and the boys join us, provided compliments on our handiwork accompany them!

Arbor Day

Oh, the tales Mrs. Sharp's trees tell outside her home: of plantings, picnics, and families who looked upon the spring observance of Arbor Day as a holiday that celebrates not the past, but looks toward the future.

Arbor Day is the gentlest of holidays; a thoughtful, reflective day that originated in Nebraska when one of the country's earliest ecologists, J. Sterling Morton, became dismayed with the wanton clearing of the Western plains by settlers. So widespread was the desolation that nineteenth-century maps of the Nebraska Territory bore the legend "The Great American Desert." To rectify the situation, Morton proposed an annual planting contest, calling the event Arbor Day. Prizes were offered to agricultural clubs and Granges that planted the most trees. Morton's scheme worked: The country's first Arbor Day—April 22, 1872—saw the planting of one million trees across Nebraska's barren prairies.

At Mrs. Sharp's house we celebrate the spirit of this noble, albeit unofficial, holiday. One Saturday in late April, according to the family's schedule, is designated "Arbor Day," which chance would have it coincides neatly with the need to tidy up the outdoors for spring planting. Victorian parents were as practical as they were sentimental.

On this festive day the family rises bright and early and, after a delicious breakfast, heads out the back door together. First we do an inventory of all our gardening supplies and tools (while, of course, straightening out the shed). Next, everyone is presented a new, clean pair of gardening gloves and perhaps a new gardening accessory, tool, or basket. We then go to work. All the children have their own trees, planted when they were babies, as well as a small patch of earth designated as their own garden. Soon they are all merrily raking up twigs and leaves. The trees are their friends, and each one gets a bright ribbon tied around its trunk to salute Arbor Day. To reciprocate, on each child's birthday, the trees lend their boughs for presents and balloons, a delightful custom that continues to charm long after childhood is supposed to have concluded. After our gardening chores are completed, made easier because of the collective effort, it is time to plant or unveil this year's Arbor Day remembrance, either a small fruit tree or flowering shrub.

If you would like to hold an Arbor Day ceremony for your family, neighborhood, or community, the National Arbor Day Foundation has a wonderful booklet available, "Come Celebrate Arbor Day!" Filled with helpful suggestions on how to plan an Arbor Day observance as well as charming plays and proclamations, it provides not only ideas but inspiration for restoration of this beloved nineteenth-century holiday.

With luck, the wind hasn't turned cold, nor has an April shower dampened the day's enthusiasm, so the family will end our Arbor Day observance with the season's first picnic on the lawn underneath the trees, now budding with the promise of spring.

A highlight of any Sharp family picnic is recitation. Dear Reader, do you read poetry to your young ones and encourage them to memorize nuggets of verse? Please do. Cultivating a love of literature as well as ease in oration is like planting a tree. You may not be able to sit in the shade immediately, but its shelter will be there for future enjoyment!

"Dear little tree that we plant today,
What will you be when we're old and gray?"
"The savings bank of the squirrel and mouse,
For robin and wren, an apartment house.
The dressing-room of the butterfly's ball,
The locust's and katydid's concert hall.
The schoolboy's ladder in pleasant June,
The schoolgirl's tent in the July noon.
And my leaves shall whisper them merrily
A tale of the children, who planted me."

—*Anonymous*

COLLECTIONS OF POEMS FOR CHILDREN

Only the rarest kind of best in anything can be good enough for the young," wrote the poet Walter de la Mare, and his anthology of poems for children, *Rhymes and Verses,* originally published in 1923, lived up to this credo. It should be on every nursery's bookshelf. Two other collections no child should do without are Robert Louis Stevenson's *A Child's Garden of Verses,* and *A Rocket in My Pocket,* a collection of over four hundred rhymes and chants of young Americans compiled by folklorist Carl Withers, originally published in 1948. Here are the street songs and playground verses for skipping rope, bouncing balls, and counting off games, collected throughout the United States. For a delightful anthology that traces the evolution of poems for American children, including many selections originally published in the nineteenth-century children's periodicals *St. Nicholas* and *Youth's Companion,* a rich resource is *The Oxford Book of Children's Verse in America.*

April.

They promised me a flower-bed
    That should be truly mine,
Out in the garden by the wall
    Beneath the ivy vine.

The box-wood bush would have to stay;
    The daily rose bush too;
But for the rest they'd let me plant
    Just as I chose to do.

Though not a daffodil was up
    The garden smelled of spring,
And in the trees beyond the wall
    I heard the blackbirds sing.

I worked there all the afternoon;
    The sun shone warm and still;
I set it thick with flower seeds
    And roots of daffodil.

And all the while I dug I planned,
    That, when my flowers grew,
I'd train them in a lovely bower,
    And cut a window through;

The visitors who drove from town
    Would come out there to see;
Perhaps I'd give them each a bunch,
    And then how pleased they'd be!

I made my plans—and then for weeks
    Forgot my roots and seeds,
So when I came that way again
    They all were choked with weeds.

K. Pyle.

Passover

For over three thousand years Jewish families around the world have gathered together in the springtime to observe one of the oldest festivals in existence—Passover, or Pesach, which commemorates the deliverance of the Israelites from slavery under the Pharaoh and their departure with Moses in search of the Promised Land. Passover is a solemn but joyful eight-day celebration that begins on the eve of the fourteenth day in the Jewish month Nisan with a festive seder dinner in the home. It is the most important family dinner of the year and the scene of many happy family reunions.

During the seder dinner, the youngest child asks four questions, beginning with "Why is this night different from all other nights?" The family then listens in rapt attention to a reading of the Haggadah that vividly recounts the Exodus from Egypt. At the heart of the Passover seder, certain foods play a role in the retelling of the famous story of how the Angel of Death flew, or "passed," over Jewish households when the first-born sons of Egypt were slain as a punishment to Pharaoh for refusing to let the Israelites leave with Moses. Unleavened bread, known as matzoh, is eaten to symbolize the haste with which the Jewish people fled into the wilderness. Bitter herbs or *maror* is served as a reminder of the harshness of slavery. *Haroseth,* a mixture of sweet fruits and nuts, commemorates the mortar the Jewish slaves used in building the pyramids in Egypt. Other ritual foods in this beautiful ceremonial meal, such as roasted egg, parsley, and lamb shank, recall Jewish history. At its essence, Passover serves as a timeless bridge linking the past with the present through ritual and remembrance.

In 1880, America's Jewish population was only a quarter of a million people. In the following three decades, however, more than two million Jews would again flee persecution in an exodus from Eastern Europe and Russia in search of a new promised land.

"For many people of all ethnic groups, holidays are the last ties binding them to their family and their tradition," writes Joan Nathan in her wonderful cookbook *The Jewish Holiday Kitchen*. "This is even more true for the Jews, given the importance of our dietary laws and the table-centered rituals involved in the Sabbath and holidays."

The first Victorian Jewish cookbook published in America was *The Jewish Cookery Book,* written by Esther Levy in 1871. Mrs. Levy's compilation was kosher, unlike two other Victorian cookbooks, *Aunt Babette's Cookbook* (1889) and *Twentieth Century Cookbook* (1897), which reflected in their choice of recipes a desire for assimilation into American mainstream culture.

The first American Jewish cookbook to promote traditional Jewish cooking was *The Settlement Cook Book,* written by Mrs. Simon Kander and published in 1901. Included for the first time were written recipes for such quintessential Jewish foods as matzoh balls and gefilte fish, a favorite delicacy since the Middle Ages. In its time *The Settlement Cook Book* influenced countless Victorian Jewish women living in America who wanted both to nourish their families in their new homeland and preserve the best of Jewish culinary customs from the old world they had left behind.

The Armchair.

MAY.

The merriest month of the year arrives bringing with it sunshine, birdsong, apple blossoms, budding lilacs, and longer days to enjoy life as spring's promise is finally fulfilled. Our days are spent outside as much as possible enjoying simple pleasures—the delights of a pretty garden, the relaxing comforts of lemonade and cookies on the front porch after school. We seem to laugh more and definitely want to play more together. Our family's festivities start the month off on a high note with the home-grown celebrations of May Day, as the children deliver baskets of flowers in the morning and dance around their Maypole in the afternoon. Mother is remembered on her special day, and finally, an old-fashioned summer begins with a Decoration Day picnic.

May Day

Of all the charming customs of former days that have passed into social oblivion, Mrs. Sharp most misses the annual observance of "a-Maying."

What merriment and good cheer are found in this simple, old-fashioned rite of spring! If you have never celebrated "the May" with your family, the time has come to resurrect this happy holiday.

The first-of-May frolic is an ancient festival originating in the English countryside before the Middle Ages. On this day children would rise early and venture out into the fields to collect wildflowers. These they would fashion into garlands and baskets of spring blossoms to be delivered in secret to friends and neighbors.

Later the children would gather around a Maypole, a large birch branch erected on the common green to which multicolored ribbons had been attached. Each child would hold on to a ribbon to perform high-stepping dances around the pole. The highlight of the occasion was the crowning with flowers of the "Queen of the May," who would then preside over the festivities of games and a springtime party of cakes and punch to which the entire town was invited.

Besides creating a Maypole, English villagers would also decorate their own homes with festive wreaths, garlands, and ribbons. An anonymous English poet describes the beloved custom this way:

It is a pleasant sight to see
A little village company
Drawn out upon the first of May
To have their annual holiday;
The pole hung round with garlands, gay,
The young ones footing it away,
The aged cheering their old souls,
With recollections in their bowls,
Or, on the mirth and dancing failing,
Their oft-times-told old tales re-taleing.

MINIATURE MAYPOLES

For a memorable souvenir, help the children make miniature Maypoles. For each you will need to have cut out a round disc (four inches in diameter) from colored posterboard. Light pastel colors work best, such as yellow, pink, or blue. Use a hole punch to make six holes around the edge and one hole in the middle (see Figure 1). Next cut streamers, approximately three-quarters of an inch wide and ten inches long, from pastel-colored crepe paper. Poke one streamer through each of the six outside holes of the posterboard disc. Glue the streamers to the top of the disc. Make small flowers to cover the top of the Maypole by twisting tiny pieces of tissue paper or use tiny artificial flowers, available at craft shops. These you'll glue to the top of the Maypole. Finally take a dowel three-sixteenths of an inch wide (available at hardware or lumber stores) for your pole. One dowel makes three poles: Each pole should be twelve inches long. Push the dowel rod through the middle hole of the disc. Secure the disc to the dowel rod on top and underneath with a little bit of modeling beeswax.

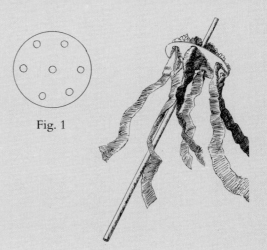

Fig. 1

Memories of a Victorian May Day

One of the most beloved of all books about life in the Victorian English countryside was Flora Thompson's trilogy *Lark Rise to Candleford*, a precious legacy from a way of life now lost forever. Here are Flora's memories of May Day:

On the last morning of April the children would come to school with bunches, baskets, arms and pinafores full of flowers—every blossom they could find in the fields and hedges or beg from parents and neighbours. On the previous Sunday some of the bigger boys would have walked six or eight miles to a distant wood where primroses grew. These, with violets from the hedgerows, cowslips from the meadows, and wallflowers, oxlips and sprays of pale red flowering currant from the cottage gardens formed the main supply. A sweetbriar hedge in the schoolmistress's garden furnished unlimited greenery.

Piled on desks, table, and floor, this supply appeared inexhaustible; but the garland was large, and as the work of dressing it proceeded, it became plain that the present stock wouldn't "hardly go nowheres," as the children said. So foraging parties were sent out, one to the Rectory, another to Squire's and others to outlying farm-houses and cottages. All returned loaded, for even the most miserly and garden-proud gave liberally to the garland. In time the wooden frame was covered, even if there had to be solid greenery to fill up at the back, out of sight. Then the "Top-Knot," consisting of a bunch of crown imperial, yellow and brown, was added to crown the whole, and the fragrant, bowery structure was sprinkled with water and set aside for the night.

On May Day the children would sing:

All hail gentle spring
*   with thy sunshine and showers,*
And welcome the sweet buds
That burst in the bowers;
Again we rejoice as thy light step and free
Brings leaves to the woodland and flowers to the
*   bee,*
Bounding, bounding, bounding, bounding
Joyful and gay,
Light and airy, like a fairy,
Come away, come away.
Come see our new garland so green and so gay;
'Tis the first fruits of spring and the glory
*   of May.*
Here are the cowslips and daisies and hyacinths
*   blue,*
Here are the buttercups bright and anemones, too.
   —*Flora Thompson, 1878–1947*

May Day Morning

Oh, let's leave a basket of flowers today
For the little old lady who lives down our way!
We'll heap it with violets white and blue,
With Jack-in-the-pulpit and wildflowers, too.
We'll make it of paper and line it with ferns
Then hide—and we'll watch her surprise when she turns
And opens her door and looks out to see
Who in the world, it could possibly be!
—*Virginia Scott Miner*

Creating May Day baskets will be as enjoyable for your children as fashioning homemade valentines. Here are three different types: tiny craft baskets, berry-carton baskets, and paper cornucopias.

The materials you will need are assorted flowers (either wildflowers or from the florist), ferns, moss, dry green Styrofoam, and containers. You will also want pretty ribbons to decorate the baskets. Other than the flowers, all the materials should be available at craft shops.

For the tiny craft baskets (three to four inches in diameter), fill the center with a small piece of dry green Styrofoam, cutting it to size so that it will fit snugly in the basket bottom. This is what you will push the stems of the flowers into so that they stay put. If you have many baskets to make, these small versions work best as they do not require many flowers. Add a pretty bow to each basket handle.

Plastic green berry baskets can be transformed into lovely May baskets. First weave a bright ribbon through the top row of the basket and tie in a bow with long tails. Line the berry basket with sphagnum moss, then place in a piece of Styrofoam cut to size. Add your flowers, filling out the bouquet with ferns.

Now tie a long (about twelve inches) ribbon handle to the top sides.

Paper cornucopia May Day baskets were the Victorian child's choice. To make them, cut an eight-and-a-half-inch square of heavyweight colored paper; patterned wrapping paper or wallpaper is also a pretty choice. With the paper facing you so that it forms a diamond, wrap the two points of the diamond together, overlapping them to form a tight cone shape. Spread glue underneath the overlapping edge to secure the cone; clip together with a clothespin until the glue dries.

Now glue some lace trim around the top edge of the cornucopia. With a hole puncher, punch out one hole on each side of the cornucopia to tie your long ribbon handle. Fill the cornucopia with flowers and ferns.

Very early on the first of May, certainly before breakfast, let the children secretly deliver their May Day baskets, hanging them on doorknobs. Should the children be seen delivering their surprise, custom dictates they must scamper back for a kiss and thanks.

If, like Mrs. Sharp's, yours is the only family in your neighborhood celebrating May Day, secretly hang a basket from your front door while the children are gone to surprise them on their return. Our family always concludes it was brought by the May Fairy.

In the afternoon, host a Maypole party. An easily portable Maypole (which can be held by an adult) can be made with a large wooden dowel (two to three inches in diameter, three feet long) available at hardware stores. Staple long ribbon streamers at the top of the dowel; if you wish, camouflage the staples by gluing a fabric bow and silk flowers around the top of the pole. As the children dance around the Maypole, weave daisy crowns and crown them all queens and kings of the May.

Should you be city dwellers, don't assume that your family can't enjoy May Day. Help the children prepare a May basket for their teachers, let them wear a fresh flower in their hair or buttonhole, take an afternoon excursion to a park if you can, and serve a May Day cake after dinner. Ice your cake with white frosting, then decorate it with a tiny Maypole made by inserting a straw into the center of the cake. Glue thin, multicolored pastel silk ribbons to the top of the straw. Pull the ribbons out to the side of the cake and add marzipan flowers to hold them to the top of the cake.

Or adapt this Victorian indoor May Day party for youngsters as described in *Popular Amusements for In and Out of Doors* in 1902. Invite children to come to your house and ask each one to bring a bouquet of one type of flower. You provide little baskets and let the little guests "use their own taste in the arrangement of the flowers . . . The hostess becomes secretary for the

whole party, writing on one side of [a] card the name and compliment of the donor and on the reverse the name of the party who is to receive the basket." Mrs. Sharp might add, perhaps, "Mama"?

Afterward serve light refreshments to your merry troop of May Day revelers, who will depart in high spirits.

Like the best pastimes, May Day is a simple pleasure. Still, its charm promises lovely springtime memories for even the most modern family.

May Day Daisy Crowns

Gather a bunch of daisies with long stems. Victorian children collected them in vast fields of flowers. You may prefer the convenience of a florist or street vendor's stand. Store the daisies in water until you make your crown, to keep them "fresh as a daisy."

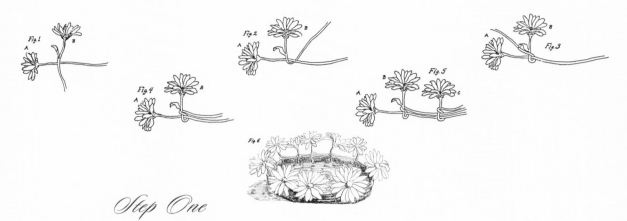

Step One

To make your daisy crown, take one daisy in your left hand and hold it horizontally, like the daisy marked A in Figure 1. Then with your right hand hold another daisy (Daisy B) upright and place its stem in front of and across the stem of Daisy A. Turn the stem of B under the stem of A and up at the back as it is in Figure 2. Bring the same stem B around and in front of its own upright part as in Figure 3. Turn it all the way around the upright part and let the stem of B rest on top of the stem of A, as in Figure 4. (In the drawing the stems are separated a little more than yours will be so that you can see each one plainly. Think of it as weaving your stems together.)

Step Two

Across the two stems of daisies A and B, place the stem of another daisy (which we'll call C) and weave it on the first two stems exactly as you wove B onto A (Fig. 5). The stem of the fourth daisy will have to cross three stems, A, B, and C. The fifth daisy stem will cross four stems, but after that you will probably have passed the stem of daisy A and you will be weaving on the subsequent daisies. It depends upon the length of the stems how many are woven over; sometimes there may be five. But it is not easy to have more than that number. Cut a stem off when it seems to be going too far around the crown.

Place the daisies close enough together to have their petals touch, or even crowd a little, because when the crown is curved and the ends brought together, the flowers will separate and leave wider spaces. When you have woven enough daisies to make your crown the proper size to fit your child's head, cut the last stems off about two inches from the last flower. With a piece of string or thin silk ribbon, tie it to the stem of daisy A.

Figure 6 shows what the daisy crown looks like when finished.

(Adapted from *Mother Nature's Toyshop* [1918] by Lina and Adelia Beard.)

What is Home without a Mother

Mother's Day

Mother's Day is an emotionally charged occasion for many families. Mrs. Sharp is sure that this was never Anna M. Jarvis's intent when, in 1907, she proposed a day be set aside for children to pay tribute to their mothers. However, when Miss Jarvis organized this annual remembrance, the original commemoration was for a mother who had passed on into loving memory.

In an effort to ease her grief, Miss Jarvis (1864–1948) arranged for a special memorial service to be held honoring her mother, providing five hundred carnations—her mother's favorite flower— as corsages.

For seven years Miss Jarvis campaigned vigorously to create a national holiday honoring mothers, winning many influential supporters, from suffragists to politicians. On May 8, 1914, Woodrow Wilson declared the second Sunday in May "Mother's Day," urging an annual "public expression of our love and reverence for the mothers of our country."

This quickly degenerated into a commercial hoopla that distressed Anna Jarvis greatly, and the poor lady spent the rest of her life arguing in letters, pamphlets, and editorials that the holiday had been intended to inspire simple loving gestures "through some distinct act of kindness, visit, letter, gift or tribute to show remembrance of the mother to whom general affection is due." Unfortunately, Miss Jarvis gave birth to an idea that, like children, grew up differently than Mother might have wished.

The new mother holding her first miracle enjoys the best Mother's Day. After that, Mrs. Sharp suspects for many women (although they are hard-pressed to admit it) the celebration of Mother's Day is a slow exercise in the law of diminishing returns.

Why should this be so?

First, mothers are rarely remembered as they would like to be, because few of our children know us as individuals with personal preferences. Usually we are so busy nurturing and meeting everyone else's needs while the family is growing up that we fail to articulate our own wants and desires. Clairvoyance is not a gift bestowed on many children.

The second reason disappointment looms is because when Mother's Day rolls around, most of us forget we are not our husband's mother. We are hurt because our husband did not remember us. Dear Reader, the day a husband annually remembers his wife with special, loving gestures is called "the wedding anniversary." Yes, it is lovely when a husband expresses his appreciation for our efforts as a mother. However, Mrs. Sharp believes it is a far better gesture for husbands to remember their own mothers rather than expecting daughters-in-law to do it every year.

Of course, in a young family Father must take on

the responsibility of helping little children prepare or obtain a small gift for Mother. But Father's encouragement should be necessary only until a child is ten years old. After that, the fledgling celebrant is on his or her own.

This means, in the course of any lifetime, there is bound to be the occasional dry year when someone forgets to remember Mama. Usually this occurs only once (the sight of Mother lying prone in the upstairs bedroom, with red, swollen eyes, has a chilling effect on even the most recalcitrant adolescent memory).

Unaccustomed as she is to giving unsolicited advice, Mrs. Sharp hesitates to intrude with suggestions on how to improve your family's observance of Mother's Day. However, one helpful hint is that if the lady of the house to be honored is offered breakfast in bed, make sure she does not have to clean the kitchen later in the day.

Mrs. Sharp's next suggestion is for her younger women friends. Dear Reader, this year decide no matter how the day turns out, from now on you will observe Mother's Day in your own special way: by reflecting on the intangible joys that come from being a mother. Celebrate yourself. Treat yourself to a lovely token of esteem, mentally toss out the past year's accumulated burden of guilt, and start anew. Remember, it is only the first one hundred years

of motherhood that are the hardest. After that, you're home free.

And for goodness' sake, do not forget your own mother!

Mothering Sunday

Long before Anna Jarvis was responsible for America's honoring Mother in May, the English were remembering their mothers on Simnel Sunday, or Mothering Sunday, which was the fourth Sunday in Lent. This observance began during the Middle Ages and was the day that young apprentices and servants were permitted an annual holiday to return to their home villages to visit their mothers. On this day, Lenten fast was allowed to be broken, and children, usually the eldest son, took their mothers a special spiced confectionery known as simnel cake, which was cut and shared by the entire family.

There are many versions of simnel cake, with each district of England claiming a particular recipe. Here is a traditional version sure to please both you and your mother.

Mrs. Sharp's Simnel Cake

¾ cup (1½ sticks) sweet butter at room temperature

1½ cups sugar

4 large eggs

2 cups unbleached flour

½ teaspoon salt

¼ cup currants

¼ cup candied fruit peel, ground fine in a food processor★

8 ounces almond paste (available ready-made in cans)

Confectioners' sugar

Candied violets or marzipan fruits for garnish (optional)

Preheat the oven to 350°. Cream the butter and sugar together until fluffy. Beat in eggs, one at a time. Sift the flour with the salt and separate into three parts, blending each portion into the egg-butter–sugar mixture thoroughly. Fold in currants and candied fruit peel and mix lightly. Grease an 8-to-10-inch round cake pan and line with waxed paper or greased parchment. Pour half the batter into the pan. Roll out half the almond paste into a circle between two sheets of waxed paper. Remove the top sheet of waxed paper and place the exposed side of almond paste on top of the batter; peel off the remaining waxed paper. Add remaining batter to pan. Bake for 1 hour and 15 minutes or until cake pulls away slightly from the side of the pan. Roll out remaining almond paste into another circle. Place on cake and return to oven for 10 minutes. Let cake cool on a rack for a half hour. To remove from the pan, run a knife along the edges and turn out carefully. Sprinkle the top of the cake with confectioners' sugar and decorate with candied violets or marzipan fruit around the outer edges, if desired. This cake also looks pretty decorated with a few fresh flowers around the sides of the cake plate.

*Note: Candied fruit peel is not always easy to find but is quite simple to make. Wash and peel oranges, lemons, and limes into long strips and place on a cookie sheet. Prepare a sugar glaze by dissolving 2 cups sugar in ½ cup water in a heavy saucepan. Swirl over medium heat until clear. Raise the heat, cover, and bring to a rapid boil, then uncover and boil 3 additional minutes. Brush the fruit peel with the glaze. After it dries, chop the fruit peel in a food processor.

It is the day of all the year
Of all the year the one day,
And here come I my Mother dear,
To bring you cheer,
A mothering on Sunday.

May.

I climbed and I climbed to the top of the tree;
    High up in the branches I stood.
Below in the field was a man with his plough,
    And I called him as loud as I could.

He stopped, and he looked at the hedges and lane,
    And no one at all could he see,
For he never once thought, as he wondered and stared
    I was up in the top of the tree.

I swung and I swayed with the tree in the wind;
    I was not afraid I would fall;
The maple seeds spread out their little green wings,
    And nobody saw me at all.

K. Pyle.

Decoration Day
(Memorial Day)

For many families, including Mrs. Sharp's, Memorial Day weekend is when the summer season officially commences. However, before she begins polishing her high-button boots or packing the picnic hamper, Mrs. Sharp thought she would reflect on the origins of Memorial Day, as the holiday was first known.

Let us return to Columbus, Mississippi, in the spring of 1866. The Civil War has been over for a year, yet Union soldiers still occupy the town. The fires of passion and prejudice that had consumed over 500,000 American lives between 1861 and 1865 still smolder in bitterness behind closed doors.

Just outside Columbus is a cemetery where both Confederate and Union soldiers killed at the Battle of Shiloh are buried. On April 25, 1866, four young women pay a visit to the cemetery to tend the graves of lost loved ones and decorate them with memorial garlands of flowers.

After decorating the Confederate graves, the women walk over to a small plot where forty Union soldiers are buried. Gently they scatter Southern magnolia blossoms on the Northern graves. The news of this unselfish, compassionate gesture spreads quickly and

touches everyone. Newspaper editorials praise this act of reconciliation and urge the nation to come together to mourn both "the Blue and the Gray."

Soon in many small towns all over the country, people were gathering at Civil War cemeteries and holding commemorative or "memorial day" services. Afterward, there would be parades led by a brass band, the volunteer fire brigade, and a review to honor America's veterans. Following the parade and patriotic orations, there would be a community picnic on the town common.

During the late nineteenth century, Decoration Day was a major American holiday and was celebrated with even more fanfare than Independence Day. This was because the Civil War had touched or altered nearly everyone's life.

Even though the country came together in spirit to honor America's war dead, the North and South still managed to commemorate independently. In 1868, General John A. Logan, commander in chief of the GAR (Grand Army of the Republic, a Union veterans' organization), designated May 30 as Memorial Day, while the Daughters of the Confederacy held firm with the term Decoration Day and the date of April 26. Today, Memorial Day is recognized as a day honoring all of those who have fought America's

Decoration Day,
May 30, 1899

re-creating the past as realistically as possible. A realistic living-history event can create the illusion that you have entered another era as your family sees firsthand the type of clothes people wore, how they cooked, what tools they used, their speech, manners, and amusements.

Usually these living-history "time machines" take the form of an organized reenactment, military encampment, festival, or program at an outdoor living-history site, such as Williamsburg, Virginia; Henry Ford's Greenfield Village in Dearborn, Michigan; or Massachusetts's Plimoth Plantation. Some living-history programs, such as the Des Moines, Iowa, Living History Farms, even provide hands-on activities for visitors.

There are thousands of living-history events taking place around the country during the summer months. A good place to begin your search for outings is through your local historical society.

Memorial Day weekend offers families an occasion to reflect on our country's past, as well as an opportunity to anticipate the fun of the summer ahead. A living-history outing, whether in your own neighborhood or farther afield, is a memorable way to celebrate this old-fashioned holiday honoring times past.

wars and is legally observed on the last Monday in May.

Now it's time to dust off the grill, as Mrs. Sharp's tradition for Memorial Day includes the family's first official backyard cookout of the season. While the chicken is barbecuing and potato salad chilling, the family also engages in a lively discussion of what our vacation plans will include this summer. Of course, there will be the requisite outings to the seashore and a respite in the mountains, but our family also enjoys annual visits to living-history reenactments or outdoor historical museums. Mrs. Sharp believes your family will, too.

"Living history" is an attempt to simulate life in another time and place through interpreting and

JUNE.

June is busting out all over as summer finally arrives. The days are hot, the roses are in bloom, and we feast on strawberries and cream. School is over, summer camp begins, picnic baskets are packed, and life begins to revolve around the front porch and swimming pool as much as possible. At Mrs. Sharp's we celebrate life with Father this month and look forward to an old-fashioned Midsummer Night's Eve and fairy revels.

Victorian Ice Cream Social

*S*ummer afternoon—summer afternoon; to me those have always been the two most beautiful words in the English language," observed Henry James. With this kindred spirit, Mrs. Sharp welcomes the first glorious June afternoon.

There can be little doubt that with the exception of Christmas, summer was the season Victorian families loved best. For children it conjured up visions of parades, picnics, and fireworks, romps in swimming holes, baseball games, catching june bugs, homemade ice cream, ice-cold watermelon, and frosty glasses of lemonade. For their parents, the summer meant family outings in the countryside, excursions to trolley parks, and, perhaps most important of all, a chance to take part in a brand-new fad sweeping the country—the two-week summer vacation.

For Mrs. Sharp's family, June's first joy begins when school bells toll adieu. After nine months of car pools, strict schedules, homework, tests, science projects, school box lunches, and parent-teacher conferences, Mrs. Sharp and the children need a carefree occasion to wipe the slate clean for three months and get ready to celebrate the "good old summertime." Don't you, dear Reader?

Mrs. Sharp's tradition to mark this annual rite of passage is an old-fashioned "School's Out/Summer's In" ice-cream social. On the last day of school the children invite their friends over for a fun-filled extravaganza of excess: do-it-yourself ice-cream sodas and sundaes. What makes this afternoon party so appealing is the blending of ages as family, friends,

classmates, and special teachers mingle in a wonderful mélange of informal frivolity.

Ice cream has been synonymous with American summers for two centuries. George Washington, Thomas Jefferson, and Dolley Madison served it at dinner parties. In 1846, however, an inventive Victorian homemaker, Mrs. Nancy Johnson, made ice cream accessible to everyone when she patented the hand-cranked ice-cream freezer.

But in the days before refrigerators, frugal nineteenth-century homemakers could not often permit a costly and easily perishable commodity such as ice to be used for the making of a dessert. This is probably why ice cream making came to be associated with an occasion calling for a special indulgence, such as a holiday or an event like an "ice cream social," a favorite Victorian summer entertainment.

By the 1870s, commercially made ice cream was available during the summer months at "ice cream parlors." At the Philadelphia Exposition in 1874, a new American confection—the ice cream soda—was born when the soft-drink concessionaire ran out of the heavy cream he normally used in a drink made with fruit juices and carbonated soda water. In desperation he substituted vanilla ice cream, to the happy hurrahs of his customers. Ice cream sodas so tickled America's fancy that by 1890 editorials wondered if this addiction wasn't undermining the moral fiber of society. To counteract this, laws were passed forbidding the sale of ice cream sodas on the Sabbath. An enterprising soda fountain proprietor got around this by leaving out the carbonated water and calling his

ice-cream-and-fruit concoction "a Sunday soda," which was soon shortened to "sundaes."

Today, of course, children believe ice cream comes from the grocery store freezer. Depending on the number of people invited over to make sundaes at your School's Out/Summer's In social, it is probably just as well and convenient that it does.

Saying good-bye to schoolmates and teachers can be an emotional occasion even for young children. Make sure you have an address book available in which to write down everyone's address, telephone number, and E-mail address. As a party activity and for take-home favors, give out autograph books—or make them. For each book take five sheets of plain

white 8½-by-11-inch paper, fold them in half, and cut them to make ten single pages. With a hole punch make two holes on the left-hand side of the pages and tie the book together with a twelve-inch piece of ribbon or yarn. If you like, use a piece of stiff art board as a cover and decorate it with a group picture of all the guests, either an instant photo taken at the party, or one you can send each guest a copy of later in the summer, as a nice way of keeping in touch.

Begin the summer with style by lingering in the long afternoon of the nineteenth century at an ice cream social. The memories you can create for your family are bound to become precious school-day souvenirs.

June.

The robins and blackbirds awoke me at dawn
Out in the wet orchard, beyond the green lawn,

For there they were holding a grand jubilee,
And no one had wakened to hear it but me.

The sweet honeysuckles were sprinkled with dew;
There were hundreds of spider-webs wet with it too,

And pussy-cat, out by the lilacs, I saw
Was stopping and shaking the drops from her paw.

I dressed in the silence as still as a mouse,
And groped down the stairway and out of the house.

There, dim in the dawning, the garden paths lay,
Where yesterday evening we shouted at play.

By the borders of box-wood, and under the trees
There was nothing astir but the birds and the bees.

And if all the world had been made just for me,
I thought, what a wonderful thing it would be.

K. Pyle.

Summer Camp

This month many families will answer the call of the wild as children are packed up and shipped off to a uniquely American institution: summer camp.

For more than a century, summer camp—a sentimental potpourri of fresh air, pine, calamine lotion, toasted marshmallows, and ghost stories around a blazing campfire—has meant a coming of age for children. Generations of hopeful parents have viewed this annual adventure as an investment in the intellectual, emotional, and creative growth of their offspring.

While the first planned outdoor summer encampment for boys was organized in 1861 by Frederick William Gunn, the realities of the Civil War gave new meaning to the word *encampment,* and organized outdoor recreational pursuits for youths spread slowly over the next two decades.

In 1885, Sumner Dudley, a member of the Young Men's Christian Association, dreamed of a network of summer YMCA camps across the United States and arranged a modest camping expedition for seven city boys to Orange Lake, near Newburgh, New York. Dudley's small camping experiment was a huge success: By the turn of the century that lone pitched tent on Orange Lake grew to 167 organized YMCA camps.

Organized camping's pioneers covered a wide (albeit mostly male) spectrum: educators, physicians, clergymen, and social workers, who campaigned vigorously for all children to spend time in the outdoors, believing it to be a remedy for almost everything that ailed America, from consumption to juvenile delinquency. In 1902, the first camp for young women, Camp Kehonka in New Hampshire, was established.

Still, Mrs. Sharp remembers that for decades each summer, articles in women's periodicals posed the provocative question, "Shall We Send Our Daughter to Camp?" Modern parents no longer ponder this issue, of course. But despite how enjoyable camp may be for many children, for some it is a period of loneliness and anxiety, especially if they are first-timers. Helping your child to overcome homesickness can be the key to a successful camp experience for both of you. Confront the problem head-on and assure your child that other children feel homesick as well. But emphasize that homesickness comes and goes; keeping busy is the best remedy.

Mrs. Sharp's tradition for helping a child feel connected while apart is a steady stream of envelopes and packages at mail call. Begin by sending your first letter before your child leaves home so that it will be there to welcome him. Camp counselors admit there is no more poignant memory than the sight of young children walking away empty-handed at mail call. If you would like to receive mail from your camper, be sure to send him to camp with a stationery kit that will encourage keeping in touch: colorful stationery, funny note cards, pens, pencils, stickers, and *self-addressed stamped envelopes.* Tuck in a supply of extra stamps to encourage notes to other friends and family. Put everything in an inviting folder with a flap and pack it in the suitcase.

Another camp custom children particularly look forward to is receiving camp "care packages" filled with books, puzzles, games, and other novelties (most camps do not want parents to send food to your camper). Plan on one care package per two-week stay and try to have five to six different items per package. Try to pick up unusual gift items as you see them and put them away several months before your child goes off to camp. Perhaps wrap each gift in colored tissue paper,

and include an extra gift for a special bunkmate.

"Now I see the secret of making the best persons," Walt Whitman observed. "It is to grow in the open air, and to eat and sleep with the earth." If you have a child attending summer camp, careful planning, positive encouragement, and support can make all the difference between going away and being sent.

A Victorian Midsummer Night's Dream

The celebration of Midsummer Night is a magical adventure of imagination and whimsy young children can embark upon. This ancient festival celebrates the summer solstice, and while it is barely noticed in America, it is still celebrated in England and Europe. It is observed either on June 21, the longest day of the year, or June 24, the official Midsummer Day, which is also the feast of Saint John the Baptist.

If you want to introduce this delightful summertime custom into your family's repertoire of pastimes, begin by telling your children that legend says that on Midsummer Night, the fairy realm holds its annual revels and is visible to human eyes (if you're lucky enough to notice), as William Shakespeare reminds us in *A Midsummer Night's Dream*.

And the fairies expect a party. Of course, everyone knows fairies are perfectly capable of providing their own refreshments. However, Mrs. Sharp discovered a secret long ago, which she passed down to her children. Any human child who prepares a feast for the fairies on Midsummer Night will be well rewarded. This enchantment comes but once a year, like Christmas, and is precious. For the magical bounty the fairies leave behind is like no other treasure.

First some caveats: The fairies leave presents only for the child who is kind enough to provide a party for them, whether in a suburban backyard garden or, for city dwellers, on the balcony or dining room table.

Help the children prepare small treats and decorations; their little hands can also keep busy setting up tables or picnics with doll dishes in the garden for the fairy feast.

As for the gifts (which need not be extravagant, just inventive) the fairies leave behind, they always arrive specially wrapped, in brightly colored ribbons and netting (inexpensive and available at the dry-goods store) or in gold foil. Suggestions include books of fairy tales; a crystal mineral piece, perhaps in its own special pouch; tiny crystal animals or a crystal necklace; small wooden animals or puzzles; dried flower wreath crowns with ribbon streamers; magic wands and capes; or unusual art supplies.

If you would like to step off the dreary treadmill for a nostalgic interlude, Mrs. Sharp knows your family will enjoy the pleasures of this old-fashioned summer tradition for many years to come.

Night-time stars and bonfires bright
Families and friends sing on good St. John's Night
Summer sun, the sweet smell of hay,
And Children all dancing on Midsummer Day.

At Midsummer time the fairies come out,
If children could see them with glee they would shout!
On Midsummer's Eve even gnomes try to dance,
In fairy-ring revels they awkwardly prance.
On Midsummer Day elves and fairies all fly
From acorns and buttercups up to the sky.

—*Mala Powers*

Celebrating Life with Father

Each year about this time it occurs to Mrs. Sharp that it could not possibly have been a woman who thought to set aside the third Sunday in June to celebrate life with Father. That's because Father's Day comes so close to Mother's Day that the memory often stings in comparison. Dear Reader, as you attempt to outdo yourself in making Father's Day a happy, memorable event in your home, please refrain from recalling the highlights of your own special day. The celebration of Mother's Day and of Father's Day is an excellent example of comparing apples and oranges. In the salad of life, each fruit has its own distinctive flavor.

"What is it men would sincerely like for Father's Day?" Mrs. Sharp once inquired of her husband, who is not keen on duck-motif knickknacks or brown-plaid thingamajigs. Although Mr. and Mrs. Sharp have been married for over a century, the celebration of Father's Day is really quite a new occasion, only becoming an official national holiday by an act of Congress in 1972. During the Victorian era, for most families, the commanding presence of "Father" dictated that every day was Father's Day.

"My dear, fathers want exactly the same thing that mothers do. Acknowledgment of their efforts on behalf of their beloved family and recognition by the

family of the father's role, whatever that is these days," Mr. Sharp responded briskly as he carried down another load of wash to the basement.

Quite so. Which is why Mrs. Sharp's tradition for helping our children observe Father's Day is an annual scrapbook of appreciation recounting all Dad did with, and for, the children during the preceding year. Did Father help someone with a school project? Read through the entire oeuvre of *Winnie-the-Pooh*? Teach a child how to ride a bicycle, swing a bat, or tie a shoe? Good-naturedly allow yet another stray animal to become a family pet? If he did, encourage the children to show their appreciation with a loving memory book containing photographs, funny captions, cartoons, and drawings commemorating their year together. Have each child write (or dictate) a letter to Dad thanking him for all he does and letting him know how much he is loved.

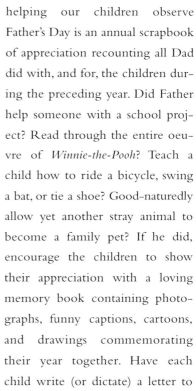

(Yes, dear Reader, Mrs. Sharp agrees, this token of esteem would also be a perfect gift for Mother's Day. But someone has to help the children organize this project during their younger years.)

"It is a wise father that knows his own child," Shakespeare reminds us. Mrs. Sharp reminds her dear Reader that wise wives and happy children know Father is very sentimental.

Entertainments from the Past
A Strawberry Regale

During the Victorian era, a favorite summer amusement on warm June evenings was the community's annual strawberry fete or festival. Usually these eagerly anticipated outdoor socials, sponsored by churches or schools as fund-raising events, featured an abundance of fresh-picked strawberries, whipped cream, cakes, pies, tarts, and ice cream.

By the turn of the century the holding of a strawberry fete or "regale" had been turned into an art form. Mrs. Nellie Mustain describes how to give one in her book *Popular Amusements for In and Out of Doors,* published in 1902.

First of all, for decorations, Victorian women were instructed to "secure as many old-fashioned garden flowers, also a profusion of vines, if possible—the strawberry vine, or the potentilla, that can be found in quantities in fields and lanes. With these the rooms should be profusely decorated." For instance, garlands of vines were recommended to run from corners of the room to the chandelier, white curtains could be looped with vines, and a potted strawberry plant in fruit or flower should be placed in the center of each table.

As for the food, "strawberries in every style and form will furnish the refreshments for the occasion; strawberry ice cream, strawberries and cream, strawberries and ice cream, strawberries and whipped cream, strawberry whip, fruit lemonade, strawberry shortcake and strawberry sherbet."

While Mrs. Sharp hasn't attended as lavish a strawberry regale as Mrs. Mustain's since before World War I, June still calls for one at the Sharp household. The day before we head out to a local berry-picking patch for the berries. Picking berries with children is one of the simplest amusements but is always as anticipated as the eating. We make sure we pack our sun hats, berry baskets, and a thermos of cold lemonade, then head out together early one morning before the sun is too hot. We fill our baskets to the brim so that there will be more than enough for strawberry shortcakes, muffins, homemade ice cream, and preserves. Even though today it is possible for us to obtain strawberries year-round, strawberry shortcake before a fireplace in January simply doesn't taste the way it does on the veranda in June.

Mrs. Sharp's Simply Scrumptious Strawberry Shortcake

This is a Victorian-inspired recipe for pound cake. The cake is moist, rich, and delicious.

3 cups all-purpose flour, sifted three times

½ teaspoon baking soda

½ teaspoon salt

1½ cups sweet butter (3 sticks) at room temperature

3 cups sugar

7 eggs at room temperature

8 ounces sour cream

2 tablespoons brandy

2 tablespoons vanilla

2 quarts strawberries

1 quart whipped cream

Preheat oven to 325°.

Sift the flour with baking soda and salt and set aside. Cream the butter at a medium speed with an electric mixer until it resembles whipped cream. Dribble sugar into the creamed butter 1 tablespoon at a time. Add eggs, one at a time, and continue to beat until mixture is light and fluffy. Add flour to this mixture ½ cup at a time and mix well. Add sour cream; beat well. Add brandy and vanilla.

Grease and flour a large tube or angelfood pan. Pour mixture into pan and bake for 1½ hours. This cake will rise very high. Remove cake and let it cool thoroughly.

In the meantime, clean and hull 2 quarts of strawberries. Place ⅔ of the strawberries in a bowl and sprinkle with sugar. Slice the remaining strawberries in half.

Prepare 1 quart of homemade whipped cream. When the pound cake is completely cooled, slice it into three layers. Ladle some of the strawberries and sugar mixture onto the first layer of cake. Top it with a layer of whipped cream. Add the second layer of cake and repeat. Finish the cake by decorating the top layer with whipped cream and garnish with whole strawberries.

JULY.

Come celebrate life, liberty, and the pursuit of happiness this month as our family revels in the summertime joys of an old-fashioned Independence Day—parades, picnics, and fireworks. Next we're off on our family vacation and excursions to the seashore. Finally, like most Victorian families, we'll celebrate Christmas in July. Would you care to join us?

The Pursuit of Happiness:
An Old-Fashioned Independence Day

The glorious Fourth of July is America's greatest patriotic holiday. Because it is the anniversary of the day the Declaration of Independence was adopted, it became known as Independence Day. Over the past two centuries the customs surrounding the Fourth of July—parades, picnics, and fireworks—have become as familiar as the candles on our own birthday cake and have changed little.

For most of us, the Fourth of July is more than a holiday; it's a state of mind. That's because there exists in America's collective unconscious an image of the quintessential Independence Day celebration: American flags waving in the hot summer breeze, the snap of a Sousa march, white bandstands festooned in red-white-and-blue bunting on village greens, picnic tables covered in gingham tablecloths and set up underneath tall shade trees, groaning under the weight of a score of straw picnic hampers.

Elegant ladies stroll this mental landscape in long white linen, parasols, and red-ribboned straw boaters, while children frolic in navy sailor suits and dresses, babies romp in bloomers, and gentlemen are permitted to strip down to shirts and suspenders for a game of baseball or a three-legged sack race. Finally, twilight gives way to showers of shooting stars, exploding into black-ness along with the rockets' red glare as blue bombs burst in air.

If you've ever wondered where this idyllic Fourth of July scene came from, you might be charmed to discover that it first appeared in fiction penned for the pages of Victorian ladies' periodicals. Just as we today are influenced (even if we won't admit it) by what we read in our women's magazines, so were our foremothers, who became inspired to re-create for their own families the nostalgic or "old-fashioned" holidays depicted in magazines such as *Godey's Lady's Book* or *Demorest's Family Magazine*.

Homegrown History

Unfortunately, the history of our American holidays has remained largely unwritten, being for the most part homegrown and oral. But history can come alive for children in family celebrations, especially when it is told as a story. Did you know, for example, there really was an Uncle Sam? Here's his story:

After serving as a soldier in the Revolutionary War, Sam Wilson began a meatpacking business in Troy, New York. Known for his honesty, common sense, and friendliness, everyone in Troy called him Uncle Sam. When the War of 1812 broke out, Sam

Wilson became a sutler, or supplier, of meat to the army. As the story goes, one day a reporter writing about the war efforts visited the Wilson butchery. There he noticed that all the barrels of beef were stamped with the initials "U.S." When he inquired as to what the initials stood for, a clerk told him, "Why, for Uncle Sam, of course." Very soon, the story of the army's "Uncle Sam" began appearing in newspapers all across the country and the association caught on, as everything the army used from cannonballs to blankets was referred to as "Uncle Sam's." During the 1830s, Uncle Sam appeared for the first time in newspaper political cartoons depicted as a young man. In the 1840s, a Victorian performer named Dan Rice made Uncle Sam larger-than-life by portraying him walking on stilts and giving him a Stars and Stripes costume. But the well-known image of Uncle Sam with gray hair and a beard was created by the cartoonist Thomas Nast, who first drew him in 1869.

Sharing stories—both folklore and history—about holidays increases a family's enjoyment for young and old alike. A wonderful resource to introduce children to the origins of our patriotic symbols is the book *Fireworks, Picnics and Flags: The Story of the Fourth of July Symbols* by James Cross Giblin.

Set the Mood for Celebration

Mrs. Sharp's Independence Day celebration begins with a candlelight breakfast that lives up to the holiday: blueberry pancakes with strawberry syrup. Soon, it's time to pack up the family to attend Takoma Park's annual Independence Day Parade—a tradition since 1889.

After the parade, the family heads to the annual Independence Day picnic. Time was, when America lived in small towns where everyone knew your name and you knew theirs, the entire community would come together for a grand Fourth of July picnic. Those days might seem gone forever, but there's no reason why the spirit of the community picnic cannot continue in your own backyard with a covered-dish gathering of neighbors, all contributing their best recipes.

An Old-Fashioned "Cooperative" Picnic

Let Mrs. Sharp take you back to one such cooperative Fourth of July around the turn of the century. Among the trees in the backyard was a clearing for the children's games, and the supper was prepared on an improvised board table of generous dimensions on the adjoining front lawn. Bunting in the three patriotic colors was carried from branch to branch of overarching trees to make a pretty canopy top over the long table. The girls had gathered together quantities of flowers, and these were arranged over the white table cover in the form of a large star-shaped centerpiece: an outline row of poppies rested on a fringe of ferns; inside it came several rows of daisies, then blue cornflowers. In the center of the blue flowers stood a quite realistic toy figure of Uncle Sam.

The dishes used were blue and white ware, and for the distinctive red touch, there were large glass dishes filled with currants, strawberries, and raspberries. The menu consisted of an appetizing assortment of hearty sandwiches, a variety of salads, baked ham, and fried chicken. Stone crocks held freshly squeezed lemonade; there was also ginger beer and mineral water to drink. A separate table draped in crisp blue gingham was provided for the assorted cakes, pies, tarts, and strawberry ice cream served in blue dishes.

Little flags decorated every possible dish, and each person at the table found at his plate a small flag as a souvenir.

Supper was served promptly at six, so that when it was finished there would be time for music, games, and the evening's finale.

After supper it was time for the games. A large flag was tacked to the outside porch of one house within easy reach of all. Over the stars had been pasted a square of dark-blue cloth. Each person was given a white paper star, and after being blindfolded in turn, he or she was twirled around, then told to pin the star in its proper place on the flag. This proved to be a merry undertaking.

After that came assorted relay races pairing children with adults and pitting the ladies against the gentlemen in various teams. When everyone had happily exhausted themselves, the participants all adjourned for ice-cold watermelon. By now twilight was approaching and the patriotic strains of "The Star-Spangled Banner" could be heard, played on small horns, whistles, drums, and harmonicas.

At nightfall everyone gathered together to watch a municipal fireworks display held in a large clearing away from buildings. Ending the Fourth of July in a parent's arms looking up at fireworks exploding in the dark sky is a memory no child should grow up without, in times past or today.

A Great Deal to Celebrate

One of the satisfying elements about celebrating the Fourth of July as a family holiday is that even if our personal experience varies—if we are barbecuing on the beach or the patio of an apartment building or enjoying a brass band concert in front of a village bandstand—it doesn't really matter. Mrs. Sharp thinks this is because when as a nation of individuals we come together with family and friends to celebrate Independence Day, it's more than the birthday of even a country. For what we really celebrate in our hearts is the birthday of an ideal and, like our forebears, a deeply personal vision of contentment.

And really, we do have a great deal to celebrate, dear Reader, don't you agree? For where else on earth is there a nation that sets aside one day a year to exalt life, liberty, and the pursuit of happiness?

MAY MRS. SHARP BE OF ASSISTANCE?

Having attended more than a century's worth of parades, may Mrs. Sharp pass on a few gentle suggestions that will make the difference between enjoying the parade and enduring it? Her parade survival kit includes a thermos of cold lemonade, as well as tempting snacks from home, since children at parades seem to require endless amounts of liquids and food. We also pack paper fans, small flags to wave, napkins, and a wet washcloth in a plastic sandwich bag for wiping sticky hands and faces (much more refreshing than those commercially packaged wipes). You might also want to bring folding chairs and/or a blanket to sit on.

July.

Past the meadows, parched and brown,
We drove across the hills to town
    To see the big parade;
The sunny pavements burned our feet.
It was so noisy in the street;
    That Tommy felt afraid.

Through the crowds, with fife and drum
And flags, we saw the soldiers come,
    And boys marched either side,
And one big fat man rode ahead
Who had a sword, and Billy said,
    "They're captains when they ride."

They carried flags, red, white and blue.
I wished I was a soldier too;
    Then when the big drum beat
The people all would run to see,
And little boys would stare at me
    As we marched up the street.

K. Pyle.

Traveling with the Children

Ah, the family vacation! What fertile memories contemplation of this annual custom conjures up: a moving garbage dump, incessant choruses of "Are we there yet?" (begun three blocks from home), sibling assault and battery, comfort stops every fifteen miles, and . . .

As humorist Robert Benchley observed: "There are two classes of travel—first class and with children."

If the above describes your last family vacation, Mrs. Sharp urges her readers to take heart. Why? Because family vacations can preserve sanity and unity. A family vacation affords parents and children the time and opportunity not just to get away from it all, but to get it all together. This summer, traveling with your children can be such a pleasure you'll look forward to it.

Impossible, you say, dear Reader?

Happy trips with youngsters are not only not impossible, they can be fun. This is because children add a new perspective to our travel. First of all, children make friends more easily than adults do. They're not as intimidated, so they open up new worlds for their parents. Vacations with children can also be more leisurely since ten-hour sight-seeing jaunts are out of the question. Families traveling together are more selective about their activities.

One reason family vacations have such bad reputations is that in the past, parents usually found themselves "making do" at hotels and resorts that barely tolerated the presence of children. The baby boom and the resulting lucrative market have changed all of this. The travel industry finally realizes that modern parents travel with their children. Many vacation resorts and hotels now offer an abundance of children's programs geared to various age groups, interests, and budgets.

After a century of traveling with a family, Mrs. Sharp believes the three most important rules to a happy and successful family vacation are that parents have the right attitude beforehand, that you can truly afford the vacation you have chosen, and that you do your homework before leaving home.

The right attitude simply means you intend to enjoy this vacation time together as a family. Toward this end, whether you're toting a toddler or taking along teenagers, the more you can involve the children in planning the vacation, the more successful the trip will be. Parents need to sit down and take into consideration the needs and interests of each family member, starting with the youngest child and working up. The youngest child is normally the hardest one to satisfy and has the most needs. You have to make sure that you can find cribs, high chairs, and booster seats. For preschoolers you must remember to give careful thought to any activity that requires a great deal of standing in line, as preschoolers are not known for their patience.

On the Road Again

While it is wonderful that the travel horizons of modern families have broadened considerably since Mrs. Sharp's day, summer is still usually synonymous with car trips. Anyone who has ever traveled more

than fifty miles with young children cooped up in a car understands that it is essential to pack activities to amuse the rising generation while riding.

One of Mrs. Sharp's traditions for car trips is "happy trails kits," designed to keep parents happy while preventing the backseat occupants from getting too restless. The kits, one for each child, hold both new surprises and tried-and-true favorites. Depending on each child's preference, we use a backpack, duffel bag, or small plastic suitcase (available at toy stores) to hold the contents.

To get more mileage out of the items, Mrs. Sharp likes to wrap each novelty individually in colorful tissue paper; the children are permitted to open a package each hour. If the trip is going to take several days, she'll ration the surprises to last the duration, at night refilling each bag to be ready in the morning.

Victorian mothers used to make up a special travel toy called the Magic Ball, a little novelty that still has the power to amuse even modern children. One Magic Ball would be made for each child. Inside a ball of yarn we would insert little novelties, continually wrapping the yarn around them, so that as the children unraveled the ball of yarn, they would discover another small toy. Using a roll of crepe paper to create a Magic Ball also works well.

Every child will enjoy creating a travel diary. Get artist's sketchbooks and glue sticks and let the children paste in menus, place mats, ticket stubs, and other paper mementos. Bring along a supply of stamps and have the children mail postcards home to themselves with their travel impressions. When they return, they can add these special (and inexpensive) souvenirs along with photographs to their travel log. Each young traveler will also appreciate a map (a clear photocopy will do as well), with the route, along with cities and landmarks, marked out in colored marker.

In each kit Mrs. Sharp includes new crayons (perhaps in amusing shapes, such as dinosaurs or teddy bears), colored felt-tip markers, drawing paper attached to small clipboards, age-appropriate activity books such as coloring books, hidden-pictures games, connect-the-dots puzzles, mazes, and crossword puzzles. Colorforms or press-and-peel reusable vinyl sticker sets are always welcomed. After the paper and activity books are used up, bring out old-fashioned magic slates, which still have the power to charm, especially in a car. For older children, magnetic games and puzzles are also available.

THE ANNUAL HOLIDAY

The practice of taking an annual holiday is becoming more and more general . . . and is beginning to be regarded rather as a necessity than a luxury. Reduced railway fares and cheap excursions have made a change of air possible to people with limited incomes and large families; and a seaside trip or visit to the country has been brought within the reach of many who formerly spent their lives from year's end to year's end in close streets and smoky towns. In these days of high pressure, life in large towns becomes yearly more wearing and more exhausting; and a change is needed, not only of air, but of occupation and of thought, to restore lost energy, and calm excited and overwrought brains. . . . [However] over and over again nowadays we hear on all sides that it is most absurd for all the members of the family to try to spend their holiday together. The seaside, the right place for the children, is, we are told, very dull and quite unbearable for the father of the family; though the fact that it is quite as dull for the *mother* of the family is often overlooked. If the sea-air or quiet country place is an absolute necessity for the children and the mother, it should be also the lot of the father; though if it can be managed occasionally for parents and children to take their holiday apart, no doubt both mother and father will be greatly benefited thereby.

"In settling the holiday, the children's good is usually the first thought; and none can object to this. The only thing to be borne in mind, and it often does need to be borne in mind, is that the mother should not always be the one to be sacrificed. She is sometimes more in need of a change than the children; and she cannot get any real rest if her cares and duties are increased, instead of being lightened, by the temporary change of family residence."

—*Cassell's Book of the Household, 1889*

Be sure to tell stories about the country through which you will be traveling. Many libraries have liberal lending policies for vacationers and will be happy to recommend regional guidebooks and stories for you to take along to read aloud. Youngsters also enjoy hearing stories about their parents' family vacations as children.

Singing together is a great family car-trip activity that releases tension and helps everyone relax. What's more, singing together reveals a parent's playful side to children, providing a reminder that the reason the family is on vacation is to have fun. Packing along a cassette player or CD with a varied assortment of story and song tapes will also break up the trip. Be sure to bring along a supply of extra batteries and headphones for when the adults are ready for quiet time and the children still want to listen.

For long car trips, a well-stocked insulated hamper can make a real difference. Fill the hamper with bags of ice and keep beverages chilled. Pack snacks, but limit your selection to nonsalted foods (salted foods make children thirsty and increase the number of comfort stops).

Mrs. Sharp also likes to pack a first-aid kit, a sewing kit, a can opener, a jackknife, a flashlight (again with extra batteries), tissues, paper towels, and an assortment of plastic bags (garbage and zipper-lock storage bags). Extension cords and a night-light (for strange motel rooms) have come in handy. She also always likes to pack a complete change of clothing for each child separately from the suitcases in case of spilled drinks, car sickness, or wet pants.

With preparation and planning, a family car trip offers a wonderful opportunity for memory-making quality time together. As Mr. Toad reminds us in *The Wind in the Willows,* the lure of the open road is irresistible: "Travel, change, interest, excitement! The whole world before you and a horizon that is always changing! Hurrah for the Open Road!"

Finally, remember there is no such thing as the "best" family vacation. The best family vacation is simply the one that works best for your family.

But what works best for any family vacation, Mrs. Sharp has discovered, is to remember to pack patience, flexibility, and good humor along with the travel guides. Dear Reader, don't leave home without them.

Christmas in July

When unexpected surprises come our way, we often refer to the occasion as resembling "Christmas in July." Of course, dear Reader, you've heard this old expression many times, but do you know its origins?

Observing Christmas in July was the custom of resourceful Victorian mothers who started thinking about Christmas long before Thanksgiving. This is because a century ago we made the majority of our gifts. By the end of the summer, Victorian families were almost done with their holiday gift making, which we began planning at a quarter past June.

"It is not necessary to deluge children with costly gifts. Capital scrapbooks can be made by children. Old railway guides may be the foundation," Mrs. M. E. Sherwood observed in her gem of an amusement book, *The Art of Entertaining,* published in 1892. "Happy is the child who has inherited a garret full of old trunks, old furniture, old pictures, any kind of old things."

While contemporary parents may not have a pile of old railway guides readily available, it is still possible to entertain children with an old-fashioned pastime when the summer doldrums appear: Encourage them to begin making their own holiday gifts.

Summer affords us a wonderful bounty of present-making materials as well as the luxury of time to begin our work. From the garden we can gather flowers to make potpourri or dried-flower bouquets. Vacations at the seashore inspire gift ideas such as seashell picture frames; kids in the kitchen can have fun preparing spiced-tea bags, nine-bean-soup mix, and preserves. Celebrating Christmas in July also affords us plenty of time to plan and execute larger holiday projects, which the family will enjoy working on together during the autumn months.

Mrs. Sharp's tradition to get everyone in the gift-making mood is by having a birthday party on July 15 for the Reverend Clement Clarke Moore, the author of "A Visit from St. Nicholas" (also known as "The Night Before Christmas"). We read his poem aloud over afternoon tea and then enjoy birthday cake. From the library Mrs. Sharp has collected various craft volumes and Christmas books. You will be pleasantly surprised to discover there is always a wonderful selection of holiday-project books available at libraries during the summer months, perfect for taking on vacation.

Creative handiwork is a gift that brings joy and satisfaction to both children and adults, whether they are givers or receivers. You need not be an experienced craftsperson to create something lovely—just willing to invest the time and energy.

Once families made everything they needed, from candles and soap to clothing and food. Today, children barely realize that things can be made by hand. When adults encourage children to become aware of the process of creating, the sense of purpose becomes as important as the object itself. Vacation time offers us this wonderful opportunity. Celebrating Christmas in July keeps youngsters as busy as Santa's elves, while nurturing a gift that will last a lifetime: their creativity.

At the Seashore

In childhood's scrapbook, summer provides some of the most cherished pages. For many of us, a favorite summer memory is the annual family excursion to the seashore. You might say, "Mrs. Sharp, we go to the beach every summer. What's so special about that?"

Yes, dear Reader, many of you do. But do you take advantage of the deliberate memory-making opportunities available to you in the annual ritual of sand and surf?

In our imaginations, let us return to the seashore in search of precious memories: heat shimmering above brilliant white sand, clusters of gaily colored umbrellas dotting the seascape, the salty, cooling tang of sea air. The children run freely, feed seagulls, search for hermit crabs, and build sand castles.

Mrs. Sharp digs a deep hole for her feet and watches the incoming tide wash over her ankles. Soon the children are pulling a flotilla of tiny boats in Mother's pond, each one made from half of an English walnut shell. To make these little boats, carefully open an English walnut and remove the kernel. Next take a bit of beeswax, place it in the bottom of the shell, and, if you like, insert a toothpick that flies a tiny paper triangular flag. Glue a piece of thread to the empty shell so the children can pull the boat.

The sun is hot, so the family retreats to the welcoming shade of our umbrella. Soon it is time to unpack a delicious picnic lunch; our sandwiches taste so much better at the beach than at home, even if they do have a little sand in them.

After lunch we saunter along the shoreline to collect seashore treasures: shells, smooth stones, and beautiful pieces of driftwood. Later in the afternoon the children will fly their kites.

But what is this, dear Reader? Your beach excursions are not so idyllic? Your memories are of wet bathing suits, mountains of soggy towels, sand castles on the couch, and everyone in the family on vacation but you? You say the last time you sat down on the beach long enough for the tide to wash over your feet dates back to B.C. (Before Child)? That you spend your beach hours making sure the children don't get sunburned, don't drown, don't wander off? Your nights are equally memorable: Get everyone clean and showered, prepare dinner, organize the evening's entertainment, come back to clean your charming seaside cottage, drop into bed exhausted, only to awaken ready for another restorative day at the beach?

Permit Mrs. Sharp to share with you a truth she has learned after a century of trips to the seashore:

The annual family beach trip may be a change of scene, but for Mother it is certainly not a vacation. Having admitted this, let Mrs. Sharp add, she wouldn't dream of missing one.

A practical suggestion to help make a beach vacation less stressful is to pack a plan for the family as well as the suntan lotion. At a beach house, chores still have to be attended to; assigning the children vacation jobs before leaving home distributes the workload. Older children can take turns being completely in charge of dinner; younger ones love to sweep sand, especially if they have their own child-size broom. Children as young as four can be taught to hang up dripping bathing suits and to keep track of their own towels. Finally, dear Reader, while it is true we carry our habits with us wherever we go, most of us can relax our housekeeping standards while on vacation. Certainly Mrs. Sharp does.

Some of the most enjoyable seashore memories are created when parents and children abandon familiar roles and become beachcombing companions. Learning together is a wonderful (and permanent) glue for keeping happy families intact. Take time to wander the beach with your children collecting shells. Build a sand castle together. The beach offers myriad opportunities to both amuse and instruct adults as well as children.

"Nature, like a kind and smiling mother, lends herself to our dreams and cherishes our fancies," Victor Hugo observed, perhaps after an excursion to the seashore. With the right attitude and preparation, a family beach vacation will reveal just how right he was.

*A*ugust arrives, bringing with it sultry summer days punctuated by thunderstorms and the whines of bored children. Mrs. Sharp's surefire antidote in the form of homegrown fun? Eureka entertainments, nature's novelties, family outings, and preserving summer's memories.

AUGUST.

Eureka
Entertainments

What, pray tell, are the varied experiences of the home circle during August? Mrs. Sharp shudders to think. Forgive me, dear Reader, but if ever there is a month that needs the assistance of good old-fashioned recreations, amusements, and helps, it is August. You've returned from your family vacation. The heat is oppressive; the pool is overcrowded. The older children have returned from summer camp, and each morning there is a mutiny among the younger members of the household, who refuse to get on the day-camp bus. It is of scant consequence to their little minds that Mother and Father paid in full (nonrefundable) for Session IV last March.

"We have nothing to do," they whine, informing you they are bored with camp, bored with the pool, bored with summer, and bored with being your children.

Ah, the burden of pint-size ennui. Mrs. Sharp also suspects she knows someone else who is bored with being the family's recreation director. Could this be why you're facing the dog days of August with fear and loathing? Fear not. Help is here with one essential caveat: All outdoor activities are off when the temperature hovers at the century mark. As far as Mrs. Sharp is concerned, when it's ninety-five in the shade, happy families stay indoors. If you feel the need, put a positive spin on the activity and call it a "Matinee Party"; let the children invite a few friends over for the afternoon, and sit them down with a stack of movies, popcorn, and sodas. Next, you go upstairs, lie down with a wet cloth over your eyes, and tell them not to call you unless it is a matter of life and death. This, too, shall pass.

However, if you can get outdoors, August offers perfect opportunities for family togetherness: field trips, outings, or offbeat home amusements. Here then, some tried-and-true solutions.

Theme Parties

Theme parties are just the prescription when the summer blahs hit.

One of Mrs. Sharp's favorite Victorian resources for theme parties was a little book published in 1894 entitled *Eureka Entertainments*. She suspects the title came from answering the question "How shall we amuse the children?" Modern mothers can find just such a resource in *The Penny Whistle Party Planner* by Meredith Brokaw and Annie Gilbar. While this book provides plans for twenty-three theme extravaganzas aimed at birthdays, scaled-down versions work well year-round. But be forewarned: If you take every one of their detailed suggestions to heart, especially in August's heat, you'll faint. Some of the *Penny Whistle Party Planner* suggestions that adapt well for August backyard get-togethers include "Backyard Beach Party," "Pirate Treasure Hunt," "Magic Party," "Space Fantasy," "Take a Trip Party," and "Western Round-Up."

Create a Memory Garden

Hot, sultry August afternoons may prevent us from working outdoors in the garden, but they do provide us with the perfect opportunity to weed through and prune back personal-memorabilia collections that propagate faster than kudzu. Give each child his or her own photograph album and a large storage box. Blank artist's sketchbooks make wonderful scrapbooks, and large cardboard portfolios to preserve precious drawings can be found at artist-supply stores. Let the children sort through their personal souvenirs and artwork, saving the best, dating them, and adding any written memories or comments (now, while they remember them).

The Circus

The first American circus was P. T. Barnum's Great Traveling Museum, Menagerie, Caravan and Hippodrome, which began traveling across the country's newly expanded railway system in 1871. It took a hundred railroad cars and three colossal tents to display Barnum's assemblage of impossible feats that dazzled your Victorian great-great-grandparents.

It won't take nearly as much effort for your children to organize their own circus. The planning alone should occupy them for at least a day. Encourage them to really revel in their prodigious preparations. Round up neighborhood pets for the animal acts, recycle Halloween costumes for the performers, and hire a twelve-year-old to stick with the project as baby-sitter/ringmaster. Circus music and sound effects can be found on records and tapes at your local library. Following the finale, have a party and serve only circus food: hot dogs, popcorn, ice cream cones, and soda.

All the World's a Stage

Victorian children adored putting on theatricals. Encourage your youngsters to produce their own pint-size version of "summer stock" out of doors. Or suggest a puppet show. Help younger children by recommending a fairy tale or story they know well. Don't be daunted if you haven't enough hand puppets or marionettes available; dolls and stuffed animals are always willing to go onstage. Again, hire a baby-sitter to oversee rehearsals (or have an older sibling assist) and act as narrator.

Novel Ideas

Literary games (known as brain games) were favorites of Victorian families, who frequently read novels aloud to one another and then played word games based on the novels. One of Mrs. Sharp's favorite traditions for August amusements is a quiet, literary-inspired doorstep party. When the coolness of evening descends, we begin our entertainments by either cooking meals or engaging in activities from our favorite novels. Four novels set in the Victorian era that offer delicious menus are *Gone with the Wind* (the Twelve Oaks barbecue—roast pork, pound cake with whipped cream, and beaten biscuits); *The Adventures of Tom Sawyer* (the camp fish fry—fried catfish and corn bread); *Little Women* (an outdoor tea of assorted cookies and apple turnovers); and Edith Wharton's *The Old Maid* (the "potluck" Victorian supper party of "oyster soup, broiled bass, stuffed goose, apple fritters and green peppers, followed by one of Grandmamma Ralston's famous caramel custards . . .").

For activities, why not a Robert Louis Stevenson *Treasure Island* outdoor treasure hunt, an *Alice in Wonderland* croquet match (with mallets rather than flamingos), or follow Winnie-the-Pooh's example and search your backyard for the feared Heffalump, a mythical beast of Loch Ness monster proportions. You provide the clues, courtesy of A. A. Milne (such as footprints going in opposite directions), until finally, a huge "Heffalump" is discovered.

Create your "Horrible Hoffamlump" or "Hellible Horralump" or "Hoffable Hellerump" out of a watermelon base, a cantaloupe head, marshmallow ears, and candy eyes, nose, and mouth. Licorice or string-candy hair and beard completes his ghastly array. And of course, everyone knows the only way to get rid of a Heffalump is to eat him.

Backyard Camping

"Much wholesome pleasure and rest" can be derived from "a Camp Party made up of a number of families in the same neighborhood," Mrs. N. M. Mustain suggests in her compendium *Popular Amusements for In and Out of Doors.* If you want to have your own old-fashioned campfire party in the backyard, use a grill (instead of a bonfire) to cook two quintessential summer sensations: doughboys and s'mores. To make doughboys, wrap raw bread dough like a cocoon around a skewer. Hold it over the flame until it's brown. Remove and fill the hole with a pat of butter and half of a grilled hot dog. For s'mores, toast marshmallows, then make a sandwich of two graham crackers, marshmallows, and a slice of thin chocolate bar.

With your own *Eureka Entertainments,* long after this summer has passed, your youngsters will remember home as the place where some of their happiest and best hours were spent. So will you.

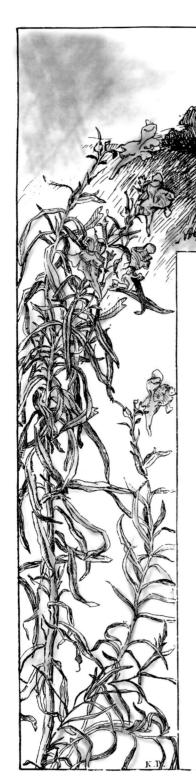

ugust

Deep in the wood I made a house
    Where no one knew the way;
I carpeted the floor with moss,
    And there I loved to play.

I heard the bubbling of the brook;
    At times an acorn fell,
And far away a robin sang
    Deep in a lonely dell.

I set a rock with acorn cups,
    So quietly I played
A rabbit hopped across the moss
    And did not seem afraid

That night before I went to bed
    I at my window stood,
And thought how dark my house must be
    Down in the lonesome wood.

                K. Pyle.

Nature's Novelties

Today's children are inundated with toys, but Mrs. Sharp has observed that many do not know how to "play." Most store-bought toys do not encourage a child's creativity, but instead his passivity.

Children never lack toys to play with if they learn how to create them from the endless resource of their imagination. Nature's many materials—pods, seeds, nuts, flowers, sticks, and vines—are summer's abundant, inviting alternatives.

Think back, dear Reader, to the long-ago summers of youth. Do you remember the happy, carefree hours when you were entertained by Mother Nature's playthings: hollyhock dolls, cucumber boats, Mr. Jack-in-the-Pulpit's lectures, morning-glory maidens, peach-pit baskets, weeping-willow whistles, acorn doll dishes, coconut cradles, and sunflower parasols, just to name a few? Do you remember the fun of sticking maple-seed pods onto your nose in spring?

Much has changed since Victorian times, but not the inexpressible joy children derive from the games, homemade toys, rhymes, and traditions of Mother Nature's nursery. For all this loving nanny requires, even of your very modern child, is a merry heart, imagination, and time enough to be happy—summer's gift to the child in all of us.

This month, dear Reader, encourage your children to explore the old wonders of natural amusements, and to open their eyes to the world around them. You'll find that natural materials to be recycled into toys can be discovered almost everywhere: in a park, on a playground, or on a walk at a nature center.

The Flower Dolly

One ephemeral entertainment of summers long ago was the gaily dressed flower doll. In Mrs. Sharp's memory, no such dolls were ever as beloved as these pretty, perishable beauties, fashioned with wit and wonder from common garden flowers and all the more precious because their visit with us was so fleeting. Would you like to make a Victorian flower doll for your children? You will need assorted trumpet or bell-shaped flowers in complementary colors—brilliantly tinted hollyhock or Canterbury-bell blossoms work best for our lady's overskirt and waist; next, a morning glory or petunia in full bloom for her ruffled petticoat; a snapdragon blossom for her head or a daisy with facial features etched in; straw-broom sticks stuck through phlox are her arms (which besides being fetching will hold her together). Top her off with a gaily colored nasturtium bonnet, and for the finishing flourish let your flower dolly carry a delicate daisy parasol to protect her from the sun! But do not limit your or your child's imagination to only these flowers—any blossom in your garden is willing to be pressed into such precious service.

And should you not have a backyard garden, by all means, please do not be discouraged. A simple bouquet of flowers obtained at the corner vendor's will provide you with ample supplies to charm your children abundantly.

The Tale of the Pansy King

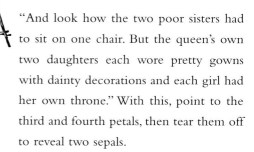

Another favorite flower amusement Mrs. Sharp's children adore is the story of the Pansy King. Take a pansy, hold it aloft, and tell your youngsters this tale:

"Once upon a time, there was a little flower

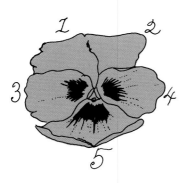

king with two lovely daughters. The king's wife had died and so he searched for a new queen to mother his children and be his companion. But alas, the king married a woman whose beauty was only skin-deep. She revealed this in many ways, such as allowing only her own two daughters to dress as princesses. With disdain, she dressed the king's two daughters in very plain gowns and even made them share a chair."

At this, point to the pansy's top two petals. "See, little ones, their gowns have no trimming." Now tear off both petals, revealing a single sepal (a small under-leaf on the stem), which had supported the two petals.

"And look how the two poor sisters had to sit on one chair. But the queen's own two daughters each wore pretty gowns with dainty decorations and each girl had her own throne." With this, point to the third and fourth petals, then tear them off to reveal two sepals.

"But to show you just how selfish this queen truly was, why, just look at her own gown. It has the fullest skirt with a flounce and the fanciest design." Now point to the fifth petal.

"And how many thrones do you think this greedy queen kept for herself? Why, two!" And with this, tear off the last petal to reveal two tiny sepal thrones, to the squeals of delight from your listeners.

And where was the king during all this time? your children might ask. "Why, right here," tell them, pointing to the stem, "down in the basement with his feet in a foot tub. And such a funny little tub, too, for it's so long and narrow that you wonder just how he manages to get his feet in it. But indeed he does! And to keep him warm, look here, his sweet daughters have knitted him a wee yellow scarf, which he wears around his neck."

The naturalist Charles Darwin, near the end of his life, wrote to his children: "When you were very young it was my delight to play with you all, and I think with a sigh such days can never return." Perhaps, dearest friends, such days of delight can just be beginning this summer for your family.

Family Outings

Victorian families did not travel together as frequently or as widely as families do today, but that is not to say that we did not have special traditions associated with vacation time. We called them family outings.

A family outing is any excursion that can easily be done in a day or less. Such excursions can relieve summer doldrums or brighten the spirits of the grayest winter day. It can be as simple as a walk in the woods with a picnic, a field trip to the zoo, an excursion to a museum, a visit to a farm (perhaps to pick our own fruit and vegetables), or an all-day "out-and-about" to diverse destinations such as historical sites or theme parks that are within one day's drive of home.

There are four elements to family outings, dear Reader, that recommend them highly: the anticipation, the actual trip itself, the memories, and the ease.

But Mrs. Sharp would like to remind you that in life, attitude is all. This is true whether you're planning family activities or just getting through the day with a semblance of grace. But perhaps nowhere is the right attitude more necessary than when carrying off "spontaneous outings" with children. Mrs. Sharp believes that in the life of every child there should be an abundance of surprises—whimsical occurrences that punctuate the dreary daily routine.

Spur-of-the-moment surprises make children happily resilient and open to life's wondrous adventure.

Of course, Mrs. Sharp's surprises appear impulsive; the children do not know in advance, but the grown-ups do because we plan them. There are also certain conditions attached to our spontaneous outings.

Rule No. 1: Novelty is essential.

Rule No. 2: Anyone who doesn't like it stays home.

All novelty really requires of us is just a slight adjustment in presentation. Mrs. Sharp frequently increases the animation in her voice, as in "Isn't this terrific? Aren't we going to have a wonderful time!" And what do you know? We do. So will you.

Here is an outing you might like to try in August. If merely the thought of twilight picnics bores the family, get them up early for a Bicycle Breakfast. Pack a simple breakfast picnic (muffins, fruit, juice boxes, individual servings of cereal, milk, a thermos of tea or coffee), then ride out together to the closest park. Getting up early together before the heat of the day, when it is peaceful and still, is an exhilarating experience for families. Trust Mrs. Sharp, everyone will adore this outing. The family will also think you're so clever.

We all want to spend more time together with our families. The way to do it is to pencil *Family* into our schedules and then keep a date with those who mean the most. Whether you stay close to home or venture farther afield, planning regular outings together is like sweat equity: an inexpensive investment in a home-grown enterprise that will reap a big return in the emotional surety of your strong family.

Preserving the Summer

If there is any tradition so resonant of yesteryear that has fallen through the cracks of contemporary domestic life, it is preserving: the cooking and storing of food. Time was in Mrs. Sharp's day, every "proper" home had a well-stocked larder to tide the family over during the winter months.

At the end of August, farmers' markets and roadside stands are overflowing with nature's bounty. Seductively they invite Mrs. Sharp to preserve edible memories. You might like to join her.

Before you swoon, dear Reader, do not think Mrs. Sharp is entreating you to slave over a hot stove putting away a hundred jars of zucchini marmalade (between car pools, finishing next year's projected office budget, attending your son's baseball team's championship finals, and leading your daughter's Brownie meeting). Take a deep breath. Relax. Mrs. Sharp has discovered how we can preserve the summer *and* our sanity.

Those same roadside stands and farmers' markets that overflow with fruits and vegetables also sell preserves, jellies, mustards, herb vinegars, and all the comestibles Mrs. Sharp has spent her entire life "putting away." Today all these goodies are being prepared by some savvy entrepreneurial mother with her own home-based business. Let's contribute to her success and our ability to enjoy the tradition of preserving by visiting one. To get into the mood, Mrs. Sharp brings a large shopping basket with a handle to the farmers' market. She then purchases a dazzling assortment of delectables. After all, Mrs. Sharp's family adores the luxury of homemade strawberry jam in January. But the jam doesn't have to be made in Mrs. Sharp's kitchen.

After she returns home, the children help Mother clean out and organize a kitchen cupboard that has been designated "the larder." While we're at it, we might as well straighten out the kitchen cabinets together. Chores that seem overwhelming are made easier when we work together as a family.

Next, we repaper the shelves with pretty new shelf paper. Mrs. Sharp then brings out some charming fabric: colorful calico, festive florals, and bright plaids. These we cut into large circles (to fit the jar tops) with pinking shears. The children put them on the jars, securing the fabric with rubber bands and ribbon. They also like to stick on their own labels. Finally, we stack our beautiful bottles and jars on the shelves, basking in the delight of a fancy pantry. To Mrs. Sharp, there are few things in life as sublime as the larder shelf laden with goodies. Although she doesn't for a moment long again for the time when August's heat was generated indoors instead of out, Mrs. Sharp's wonderful cupboard does encourage her to dabble in preserving some summer memories for fun. If truth be told, her temptation inevitably comes from preparing some Victorian viands—fruit honeys, cordials, and compotes—for pleasure. And she can indulge herself in the joy of "putting away" selective morsels now that the hard work of stocking the larder has been done by someone else.

None of us today, dear Reader, has time to do everything—whether it's preserving jam or memories. When we realize that setting priorities is not a compromise but the way to find the time to accomplish what's really important for ourselves and our family, it's easy to preserve precious moments of daily life to be recalled and savored in the months and years to come.

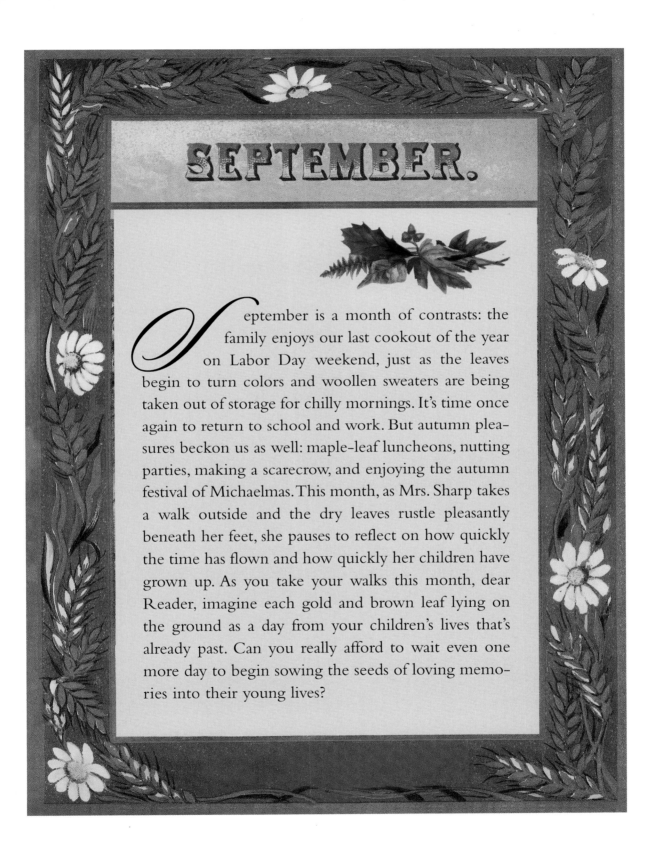

SEPTEMBER.

September is a month of contrasts: the family enjoys our last cookout of the year on Labor Day weekend, just as the leaves begin to turn colors and woollen sweaters are being taken out of storage for chilly mornings. It's time once again to return to school and work. But autumn pleasures beckon us as well: maple-leaf luncheons, nutting parties, making a scarecrow, and enjoying the autumn festival of Michaelmas. This month, as Mrs. Sharp takes a walk outside and the dry leaves rustle pleasantly beneath her feet, she pauses to reflect on how quickly the time has flown and how quickly her children have grown up. As you take your walks this month, dear Reader, imagine each gold and brown leaf lying on the ground as a day from your children's lives that's already past. Can you really afford to wait even one more day to begin sowing the seeds of loving memories into their young lives?

Back to School

It seems hard to believe, but in a few days it will be time again for Mrs. Sharp to prepare the children for another wonderful school year. How the summer days have flown by!

Preparing to go back to school can be one of the most pleasurable aspects of the summer, dear Reader, if you transform your preparations into family traditions. The key ingredient? Make returning to school an event everyone looks forward to.

The first thing Mrs. Sharp does is to make an assessment of each child's wardrobe. This is done with each child alone. Try on everything to see what fits and what is suitable for this year. Then decide if anything can be passed down to smaller children

or received from an older sibling. Now, armed with pen and paper, make a list—with the child present—of what items are needed to complete each outfit. List the colors and all the accessories, such as socks and belts. For convenience, I try to see that each child has five different school outfits, one for each day of the week. Show your younger children which shirt goes with which pair of trousers or skirt and get the child's approval of this coordination at this time—a tip that will do wonders to ease your early morning dressing time after school begins.

Next, plan to take the child shopping for his or her back-to-school wardrobe. Take each child with you on a separate shopping excursion, if at all possible. This outing is best undertaken in the morning (after a hearty breakfast) when we are all in good spirits. Before you go, sit down with your child and make out an old-fashioned budget, explaining what a budget is and how much money you have set aside to spend on clothing. If possible, buy one completely new outfit for the first day of school.

If you are planning to order some of the children's clothing from mail-order sources—a wonderful time-saving convenience—then sit down with your child, have some milk and cookies, and shop through the catalog.

If you are handy with a needle and plan to sew your children's new school clothes, include them in the planning stage as well by letting them help pick out the patterns and fabrics.

And of course, besides school clothing the children need back-to-school supplies, such as new lunch boxes, knapsacks, and other accoutrements from pencils to hair bows. Again, make a list of what you are going to buy before you leave the house. Plan on a separate shopping trip for the school accessories. It can be too confusing combining school supplies with clothing, especially if you must bring along two or more children on the shopping trip. All of these suggestions may sound elementary, dear Reader, but they were learned at the school of hard knocks.

Mrs. Sharp's last tradition for our back-to-school shopping expedition—that is, if we are all still speaking to one another—is to stop off for either lunch or ice cream sodas to celebrate!

The First Day of School

You can make the first day of school a special event by planning on serving the children's favorite breakfast and by having the camera ready for pictures (buy a Polaroid camera when you purchase school supplies). Tuck something extra into the lunch box, such as a note with love and best wishes for a wonderful school year from Mother and Father. That evening plan on enjoying a festive dinner together with a special dessert, and catch up on all the exciting news. Mrs. Sharp then presents the children with the school scrapbooks. On the first page they find mounted a picture taken that morning (with an instant camera) with a funny caption to start them off.

Our family's other successful back-to-school tradition includes reminding the children that we lay our clothing out the night before, down to socks and shoes, and reestablishing the front-door-basket system of organization. The door baskets—each one labeled with a name and one for each family member—are where the family places their books, hats, mittens, lunch-money purse, etc., before retiring, so that there is no searching in the morning. If you have not used the front-door-basket or box system before, you

might want to make integrating it into your family life an event by unveiling the new system the night before the first day of school.

"Be patient, worn mother, they're growing up fast," a Victorian poem reminds us. "These nursery whirlwinds, not long do they last; A still, lonely house would be far worse than noise, rejoice and be glad in your brave girls and boys!"

Our children do grow up so quickly. Making the most of returning to school by helping them celebrate is a tradition no youngster should grow up without.

MAY MRS. SHARP BE OF ASSISTANCE?

During the last week of August and the beginning of September, many stores have sales on art supplies and stationery products. This is an excellent and economical time to stock up the Rainy Day Cupboard with craft items. However, this is one shopping trip to do alone, or the items to replenish the Rainy Day Cupboard inevitably will end up in the school bag. At this time, also purchase a plain artist's sketchbook for each child, which will become the child's school-days memory scrapbook for that year.

Labor Day

The first Monday of September the season changes officially from summer to autumn with "Labor's Holiday," as Labor Day was known during the Victorian era. This holiday grew out of organized marches of working men and women during the 1880s to protest the intolerable working conditions in America at that time: very little pay for brutally long hours, unsafe and unsanitary conditions, and the great wrong of child labor in sweatshops. In 1894, Labor Day became an official American holiday, and from that time until World War I, it was celebrated with lavish community picnics, grand parades, and oratory. Everyone took the day off from work and enjoyed the fruits of their labor: recreation.

Of course, these traditions have long since passed away, and today Labor Day is viewed primarily as the official end to summer. Vacation is over, the children need to get ready for school, stores begin to display winter clothing. Once again, it's back to work.

Work is a recurring theme at Mrs. Sharp's house these days and she suspects—with fifty million mothers of school-age children working outside their homes—she's not alone. There's homework, office work, and perhaps our most important work, raising and nurturing a family. Labor Day provides us with an opportunity to reflect on better ways for our family to work together.

One practical tradition is a Labor Day annual review of family chores. With a new school year, we try to distribute different jobs to keep the household running smoothly. Quality time spent together as a family can occur while working together, not just while having fun. Household chores teach children valuable lessons that increase confidence and esteem.

Mrs. Sharp also believes that when parents and children work together, these times also provide occasions for conversation on topics that might otherwise be difficult. Younger children need and want face-to-face contact when talking to Mother or Father, but teenagers don't. They much prefer seeking advice the way Dorothy sought help from the disembodied Wizard of Oz. It is far easier for older children to open up while drying a dish, folding clothes, or raking leaves.

But the week before or after Labor Day also offers pleasurable opportunities for a parent-child field trip, such as a visit to Father's and/or Mother's place of employment. The seven-and-under set are very curious about what their parents do all day and where they do it. For all they know we might as well be disappearing into a black hole (and they could be right).

If you have not yet talked with your youngsters about the type of work you do, try to explain what it is you are attempting to accomplish each day. Mrs. Sharp gently recommends you ruminate on the esoteric purpose of your occupation in the grand scheme of life prior to explaining it to your children, or there's no telling how the conversation might end up.

If you can arrange it, work-related field trips are more enjoyable on a regular workday, so that you can introduce the children to some of your colleagues. By bringing them to the place where you spend one-third of your life, the children get a better sense of you as a person, rather than as just their parent. A nice way to finish the trip is to take the children to the place where you eat lunch regularly (the company cafeteria, a favorite restaurant, or the park with a brown bag lunch).

Another enjoyable Labor Day family tradition is to trace the work history of your family. Begin by interviewing the oldest member of your family (grandparents and great-grandparents) to discover what types of work they and their parents did.

As you trace the occupations of your own family, you will weave together fascinating threads of personal history. Perhaps several generations back your family worked on a farm, then moved into the city. You might discover occupations in your family's past that no longer exist. Mrs. Sharp keeps a special book about our family's work history; each year we try to add one more relative's story.

Very soon, adding to this annual Labor Day project will become a treasured family custom and legacy, made all the more precious because you "worked" on it together.

September.

We made ourselves a castle
        Once after school was out;
We raked the leaves together
        To wall it all about .

We made a winding pathway
        Down to the school-yard gate ,
And there we worked with might and main
        Until the day grew late ;

Until one bright star twinkled
        Above the maple tree ,
And lights shone down the village street
        As far as we could see .

We planned that every recess
        We'd come out there to play ,
But in the night it blew so hard
        Our castle blew away .

                        K. Pyle .

Grandparents' Day

On the second Sunday in September comes Grandparents' Day—a holiday that has been formally observed only since 1978. Mrs. Sharp believes it is a holiday that should be enthusiastically embraced.

During the Victorian era, grandparents were a strong physical and psychological presence in the lives of their grandchildren, who knew Grandma and Grandpa intimately since most families lived close to one another—if not sharing the same house, then just a short buggy ride away.

Today the traditional extended family seems to have disappeared with the dinosaurs. Most grandparents are separated from their children and grandchildren by geographical distances; some are separated by the psychological distances of divorce and remarriage. Many youngsters know their grandparents only through occasional visits, brief, awkward phone conversations, and as a name on a present.

When Mrs. Sharp thinks back over this last century, the most startling change in the way we live is family roles. Granny no longer sits in her rocker crocheting booties. She's likely to have opened up her own children's clothing boutique.

But one thing has not changed since Mrs. Sharp's day, and that is the vital link of love that binds the

generations. Certainly Mrs. Sharp believes that nobody deserves remembering more than Grandma and Grandpa. But she also believes that instead of a card or bouquet, what grandparents—if they were asked—would say they really want is a way to become part of their grandchildren's lives year-round.

Unlike preparing for impending parenthood, for which there are literally thousands of resources to help expectant parents—books, magazines, and classes—up until recently there have been few resources that tell people how to behave when they become grandparents or what to expect: of themselves, their children, and the new addition to their family. One day the telephone rings with some exciting news, and suddenly there is a flood of questions.

Some of the questions Selma Wasserman, author of *The Long-Distance Grandmother: How to Stay Close to Distant Grandchildren,* found herself asking when she discovered she was about to become a grandmother for the first time included: "Do grandmothers have to dress differently? Should I let my hair go to gray? Is it unseemly for grandfathers to ride motorcycles? To fall in love? Should grandfathers help with the gardening? Be available on call as baby-sitters? Maintain a college fund? Should grandmothers offer to take the children

their grandchildren a sense of stability—an anchor of unconditional love and acceptance—in a rapidly changing world.

While there is a natural instinct to grandparenting, the biological bond between grandparents and children must be kept strong through shared time and intimate contact. This can be difficult when grandparents and their grandchildren are separated by miles. But some grandparents, like Selma Wasserman, find a way to forge this bond with both creativity and commitment. In her book she details some of the innovative ideas she's successfully used to overcome the barriers of distance. These include special ways to use the telephone (beginning when the grandchild is as young as six months), audiotapes, captioned photographs, stories, and small, inexpensive, and playful gifts that engage children in shared activities across the miles.

The reaching out to create a relationship between grandparents and grandchildren does not depend on a special occasion, even one like Grandparents' Day. What matters is a grandparent's longing to be a part of his or her grandchild's life and then doing it.

for two weeks every summer to give the parents a breather?"

Mrs. Sharp believes the answers to these conundrums and many more involving grandparenting is "It depends." That's because each question has as many answers as there are families asking them. What is important before answering them, however, is to understand one crucial premise: Never before has the natural role of grandparents—as the emotional elders of the family—been needed more. Grandparents offer

If there are grandparents and grandchildren in your family, dear Reader, perhaps they cannot enjoy the same type of relationship many Victorian families experienced when the extended family of three generations lived closely together. But there are ways to bridge the physical distances of today and keep the connection alive. Passing on family traditions is one of them.

Autumn's Work

These are perfect Indian-summer days: The heat has passed, the air is fragrant from the scent of burning leaves, and autumn colors dazzle with their beauty.

For Mrs. Sharp's family, it's time for such seasonal pleasures as apple gathering, cider pressing, hayrides, and scarecrow making.

Autumn's work also beckons us: raking leaves, preparing the garden for winter, stockpiling wood, not to mention grocery shopping, laundry, dusting, and vacuuming. The family's free time together seems so short, the chore list so long.

But over the years Mrs. Sharp has discovered the secret for transforming any chore—from preparing school lunches to raking leaves—into a perfect opportunity for family togetherness.

It's called planning.

For example, this is the Sharps' family plan for a fall Saturday. After breakfast, everyone has an hour's worth of household tasks. With fourteen of us cleaning different parts of the house, in a short time an entire day's work is completed.

Next, we head outdoors together to tackle Mother Nature's job list. Of course, the younger children play in the leaves as much as they rake them, but all know the yard work must be completed before the afternoon's amusement begins.

Maple-Leaf Luncheon and Nutting Party

For the luncheon, the children collect large maple leaves to make party crowns. Use six or seven leaves of approximately the same size for each crown. They should be soft and pliable. Remove the stems, but do not discard them. Take two leaves and slightly overlap them, then join the two together by using the stem much the same way you would a straight pin. Continue doing this until you have made a suitable length to surround the head, like a crown.

Next, the children make leaf drawings. Place tracing paper on top of a leaf, skeleton side facing up. Instruct the children to rub crayons gently over the paper. The shapes of the leaves with their patterns will become visible, creating "stained-glass" nature pictures.

Now it's time for lunch, served outdoors. A hearty autumn vegetable soup is served in scooped-out, slightly underripe pumpkins. Mrs. Sharp also serves brown-bread sandwiches cut into the shapes of leaves and acorns using cookie cutters. For dessert we have butter pecan ice cream and apple tart.

After the family has feasted, everyone is ready for an old-fashioned nutting party—a leisurely walk in the countryside where we collect an assortment of different nuts—acorns, chestnuts, and hickories. (If necessary, Mrs. Sharp will hide store-bought nuts along the chosen party route, in advance of the walk.) If you don't care to venture far afield, the backyard is quite suitable for your nutting party.

The child who fills his or her individual basket first is called "the little brown squirrel," the child who has the largest assortment of nuts becomes "the little red squirrel," and the rest of the children become "little gray squirrels." After the game, we place the nuts near the trees for the real woodland creatures and retire to a blanket to tell stories about the squirrels' exemplary habit of gathering and saving.

You might say: Really, Mrs. Sharp, all your family did was clean up the house, rake leaves, have lunch outdoors, and take a family walk together. This is tradition?

Of course, dear Reader. Traditions are simple but festive homegrown celebrations that cement your family together with the mortar of loving memories.

Plan a maple-leaf luncheon and hold a nutting party to see for yourself.

Things to Make with Autumn's Treasures

As the children go on nature walks, they will want to bring home "treasures" to display. Learn from them, dear Reader. Let your eyes roam the woodside looking for treasures just as your little ones do.

The first sight that catches our attention is the foliage. Victorian women adored decorating their homes with natural materials and during the autumn months would create large and elaborate bouquets using leaves as the foundation. You can, too. Select large branches, when the leaves have first turned their beautiful crimson, orange, and gold and before they start to fall, just as you would bouquets of flowers.

Victorian women anticipated the annual activity of preserving leaves. To do so:

Split the stems of your branches about three inches from the bottom; stand them in a bucket of warm water for several hours. If any of the leaves begin to curl, remove them. Then prepare a solution of glycerin (available at pharmacies) and water by combining one part glycerin with two parts water. Bring the solution to a boil, simmer gently for ten minutes, and let it sit until completely cool. Cut the bottom of your branch stems at a very sharp angle and stand your branches in the mixture, storing your container in a cool, dark place until all the glycerin mixture has been absorbed. This will take about a week to ten days. When you first notice tiny beads of glycerin forming on the leaves, remove them from the solution, wipe down the leaves with a damp paper towel, and dry thoroughly. Now your leaves are preserved and will look fresh for several seasons. "It is needless to enter upon suggestions for the appropriate use of autumn leaves," Mrs. J. R. Rees observed in *Appleton's Home Occupations,* published in 1882. "They are universally known, and whether they serve as ornaments alone, or are used in combination with berries and burrs, they are always graceful, appropriate and beautiful." Mrs. Sharp could hardly add more.

What else do we see? Bunches of goldenrod, rich-brown cattails, vines of bright-orange bittersweet berries, and that wonderful old-fashioned favorite, the honesty plant with its white, satiny pods. Collect them to have a glorious dry bouquet that will keep all winter without fading (just don't place it in water).

Do we see nuts—acorns, conkers, fir, and pinecones—lying about? Collect them, for with a bit of glue, felt pieces, and sheep's wool you can create tiny animals, autumn fairies, and simple gnomes for the children to play with.

To make autumn's fairies: Take colored tissue paper (in autumn colors) and twist a little shape around a tiny wad of cotton batting or sheep's wool for the head. Now glue on wings of the honesty seeds and place them into a half walnut shell.

Acorns make tiny animals when you glue two together, adding a bit of black felt for a tail and feet.

With a black marking pen, draw on a face. For the animals' woodpile, select a fine twig and cut it into a dozen two-inch pieces. Pile them up like a cord of wood and glue them together. Acorns also make charming tiny fairy tea sets when you separate the cups from the nut.

Take pinecones and transform them into woodland gnomes with felt capes and cone-shaped hats. Add a bit of sheep's wool to use for the beard.

Sheep's wool is a lovely craft material for children to use as it is very soft, pliable, and can be easily formed into many shapes. When it is used as a stuffing, the dolls and toys are soft yet well shaped. But sheep's wool can also easily be dyed and used for other projects: It can be made into nests or draped over pinecones to form a landscape when creating seasonal scenes, which your children will want to do after their animals, fairies, and gnomes are completed! Children's imaginations can find even more uses for this craft material. For instance, we use natural sheep's wool to create clouds over our manger scene at Christmas. Another favorite activity is to create wool pictures using a variety of different-colored wool against a piece of felt.

Today's youngsters, while inundated with plastic toys and ready-made craft kits, often seem bored. Yet even the most jaded youngster will delight in the limitless possibilities of seasonal handicrafts once he is introduced to the bounty of Mother Nature's supplies. It has been Mrs. Sharp's observation, however, that parents often seem reluctant to go back to nature for their children's diversions. That is, until they discover a rich resource of imaginative pastimes in two marvelous books from England. The first, *Festivals, Family and Food* by Diana Carey and Judy Large, takes a young family on a journey throughout the year to celebrate seasonal festivals with more than 650 activities—songs, games, projects, stories, poems, and recipes. Its companion volume, *The Children's Year* by Stephanie Cooper, fosters an awareness and appreciation of the four seasons through enchanting craft projects for the family to enjoy together. Both these wonderful books are perennial favorites and are highly recommended for any parent's or teacher's bookshelf.

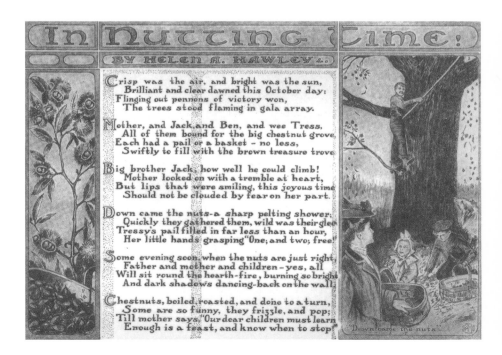

In Nutting Time!

BY HELEN A. HAWLEY.

Crisp was the air, and bright was the sun,
    Brilliant and clear dawned this October day:
Flinging out pennons of victory won,
    The trees stood flaming in gala array.

Mother, and Jack, and Ben, and wee Tress,
    All of them bound for the big chestnut grove,
Each had a pail or a basket - no less,
    Swiftly to fill with the brown treasure trove

Big brother Jack, how well he could climb!
    Mother looked on with a tremble at heart,
But lips that were smiling, this joyous time
    Should not be clouded by fear on her part.

Down came the nuts-a sharp pelting shower,
    Quickly they gathered them, wild was their glee
Tressy's pail filled in far less than an hour,
    Her little hands grasping "One; and two; free!"

Some evening soon, when the nuts are just right,
    Father and mother and children - yes, all
Will sit round the hearth-fire, burning so bright
    And dark shadows dancing-back on the wall

Chestnuts, boiled, roasted, and done to a turn,
    Some are so funny, they frizzle, and pop;
Till mother says,"Our dear children must learn
    Enough is a feast, and know when to stop."

"Down came the nuts."

Some of Mrs. Sharp's more interesting acquaintances live near The Vicarage, propped up in the garden. They are the family's "stuffed shirts," the scarecrows, which provide our garden with seasonal comic relief. Each autumn we look forward to freshening them up or fashioning new ones.

You certainly don't need to be concerned about protecting a vegetable patch to make them. Scarecrows also like to be propped up on front porches and sit on steps, too.

To make a scarecrow you will need the basics for each figure: two pairs of panty hose (for small scarecrows use children's tights), straw, string, stuffing material (either straw or leaves), scrap material (yarn, fabrics, etc.), a pumpkin for the head, a wooden T-shaped frame (made from two one-inch-wide dowels, one sixteen inches, the other twenty, formed like a cross), glue, and such appropriate adornments as clothing, hats, and acrylic paints.

Remember, just as clothes make the man, they also make your scarecrow. In Victorian days, it was customary that if a traveling man came across a handsomely dressed wooden stranger, he could feel free to exchange his own worn garments for the scarecrow's finery, which is how scarecrows always came to be seen wearing ragged, hand-me-down clothing. Father Scarecrow is usually decked out in an old pair of blue jeans, a buttoned-up shirt, preferably plaid, and an old straw hat. For Mrs. Scarecrow, an old dress, jewelry, a hat, and gloves do the trick. (You can find fetching costumes at thrift shops.) For the scarecrow children, your own youngster's outgrown or frayed clothing will do wonderfully.

Begin by stuffing a pair of panty hose; lightly stitch the opening shut with thread. Stuff a second one and sew the two waists together with a basting stitch. This is your basic body. Now put on the pants over one pair of legs. Tie string around the pant cuffs. Put on the shirt over the remaining top torso of panty hose and twist the panty-hose legs into the arm sleeves. Button the shirt and tie off the cuffs. Now stuff a bit of straw at the leg and sleeve openings for decorative effect.

Take a pumpkin and using fast-drying acrylic paints, paint on a face. Add yarn to make hair if you wish. Mrs. Sharp does not carve our scarecrow's face because the pumpkin will soon deteriorate; using paints, he'll last all season.

Next attach the body to the wooden T-shaped frame. Stick the length of the pole down the scarecrow's back and drape the arms over the horizontal part of the cross. Make a small hole approximately one inch in diameter in the bottom of your pumpkin head and place it on the top of the cross.

A family scarecrow can be a wonderful project for everyone, and like the best of simple, creative, old-fashioned pastimes, it requires only the investment of imagination and time.

Michaelmas

On September 29, Mrs. Sharp's family observes the first of the autumnal festivals—Michaelmas, which is the feast day of Saint Michael the Archangel. This is an ancient harvest festival dating back to the sixth century, but it is still celebrated today in the Celtic provinces from Cornwall in England to Brittany in France. Legend tells us that England's patron saint, Saint George, was the Archangel Michael's earthly representative. In heaven Saint Michael was the angel who threw Lucifer out for his treachery, and on earth Saint George was famous for slaying dragons and rescuing princesses.

During the nineteenth century, English harvest or Michaelmas fairs offered Victorian families a well-deserved opportunity to enjoy themselves after months of strenuous labor. These gatherings included food, music, dancing, games, and festive costume parades. Michaelmas was also considered the time to settle up accounts and pay rents. A children's verse tells the story:

Now the Harvest is in,
Grain is in the bin,
Through hard work and God's aid
The year's rent has been paid.
With Pennies to spare
We're off to the Michaelmas Fair!
—Mala Powers

In Victorian English homes the celebration of Michaelmas meant the pursuit of serious merry-making from the nursery to the kitchen as children reenacted the legend of Saint George and the dragon. Modern children will enjoy Mrs. Sharp's tradition of making a sweet-dough dragon, much better than slaying a sibling. Create him with refrigerated dough, available at grocery stores, and fill his stomach with apples and dried fruit. Use sliced almonds for his scales. No matter what he looks like, children will be delighted with the outcome.

By teatime our dragon is removed from his fiery red lair to be slain and consumed along with a selection of delicious blackberry jam from our pantry. This is the last time of the year we will enjoy blackberry jam, for legend has it that after the devil was thrown out of heaven he landed in the blackberry brambles. After Michaelmas, it is said the blackberries turn bad!

Over tea we tell the tale of Saint George, and Mrs. Sharp ceremoniously lights the parlor hearth, signaling autumn's true arrival, another Michaelmas tradition.

Soon the children are lost in play, as knights and princesses in castles far, far away. Mrs. Sharp lingers over her cup of tea, savoring the contentment that always comes when she makes a special effort to keep an old tradition alive.

Frequently Mrs. Sharp is asked by her younger friends, Are traditions worth all the time they take? Does a modern family really need to observe Michaelmas? Ah, dear Reader, you must look into your own heart to discover that answer.

OCTOBER

October arrives bringing with it a wash of wonderful color, fragrant, cool breezes, and a bounty of seasonal pleasures from apple-cider pressing to pumpkin carving. Come with us on a harvest-moon hayride, then help us make masquerade costumes and prepare for an old-fashioned Halloween frolic at home.

The Costume-Planning Party

It has been Mrs. Sharp's experience that All Hallows' Eve is a holiday that brings out either the angel in us or the witch.

Bearing this in mind, let us speak frankly about this business of Halloween costumes. Whether we like it or not, this is the time we must start planning the children's costumes or little Johnny will end up a ghost for the seventh year running. Trust Mrs. Sharp—soon everything will be picked over and there's nothing so disappointing for children or frustrating for parents than to discover that they or the store have run out of exactly whatever it is you need.

While Halloween is the children's own favorite holiday, it is the one Mother fears most. Why? Because in her heart every woman dreads the annual occasion of having her maternal gifts (or, she fears, her lack of them) so publicly displayed. We mothers have allowed costumes to become an emotional litmus test.

It takes one to know.

A true story: For Victorian families Halloween was not just a holiday, but an occasion. There were masquerade parades, harvest frolics, and All Hallows' pumpkin festivals, and each event required elaborate costumes. For months beforehand, women's periodicals featured articles detailing the minutiae of various fancy dress for our young ones. To refresh your memory, the costumes a century ago were all homemade.

Mrs. Sharp admits she's always been nimble with a thimble, but more important, she has been blessed with an abundance of common sense. Perhaps this is why her children were always happily outfitted for Halloween, usually in simple costumes of their own choosing.

Then one fateful autumn, Mr. Ebenezer Butterick's "All New 1899 Pattern Catalogue" arrived in the post. That year, a costume known as "the Ant"—a black sateen confection with six legs—was all the rage.

Suddenly, Mrs. Sharp's heart started beating wildly at the thought of cleverly outdoing herself. Imagine! One small, fabulous little ant. But Mrs. Sharp then had six young children. Imagine! Our own school of ants: six sibling insects all walking hand in hand in shiny splendor. The very thought sent shivers of excitement down her spine.

Needless to say, the ant costumes consumed Mrs. Sharp's every waking moment, and many moments when she should have been asleep. At first, the children cheered. But then they cried and became increasingly cranky. The more they fussed for Mother's attentions, the more irritable she became. *Certifiable* was a word frequently muttered by her husband. Miraculously, the home circle survived intact.

Finally, the big day arrived and what a very handsome school of worker ants paraded out Mrs. Sharp's front door on their way to win first prize at the Takoma Park All Hallows' Eve masquerade contest. And the Sharp family would have brought home the

blue ribbon, had it not been for Mrs. Henry Hollister's twins, Bertha and Buddy, disguised as a matched set of glass-bead-encrusted Etruscan vases.

Of course, the sight of those miserable children was a startling epiphany for Mrs. Sharp, who realized mothers create Halloween costumes for one another, not for our children. Dear Reader, no child ever begged Mama to turn him into an Etruscan vase. So let us continue to remind ourselves vigilantly each October just whom the Halloween costumes are for, and all will be well.

Now, armed with a notebook, pen, and measuring tape, gather the children over milk and cookies and invite them to confide what they would like to be. Discuss with each child what particular items are absolutely crucial for their character's costume, and then, leaving nothing to chance, write it down. It has been Mrs. Sharp's experience that it is always the smallest detail—especially if it is missing—that causes the biggest fuss.

And please do not fret about buying Halloween costumes. If little Johnny says he wants a store-bought costume, being possessed of your reason, you will smile and say, "Wonderful." Yet Mrs. Sharp has discovered that this is not the attitude of many modern mothers, especially if they work outside their homes. For years, working mothers have tortured themselves needlessly with the fantasy that all the little children of full-time homemakers will be wearing wonderful, handcrafted creations at the grammar school masquerade parade. Having attended more school Halloween assemblies than you will ever—thank heavens—have to, let Mrs. Sharp assure you, this is not the case. The children are not separated into two groups: store-bought and homemade.

Remember that any costume you help your child create—whether it's from your sewing machine or purchased with loving forbearance—will be treasured. The tradition worth preserving is not the homemade Halloween costume but the special time you set aside to have fun planning costumes together.

MAY MRS. SHARP BE OF ASSISTANCE?

In our house each child has twenty-four hours to change his or her mind after the costume consultation. Warn the children ahead of time and be firm! If you waver, dear Reader, you will forever find yourself in a purgatory of regret come each Halloween. Inevitably, one year little Minnie May will decide she "really wants to be a princess" instead of a fluffy kitten, even as you are up to your ears in fake-fur shreds. This domestic scene is very scary. Respond gently, but with resolve: "That is a lovely idea, dear. For next year."

The Pumpkin-Carving Party

Making a family outing of the search for the perfect Halloween pumpkin has long been one of our family's most enjoyable annual amusements. About a week before Halloween, Father and Mrs. Sharp gather up the children along with assorted cousins from tots to teens, as well as aunts, uncles, grandparents, and friends, for an excursion to our local pumpkin patch, where each person chooses his or her own Halloween pumpkin and then helps search for the official Sharp family jack-o'-lantern.

It is such a simple entertainment to be out in the fresh air sharing the bounty of the harvest with the family on a bright sunny afternoon, selecting a pumpkin each according to his fancy. And the mixture of all ages adds to the festive spirit of this tradition.

After everyone chooses a pumpkin (and mark it, please, with an initial to avoid disputes later, for back home, pumpkins never appear the way they did in the field), the collective search is on for the most perfect, most plump, most round, and most orange pumpkin, which will be carved with much ceremony the night before Halloween and crowned (with a gold-foil paper crown) King Jack.

If you should not be able to get to a pumpkin patch, do not brood. Many city farmers' markets and produce stands load up on pumpkins during the autumn. Or you can always go to your local greengrocer's and purchase an assortment of pumpkins to hide in your own backyard. It's the spirit of the tradition that counts.

When the family returns home to The Vicarage, our carving party begins. Mrs. Sharp spreads brown wrapping paper on the front porch and brings out felt-tipped markers and soft crayons so that everyone can first design their pumpkin's face before the carving.

Since only adults and older children are permitted sharp knives, Mrs. Sharp brings out a special basket of gourds, dried wheat, cornhusks, and vegetables along with acrylic paints, construction paper, yarn bits, fabric scraps, and glue sticks for the younger children to use in creating what Victorian children called "pumpkin moonshines."

Before long, the family has a fine collection of fierce and fancy Halloween pumpkin faces. But Mrs. Sharp has also been carving checkerboards, hearts, stars, and teddy bears out of some of the smaller pumpkins. After their own jack-o'-lanterns are finished, the children enjoy creating unusual designs for a festive harvesttime display that we arrange on our seasonal table in the dining room.

Now it's time for apple cider, fresh, hot popcorn, and taffy apples before everyone departs. As they always do, the children say they don't want the afternoon to end. But Mrs. Sharp assures them there is still much harvest fun to be had in the days to come.

A Brief History of Halloween

The history of Halloween comes down to us from the ancient pre-Christian Celtic festival of Samhain, which was held on October 31, the last autumn night before the cold and barrenness of winter. On this festival night—which was considered the Celtic New Year's Eve—the Druids (or Celtic high priests) believed the Lord of the Dead ruled and that the supernatural world drew closer to the physical world.

This was the night that the ghosts of the dead were permitted to return to visit their former homes for a brief reunion with the world they had left behind. Other supernatural creatures—fairies, witches, goblins, and devils—supposedly conjured magic spells on any poor humans they might encounter. Little Irish children who had to travel the dark country roads carried lanterns, carved by their mothers from turnips, that held a hot coal of turf so they could see their way clear of fairy hills or bogie bogs. The custom of trick-or-treating probably evolved from children's begging burning peat embers from houses as they walked the lonely dark roads. As well, in order to frighten these spirits away, the Celts would light huge bonfires and wear animal skins—a forerunner of Halloween costumes.

When Christianity arrived to Ireland, the church attempted to transform these pagan rites into remembrance of the good who had died by fixing two important church feast days near Samhain: All Saints' Day (on November 1) and All Souls' Day (November 2). But old rituals, especially those that speak to the fears and fantasies of our inner life, are hard to eliminate, even if the name of Samhain was changed to All Hallows' Eve (*hallow* is the Old English word for "saint"), meaning the night before a holy day.

When the Irish migrated to America in huge numbers, they brought their Halloween customs with them, trading in their lighted turnips for jack-o'-lanterns carved out of pumpkins. The night lost all of its sinister connotations and became a time for fun and frolic.

For small towns in late-nineteenth-century America, the celebration of Halloween eventually evolved into a gala affair, although it would be another century before trick-or-treating became part of our Halloween traditions.

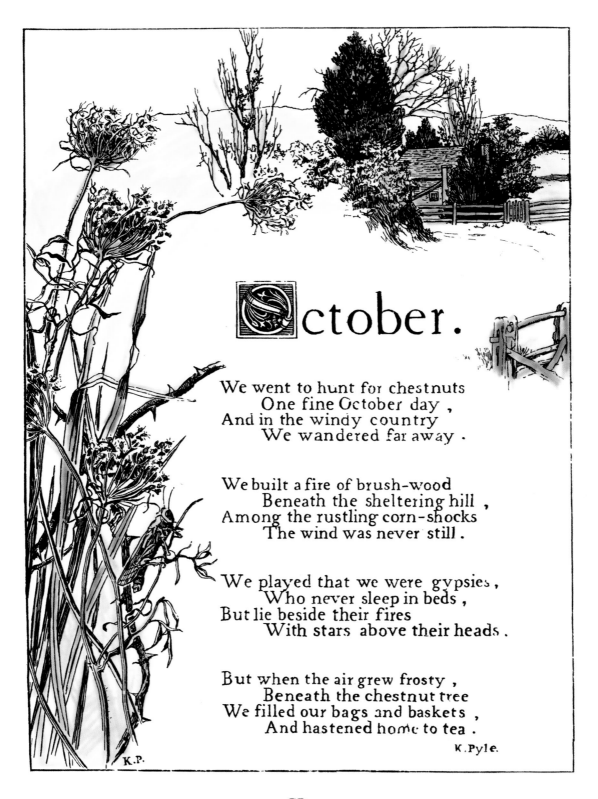

October.

We went to hunt for chestnuts
    One fine October day ,
And in the windy country
    We wandered far away .

We built a fire of brush-wood
    Beneath the sheltering hill ,
Among the rustling corn-shocks
    The wind was never still .

We played that we were gypsies ,
    Who never sleep in beds ,
But lie beside their fires
    With stars above their heads .

But when the air grew frosty ,
    Beneath the chestnut tree
We filled our bags and baskets ,
    And hastened home to tea .

K. Pyle.

All Hallows' Eve Home Frolic

Goblins on the doorstep,
Phantoms in the air,
Owls on witches' gateposts
Giving stare for stare,
Cats on flying broomsticks,
Bats against the moon
Stirrings round of fate-cakes with a solemn spoon.
Whirling apple parings
Figures draped in sheets
Dodging, disappearing, up and down the streets,
Jack-o-Lanterns grinning
Shadows on a screen,
Shrieks and starts and laughter—
This is Hallowe'en!
—*Dorothy Brown Thompson*

How shall we celebrate Halloween this year? Mrs. Sharp says it is time to turn the focus of this old-fashioned young people's holiday back to where it belongs: in the home. Of course, your young ones will want to go trick-or-treating, but you can keep this activity a short one both in time and locale—especially if you have an All Hallows' Eve Home Frolic awaiting them.

Ah, the masquerade parties we used to have at the turn of the century, dear Reader. Now here was an excuse for frolic! Halloween is a night when a magic spell enthralls all the earth, and Mrs. Sharp's home was no exception. To all our friends we sent the summons:

What does the Future hold For You?
Hallowe'en will Tell you True!
To the Vicarage that Night
Arrive at Eight
Come Prepared to Learn Your Fate!

Bewitching Beginnings

While other parties are enjoyable in the front parlor, Halloween parties are best in large, open spaces; our party flows freely among the kitchen, dining room, and, if the weather is agreeable, the backyard. To ensure the success of any Halloween party, all formality must be dispensed with; Mrs. Sharp removes all breakable items from her party rooms. These are replaced with nature's decorations: cornstalks, assorted pumpkins, gourds, and Indian corn. Large tree branches are hung with white muslin ghosts (old men's handkerchiefs or cloth diapers work well, too). To create a magical mood, red or yellow muslin (available at fabric stores) draped over lampshades will cast a harvest-moon glow inside, even if your party is in the late afternoon.

Fun and Frolic

After our guests have arrived (naturally, in costume, adults included), the games begin. Of course, we bob for apples, but we also have apples suspended from the ceiling on strings, and the boys and girls must attempt to take a bite out of their apple without touching it with their hands, which they discover—to great glee—is a rather hard thing to do. A game that never fails to amuse the children is called Nut Shower. Mrs. Sharp gathers all the children into one room, then scatters large English walnuts on the floor for a general grab (but she keeps some back so that everyone gets the same amount, either two or three walnuts). Nutcrackers are provided and the unsuspecting children sit down to crack open their nuts, then to their surprise discover the nuts do not contain kernels but little charms! Earlier Mrs. Sharp had removed the kernels and inserted small trinkets (available at party shops), then the shells were glued back together.

Festive and Fateful Food

Partners for refreshments are found in this unique way: Each little guest is given a small ball of yarn in different colors and told to wind it up to discover what lies at the other end. Since Mrs. Sharp has tied together two balls of yarn (in similar colors), what he discovers is another child: his supper partner. The yarn should be wound in and around furniture and through two different rooms so that the partners will not meet until some fun has been created by running to and fro.

For our party buffet, Mrs. Sharp serves hearty autumn-vegetable soup, assorted sandwiches cut in festive Halloween shapes, stuffed baked potatoes with a selection of fillings, popcorn balls, pecan tarts, pumpkin muffins, and witches' brew (mulled cider). Traditional Halloween foods can also be prepared: a delicious fruited yeast bread known as barm brack, colcannon from Ireland, a sweet porridge from Scotland called crowdie, and Victorian ring cake. Charms are tucked into these foods, supposedly to foretell the future: a coin for wealth, a ring for marriage, a button for a bachelor, a thimble for a spinster, a wishbone for your heart's desire. Having an assortment of fortune-telling foods gives everyone a chance for a bit of good luck.

High Spirits and Happy Hearts

After supper it is time for a few more games, all with a fortune-telling theme.

Nut Crack is one of the oldest Victorian Halloween games, and for centuries in England, All Hallows' Eve

THIS IS HALLOWE'EN

The perfect invitation sets the mood for any party and is both a joy to send and receive. You can begin to turn the clock back for an old-fashioned All Hallows' Eve Home Frolic by helping your youngsters make their invitations: grinning jack-o'-lanterns. These are simplified versions of paper "mechanicals" that Victorian children so loved.

To make them: Cut pumpkins out of orange construction paper (three and a half inches wide and three inches long). With a black marker draw in the face; place glue on the sides and bottom of the pumpkin but not at the top. Paste the pumpkin onto a piece of black construction paper (four by six inches). Now cut out a piece of bright green paper (two inches wide by four inches long), curving one end to resemble a stem. On this you will write the time, date, and address of your party. At the top of the stem, write "Pull Me." Slip the stem into the open top of the pumpkin.

Be sure to let your guests know they must come in costumes!

was known as Nut Crack Night. This is the game, testing love and loyalty, that gives the day its name: Two people place either a hazelnut or chestnut side by side on a warm grate in the fireplace. If the nuts burn quietly with a steady glow until they become ashes, it is a sign that a long and happy friendship will continue (or that a suitor will become a sweetheart). If the nuts crack and burst, it predicts the same with the friendship.

Full of good cheer, our annual All Hallows' Eve Home Frolic draws to a close with promises that we shall do it all again next year. Whether your gathering is small or large, Halloween offers us all the opportunity to remember that the most potent magic spell any parent can cast is the one that makes home the place where a family's happiest hours are spent.

Halloween Entertainments

A Halloween party is a particularly easy form of entertainment because the guests are always willing to help amuse themselves, all being eager and alert to discover what the fates have in store for them," the Victorian magazine *The Delineator* informed hostesses in 1891. Here are some of their suggestions for party pastimes:

Bobbing for Apples

No one ever thinks of celebrating Halloween without playing this game. Choose as many fine, large apples as there are persons in the company, and scratch or prick on each the name or initials of some person known to all present, placing the names of girls or women on the apples intended for all the men and vice versa. Have in readiness a tub two-thirds full of water, and in it place the apples prepared for the feminine "bobbers," who will then kneel beside the tub and endeavor to take an apple from the water with their teeth. The men are then permitted to attempt this rather difficult feat. When anyone succeeds in taking an apple from the water, the person whose name is inscribed upon it will be his or her partner for life.

Apple Peeling

Each guest peels an apple, being careful to keep the paring in an unbroken strip. To make this possible the fruit should be very smooth and in perfect condition. When all the apples have been pared, each person in turn tosses his or her strip of peel over his or her right shoulder, and one of the company who acts as oracle decides what letter it resembles as it lies. The letter named is an initial of the person's future lover.

Kaling

This is a Scottish game for Halloween and can be properly played only where there is a garden close at hand. One of the company, having been blindfolded and led into the garden, pulls up the first cabbage stalk he or she touches and carries it into the house, where a fortune-teller interprets. The comparative size of the cabbage indicates the stature of the individual's future partner for life; the quantity of earth clinging to the roots shows the amount of money that will be secured by the match; the taste of the pith tells what the temper of the expected spouse will be; and when the stalk is placed over the door, the first name of the first person entering thereafter is that of the prophesied husband or wife.

Launching Walnut Shells

This is a particularly pretty game. Split a number of soft English walnuts exactly in half, remove the kernels, and clear away the small partitions that may remain in the shells. Place a bit of heavy cotton string in each piece of shell and pour melted beeswax around it, shaping the wax into a cone or little hill, with the string protruding from the top. All the shells being prepared, the wicks of several are lighted, and the frail craft are launched simultaneously by their owners upon the "sea of life"—or, in other words, a tub of water. When a light burns steadily until the wax is all melted, and the little boat safely rides the waves made by slightly stirring the water or by gently shaking the tub, a happy and long life is assured the owner. When two boats collide, it means that the persons who launched them will meet and have mutual interests at some period of their lives. If two boats cross each other's course, their owners will do likewise. If two boats come together and continue to sail about side by side, those whom they represent will pass much of their lives together. When a boat clings persistently to the side of the tub, refusing to sail out into the center, the owner will surely be a stay-at-home. Touching frequently at the side of the tub indicates many short voyages, but when a boat sails boldly to the center, seldom touching the sides, a life filled with long journeys may be predicted. The actions of the little fleet will prove of absorbing interest to imaginative minds.

Fortune-Telling Foods

Fortune-telling foods were such an important part of Victorian Halloween celebrations that late-nineteenth-century hostesses were able to purchase inexpensive cast-iron charm sets at novelty stores. You can find charms at party shops, or you can assemble your own assortment. However, because modern incarnations will be made of plastic, do not insert them before preparing the foods!

The most popular fortune-telling foods were ring or fate cakes (use Mrs. Sharp's recipe for pound cake, inserting a ring

through the bottom of the cake after it's baked), colcannon (see our recipe for St. Patrick's Day), barm brack, and fortune-telling crowdie.

From ghoulies and ghosties and
long-legged beasties
And things that go bump in the night,
Good Lord, deliver us!
—*Old Cornish prayer*

Halloween

May each old Witch that here is seen,
Bring you Good Luck on Hallowe'en.

Barm Brack

1 package active dry yeast

1¼ cups, plus 1 teaspoon, lukewarm milk

¾ cup, plus 1 teaspoon, sugar

4 cups unbleached flour

1 teaspoon nutmeg

1 teaspoon cinnamon

1 teaspoon grated allspice

1 teaspoon salt

1 stick unsalted butter, cut in small pieces

2 eggs, beaten with a little water

2 cups mixed fruit (sultanas, raisins)

½ cup mixed candied fruit peel (lemon and orange)

Glaze: 3 teaspoons confectioners' sugar dissolved in
   3 teaspoons boiling water

In a small bowl, cream the yeast with 1 teaspoon milk and 1 teaspoon sugar until frothy. In another bowl, sieve together the flour, sugar, spices, and salt. With your hands, rub in the butter. Make a well in the center of the flour mixture and pour in the yeast, the beaten eggs, and the milk. Mix the ingredients well with a wooden spoon for about 5 minutes until a good dough forms. Add the fruit and fruit peel and work it into the mixture by hand. Cover the bowl with a clean cloth and allow it to rise in a warm place until doubled in size (about 1 hour and 15 minutes).

Knead again slightly and place in a lightly greased cast-iron skillet, cover, and again allow the bread to rise another 30 minutes.

Place in a preheated oven at 400° and bake until golden brown, approximately 1 hour.

When done, remove from pan and let cool on a wire rack. Glaze while still warm.

Fortune-Telling Crowdie

1 pint heavy cream, lightly whipped

1 teaspoon vanilla

4 teaspoons sugar, to taste

2 tablespoons rum (or ½ tablespoon rum flavoring)

4 tablespoons lightly toasted oatmeal (toast on a cookie
   sheet in a 350° oven for 7 minutes)

Charms: 1 coin, 1 ring, 1 button, 1 thimble, 1 wishbone—each wrapped in aluminum foil

Whip the cream with vanilla. As peaks form, add sugar and rum and continue to whip until well blended.

Combine with oatmeal. Chill for one hour. Just before serving, stir in charms.

When you serve this dish, have a spoon for each guest. Let them dish out a spoonful of crowdie on their plates.

Serves six; adjust proportions accordingly.

Harvest Home

At last, the hour of bewitchment has arrived—All Hallows' Eve. "The bogeyman will get you if you don't watch out," children call to one another with high-pitched squeals of nervous laughter.

But the bogeyman won't get his chance, for Mama and Papa *are* watching out. Mrs. Sharp is sure you watch closely over your young ones, dear Reader, but in concentrating on children's physical safety, perhaps you overlook how sensitive and susceptible is the young child's imagination. All the supernatural elements that give Halloween its potent magic can linger long after the holiday is over, frightening very young children, even if they do not admit it.

Think of Halloween from a small child's perspective: Normally friendly-looking adults suddenly appear in gruesome goblin garb, hideous face masks stare down from drugstore shelves, and macabre images appear on television to "celebrate" the holiday.

Believe me, dear Reader, with Halloween today, the bogeyman is the least of our worries. However, there should be a children's holiday devoted to make-believe, mischief, mystery, and magic. But of the right kind.

Bring Back That Rhapsody in Boo

What is needed, then, is a plan that provides the children with a festive holiday but one that offers a comforting sense of balance and harmony, such as our All Hallows' Eve Home Frolic.

But Mrs. Sharp's favorite tradition for children who have had too much Halloween is our family celebration of Harvest Home. This adapted tradition grew out of Mrs. Sharp's desire to reassure the children that, indeed, all ghosties and ghoulies had gone away the morning after the night before. When the children persisted that they could still see "skeletons and devils and all sorts of horrible things" hiding behind their eyes, Mrs. Sharp told them not to worry, for she had invited all the good spirits to a Harvest Home dinner that evening in honor of their day—All Saints'. Immediately the children concluded that if there were any unsavory Halloween creatures lurking about, the Sharp house was certainly not the place for them to be. At peace, they returned to play and a new tradition was born.

Reap the Rich Harvest Love Has Sown

Harvest Home was the traditional Victorian English celebration after all the gathering in the fields had been completed. Over a community feast, families would come together to rejoice in their bounty of blessings.

A Harvest Home festival for the family is similar in that we rejoice in reaping the rich harvest that love has sown. And there is really no better occasion during the autumn to have a Harvest Home celebration than the day after Halloween—on All Saints' Day, November 1.

The reason for this is that the giving of equal attention to good deeds as well as ghoulish pranks confirms a young child's instinctive sense of justice. Furthermore, by having a family party that celebrates our harvest of home blessings, we are able to pass on to the children the emotional security of loving, faith-building rituals that will ward off evil—real or imagined—better than any magic charm.

Little Saints Come Marching In

While All Saints' Day originated as a religious holiday in the ninth century, at Mrs. Sharp's house one does not have to be canonized to qualify for an invitation to dinner. For our purposes, a saint is anyone who has lived an inspiring life.

Although Mrs. Sharp's Harvest Home festival has evolved into quite an elaborate family affair—as inevitably family traditions do—that first year it simply involved setting an empty place next to each child at the table and, during dinner, conversing about what personal saints, heroes, and heroines we would invite to dinner if we could and why.

Today the children look forward to selecting their "saint" each year and learning as much about him or her as possible. The identity of everyone's guest is also a closely guarded secret, and happy hours are spent fashioning the "saints'" fancy dress.

Then on All Saints' Night before dinner, we have a little masquerade parade throughout the house—to the tune, naturally, of "When the Saints Go Marching In." Father and Mrs. Sharp then have to guess which "saint" each child is. The success of this charade usually depends on divine intervention, but the pantomime always ends in great merriment.

Finally the family sits down to a festive autumn supper. Mother lights the candles, Father (or the oldest child) pours the wine and cider, and we hold hands and invoke blessings on the meal. The family tells stories, sings the old songs, and basks in the healing power of hearth and Harvest Home. Outside, winter's darkness begins to close in. Inside we have found our own light.

The fields are harvested and bare,
And Winter whistles through the square,
October dresses in flame and gold
Like a woman afraid of growing old.

—*Anne Mary Lawler*

NOVEMBER.

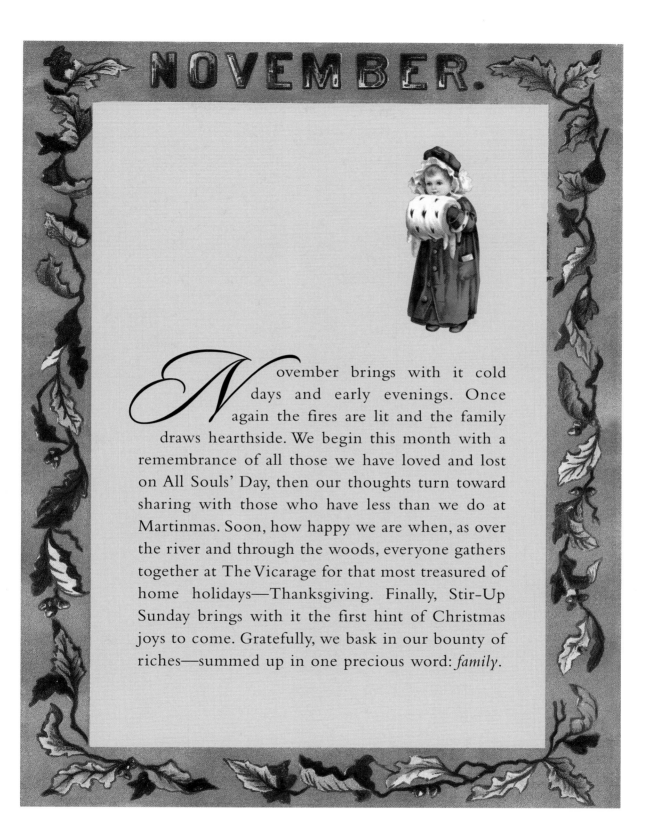

November brings with it cold days and early evenings. Once again the fires are lit and the family draws hearthside. We begin this month with a remembrance of all those we have loved and lost on All Souls' Day, then our thoughts turn toward sharing with those who have less than we do at Martinmas. Soon, how happy we are when, as over the river and through the woods, everyone gathers together at The Vicarage for that most treasured of home holidays—Thanksgiving. Finally, Stir-Up Sunday brings with it the first hint of Christmas joys to come. Gratefully, we bask in our bounty of riches—summed up in one precious word: *family*.

November

Now the cold wind rattles
   In the icy sedge,
And the sparrows ruffle
   In the leafless hedge.

Past the wood and meadow,
   On the frozen pool
All the boys go skating,
   When they come from school.

The river too was frozen;
   I saw it far away,
And wished that I could trace it,
   Skating night and day,

Up to where the ice-bergs,
   On the polar sea,
Float, like glittering castles,
   Waiting there for me.

K. Pyle.

All Souls' Day

For centuries, the souls of the dead have been remembered and prayed for on November 2, All Souls' Day. This was the day Victorian families would visit the cemetery, offer prayers, and reflect on the sweetness—and often brevity—of life.

From England comes the tradition of "soul cakes" for All Souls' Day. An ancient belief held that all unhappy souls could return to their former homes for a visit. Thus it became customary on All Souls' Eve to keep the hearth well tended and leave food, especially sweet buns known as soul cakes, on the table in case the visiting spirits were hungry.

Soul cakes were also offered to visitors and distributed to the poor who came "a'souling," praying for a household's departed relations, in return for alms and a soul cake.

In Mrs. Sharp's house, like Lenten hot cross buns, these delicious treats come but once a year and will eagerly be awaited by your family. When you serve your soul cakes, have the children sing this song:

A Soul, a Soul, a Soul cake,
Please good misses a Soul cake,
An apple, a pear, a plum or a cherry
Or any good thing, to make us merry.
One for Peter, two for Paul
and Three for Him who made us all.

Into her family's soul cakes, Mrs. Sharp inserts shiny copper pennies, wrapped in aluminum foil, for the rest of the song goes:

The lanes are very dirty
My shoes are very thin,
I've got a little pocket
To put a penny in.

If you haven't got a penny,
A ha' penny will do,
If you haven't got a ha' penny
God Bless You!

Mrs. Sharp's Soul Cakes

1 stick butter, softened
1 cup sugar
3 eggs
1 teaspoon vanilla extract
1 teaspoon lemon extract
4 cups flour
1 teaspoon cinnamon
1 teaspoon nutmeg
1 teaspoon allspice
½ cup currants
½ cup milk

Preheat the oven to 350°.

Cream the butter and sugar together (with an electric mixer), then beat in the eggs one at a time. Add vanilla and lemon extracts and mix well. Sift the flour and the spices together and then add to the butter mixture. Stir in the currants and add milk to make a soft dough. Form the dough into flat cakes and place on a greased cookie sheet. Bake for 15 minutes or until golden brown.

Martinmas

On November 11 comes the festival of Martinmas, a very old European winter celebration dating back to the Middle Ages, concerning Saint Martin of Tours. As the legend goes, a young soldier named Martin was passing under an archway when he discovered a poor beggar huddled there. It was very cold and the man was nearly naked. Although Martin was not a rich man, upon seeing the poor beggar, he took off his own cape and ripped it in half in order to cover the beggar.

The following night Martin had a dream in which he saw Christ wearing his cape. Christ said, "Martin, what you have done unto the least of your brothers you have done to me." Inspired by his vision, Martin abandoned his career in the French cavalry, became a monk, and devoted the rest of his life to helping all of mankind regardless of their station. Today he is considered the patron saint of beggars, drunkards, and outcasts.

In many European countries, particularly Germany, France, and the Netherlands, Martinmas is

celebrated with a festival of lanterns, symbolizing the light of generosity that illuminates the darkness of lack. We celebrate it in our home as well. Earlier, Mrs. Sharp has gathered together the good, serviceable clothing that the entire family has outgrown—each child is responsible for choosing something to pass on to another—and after it has been washed and cleaned and mended, we take the clothing to a nearby shelter.

Each year Mrs. Sharp reinforces the tradition of giving on Martinmas by giving a special sweater or scarf to each child. The gift is symbolic: something that will keep him or her warm both physically and emotionally.

In the afternoon the children put the finishing touches on the paper lanterns they have been working on for the past few days. Victorians enjoyed decorating with paper lanterns, which were often strung outside in great numbers to illuminate evening entertainments.

When the children's lanterns are complete, we ceremoniously light them and the children carry them once around the dining room. Afterward we enjoy a festive tea together.

Now, you might say, Martinmas sounds lovely, Mrs. Sharp, but, really, this is one tradition that is very far removed from our daily life. Well, dear Reader, perhaps not. Isn't it likely that every year you will sort through your clothing to donate to a charitable organization? Isn't it likely you will either knit or purchase a new sweater for the children each year? Wouldn't an interesting and simple craft activity brighten a few November afternoons? And aren't you looking for a tangible way to instill generosity in your children? The answer to all of these questions is probably yes. All that Mrs. Sharp has done is pull all of these elements together around an annual tradition.

Remember that you can start your own traditions with your family and you should, for that is how our legacy of love grows for ourselves and our children.

Martinmas may not be a festival you are familiar with today, but its gentle caring customs can become all the more precious in time for the lesson it lovingly imparts.

Making Paper Lanterns

Making paper lanterns is an activity that young children love. It is fairly simple, but be sure to allow plenty of time for the various steps of this project; it will occupy at least three afternoons. Don't try to rush the steps if you want your lantern to hold together.

First, take a sheet of quality watercolor paper, sixteen inches by twelve inches. Have each child paint a pretty picture with watercolors on it. Let it dry overnight. The next day, take a paper towel dipped in vegetable cooking oil and rub it over the painting. Do this several times until the paper is saturated with the oil. Let it dry overnight. The oil-saturated paper will reflect candlelight beautifully.

Now you are ready to make your lantern. First mark off eight two-inch strips, three inches from the bottom of the paper, as shown in the diagram. Cut the strips, but do not cut them off the paper. Now form your lantern by rolling the two ends of the painting together, overlapping by one inch. Glue the sides of the lantern down; clip with a clothespin until dry. Next fold up the strips of the lantern to form the base. Glue into place. Stand your lantern up and place a large rock or a mug into the bottom of it to help give it shape. Let it dry overnight.

The next day, glue a small metal votive-candle holder on the bottom of your lantern. Punch two holes on either side at the top of your lantern for your handle. Make the handle for your lantern out of a piece of yarn sixteen inches long.

On Martinmas afternoon, place a small votive candle in the metal base of the lantern and have an adult light it. The lanterns look very pretty when grouped together in the center of the dining room table for tea. The handle of the lantern is for when the children want to play with them afterward, but not, dear Reader, with a lighted candle!

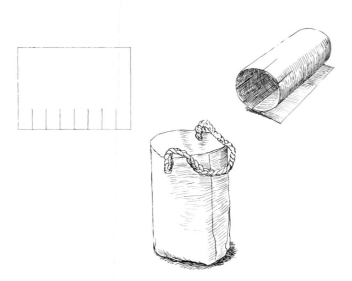

Thanksgiving

"Thanksgiving! What a world of pleasant memories the word recalls," a Victorian writer named John Tremaine observed. "Memories obscured and softened, not by the mists of time, but by the fragrant steam rising slowly from innumerable savory dishes! Oh, the Thanksgiving dinners we have eaten! The Thanksgiving cheer of which we have partaken!"

Indeed, dear Reader, what a happy holiday Thanksgiving is, as over the river and through the woods we travel back home to be together. Soon family and friends will be gathered around the groaning dining room table for turkey with all the trimmings.

But what is this we spy? A sadder-but-wiser reader who felt that her Thanksgiving dinner was rather a humdrum affair has replaced the family's traditional candied yams with an acorn-squash souf-

May you always ride on the wings of prosperity and plenty.

May you see many glad
THANKSGIVING DAYS

flé. "What? No sweet potatoes?" the family cries. "But we always have sweet potatoes at Thanksgiving."

Let us leave this sorry scene. It is one that could have been avoided and will be in your happy homes. We do not wish to become slaves to tradition, but some customs are sacred, such as your family's Thanksgiving bill of fare. If they have enjoyed corn bread, onion, and sage stuffing since Plymouth Rock, do not substitute chestnut and prunes.

"But, Mrs. Sharp," you protest. "How do we ever get our families to try anything new? If we can't even get them to eat a new dish, how will we ever get them to try a new family activity?" Subtly, my dears.

Take our soufflé, for example. Mrs. Sharp would never substitute it for the candied yams, but would place it on the table (without too much fanfare) in addition to the yams. This way the family can try it without giving up anything known and loved.

The same is true with new family activities that may someday become your children's traditions. Mrs. Sharp believes traditions are like recipes. Some we don't alter a bit because they are perfect. Others need a dash of this or that to suit our family's taste.

As with any new dish, you'll know soon enough whether the new custom suits your family and should become part of your repertoire. Did they enjoy it? Did you? Was the activity worth the effort it took to do it again? In the Sharp household, to qualify as a "tradition," an activity has to be repeated at least twice.

Still, before you can create culinary delights, you need first to read the recipe, check to make sure you have all the ingredients, then set aside the time in the kitchen.

The same principle applies to cooking up family fun: Read ahead (for inspiration), check ingredients (for information), and set aside the time (for the whole family's involvement and enjoyment). The result will be your family's just desserts: loving memories.

The Thanksgiving Day Hamper

One tradition that Victorian families shared together was to prepare Thanksgiving food baskets for the hungry. A century later this need still exists; there are many food banks around the country that would appreciate contributions. When children assist in the gathering and preparing of food gifts and then help pack a basket and deliver it, they learn the deeper significance of Thanksgiving and see how much they have to be thankful for.

In Mrs. Sharp's home we try to duplicate as much as possible of our dinner to give away, down to the baking of extra pies. Granted, this tradition involves extra effort and expense, but whatever you are able to help your children do for others—even donating a few cans of nonperishable items to a food bank—will richly be worth your trouble. Our children's Thanksgiving hamper always returns much more to our family than we could ever give away, helping our children adopt the traits of gratitude and reverence.

The Children's Contribution

A Thanksgiving tradition the children in our family particularly enjoy is setting the table, for on this festive occasion what is viewed as a daily duty is transformed into a holiday privilege. While Mrs. Sharp derives great pleasure from laying out her best china, sparkling crystal, and freshly pressed white linen for our Thanksgiving Day dinner, she knows the children need to make their contributions to the table in order to feel that the celebration belongs to them as well.

That's why the children make the table's merry place card "favors." A few days before, Mrs. Sharp gives the children a box of old photographs. They cut out heads of family members and mount them on funny figures of people and animals selected from magazines. These are then pasted on cardboard for use as our place cards. When guests ask to take the place cards home—as they invariably do—it doubles the children's pleasure and ensures that the tradition is repeated each year.

We all have much to be grateful for, dear Reader, and never is this more apparent than when we glance around our dining room table on Thanksgiving Day—such bountiful blessings have been bestowed upon us all! May this gratitude remain forever engraved on our hearts.

A Brief History of Thanksgiving

Thanksgiving is one of America's oldest and most beloved holidays. It is also our country's most misunderstood holiday.

It might come as a surprise, but most of the traditions of this holiday originated with Victorian mothers rather than Pilgrim fathers. What's more, if it hadn't been for the unrelenting efforts of one Victorian lady, we probably wouldn't be sitting down to dinner together as a nation on Thanksgiving.

In the first place, the very religious early settlers of New England believed days of "thanks giving" to God were to be set apart for prayers and fasting, not feasting and merriment. Whenever the settlers needed divine deliverance from situations like drought or illness, a day of prayer and fasting would be declared. After their prayers had been answered, a day of "thanks giving" occurred with religious services.

Gradually the religious intensity that characterized both church and state functions lessened. Then, in 1789, America's first national Thanksgiving Day observance was proclaimed by President George Washington in acknowledgment of the favors the Almighty had bestowed on the country, namely, for winning the Revolutionary War. For the next seventy-five years "Thanksgiving" was irregularly celebrated, with each state's governor fixing the date the holiday was to occur.

All of this confusion drove Mrs. Sarah Josepha Hale, editor of the Victorian *Godey's Lady's Book,* nearly crazy. Fervently patriotic and devoted to promoting the family and home as the bedrock of the nation, Mrs. Hale believed one day a year should be set aside for American families to gather together to acknowledge their blessings and celebrate the bounty of peace and plenty.

In 1827 she began what would become nearly a lifelong crusade for a uniform national observance of Thanksgiving. For more than three decades she wrote impassioned editorials and countless personal letters to every governor and ten presidents.

When her pleas fell on deaf male ears, she realized what her holiday needed was not the support of politicians but of women and their families. As editor of America's most influential nineteenth-century women's periodical, Mrs. Hale was in a position to create in her readers' imaginations a nostalgic, emotional longing for a holiday that never really existed.

She wrote: "I have thus endeavored to lay before my readers one of the strongest wishes of my heart, convinced that the general estimate of feminine character throughout the United States will be far from finding it an objection that this idea of American Union Thanksgiving was suggested by a woman. The enjoyments are social, the feastings are domestic; therefore this annual festival is really the exponent of family happiness and household piety, which women should always seek to cultivate in their hearts and in their homes. God gave to man authority, to woman influence: she inspires and persuades; he convinces and compels. It has always been my aim to use my influence in this womanly way."

Mrs. Hale's womanly way of exerting influence was to publish tantalizing Thanksgiving Day menus featuring elaborate Victorian interpretations of Pilgrim fare (roast turkey with giblet gravy, creamed baby onions, and cranberry sauce), and sentimental, heart-wrenching redemption stories (just as the family prepares to say grace, the prodigal son or disgraced daughter who had run off to the big city would reappear to great rejoicing). "Let Thanksgiving, our American holiday . . . awaken in American hearts the love of home and of country, of thankfulness to God and peace between brethren," Mrs. Hale implored her readers.

Very quickly, nineteenth-century American women embraced the holiday. Before long the celebration of Thanksgiving entered the vernacular of popular culture: Currier and Ives captured the essence of the holiday in sentimental family tableaux, and Mrs. Lydia Maria Child, a friend of Sarah Hale's and frequent contributor to *Godey's,* wrote her famous ode to the holiday, "Over the River," which is still sung today. In 1863, President Abraham Lincoln issued the first national Thanksgiving proclamation in the United States, setting the last Thursday in November as a national holiday.

The Gift of Grace

In many modern households, the demands of school and business often make the evening meal the only hour in which all members of the family are together. This is reason enough, Mrs. Sharp believes, for any parent to offer appropriate expressions of gratitude.

The next time you find your family assembled all together to dine, pause a moment to count your blessings, dear Reader, and give thanks. The ritual of a family table grace—symbolizing unity—is one of the loveliest traditions you can incorporate into your daily lives.

A century ago, Mrs. Sharp would not have thought it necessary to offer such an observation, as faith was one of the foundations for family life. Today this is not always the case.

In the Sharp household, we say a simple grace before meals, not only because of a religious need but because it provides a moment of reflection and peace. Blessing our food before breaking bread provides our family with more than just nourishment for the body. We hold hands and say together:

> For our daily food and drink,
> Our home, family, and friends,
> We give thanks.
> Blessings on the meal.

However, with a family table grace, what matters is not what is said, but whether or not you take time to say it. If your family is not yet saying grace before meals, one enjoyable way to introduce this ritual into your repertoire is to compose your own. Invite the children to each contribute a thought or phrase. This collective effort will help make your "thanks giving" very personal. Some families also like to incorporate spontaneously thanks for the best thing that happened to members of the family during the day, which often sparks dinner conversation.

Should your children often respond to your inquiry as to how they spent their day with monosyllabic muttering, you might need a bit of assistance. During the Victorian era, the dinner hour was the time for children to be seen but not heard. Today, we know how precious little time modern families spend together. The give-and-take of dinner conversation is an integral part of successful family life.

Mrs. Sharp's tradition for encouraging meaningful dinner conversation is for everyone to write down favorite or interesting quotations on index cards, which are kept in a small basket on our table. Encourage your family to cast a wide net for quotations: the Bible, literature, readings done for work or school, magazines, and newspapers. Take turns selecting a card, then use it as a theme for your conversation. You'll find that with just one thought to prime the pump, the conversation will flow easily into other topics.

When we begin to introduce new rituals into our family life, it is natural to feel self-conscious and a bit awkward as we grope along an unmarked path. But persevere. Traditions and rituals in daily life elevate the mundane with meaning. Life seems far richer after we pause to count our blessings and then offer gratitude with a grace before meals.

Stir-Up Sunday
(The Sunday Before Advent)

For Mrs. Sharp's family the holiday excitement begins as soon as the Thanksgiving Day turkey starts simmering on the stove for soup. Then we put away the everyday china to make room for the Christmas crockery and bring out the Advent Box.

You may ask, "Advent Box, Mrs. Sharp? Is this another old-fashioned Victorian tradition?"

No, dear Reader. The Advent Box is simply a cardboard box containing all the books, supplies, and materials Mrs. Sharp needs early in December in order to observe the season of Advent, including her Christmas plum-pudding recipe. You see, before Advent commences next week, the family must prepare the Christmas pudding in order to give it time to age properly. We make it the Sunday before Advent begins (usually the Sunday after Thanksgiving), a day that the Victorians called Stir-Up Sunday.

This old custom probably originated because, on the Sunday before Advent, English congregations were exhorted in church to "stir up" and "bring forth the fruit of good works," a timely reminder to the vicar's wife and other Victorian women that it was time to prepare their Christmas puddings. An irreverent choirboy's rhyme tells us what everyone was going to do after returning home from church:

Stir up, we beseech thee
The pudding in the pot
And when we do get home
We'll all eat it hot!

Eating plum pudding as the grand finale to Christmas dinner is as English a tradition as you will ever find. Yankees may think they prefer their pumpkin pies and Christmas fruitcake—but only until they taste the plum pudding! As far as Mrs. Sharp is concerned, Christmas dinner is inconceivable without it.

Despite the fact that there is not a plum to be found in the recipe, this dish does have a venerable history. It began during the Middle Ages as plum porridge, or festive gruel, and by the eighteenth century became pudding—now containing bread crumbs, spices, sugar, eggs, milk, and suet. The Victorians invented the method of steaming the pudding in a basin—in earlier times it had been boiled—and added brandy. As it had achieved perfection, there was no need for it to evolve further.

On Stir-Up Sunday, the entire family gathers together to help Mrs. Sharp, for no matter what the particular ingredients of your favorite Christmas pudding recipe, one essential part of the ritual is that all the members of the household must take a turn stirring the pudding while making a wish. Finally Mrs. Sharp stirs a lucky sixpenny piece into the spicy dough. Whoever finds it in his or her portion on Christmas Day is destined to be wealthy the following year. But we all know it really doesn't matter who finds the coin, for as the family prepares our Christmas pudding together, we realize in the laughter and happy faces around the kitchen table that our joy is the season's true treasure.

Mrs. Sharp's Victorian Christmas Pudding

½ cup candied citrus peel

2 ounces candied lemon peel

2 cups raisins

2 cups currants

½ cup almonds, blanched and chopped

2 small nutmegs grated (1 teaspoon nutmeg)

1 teaspoon cinnamon

1 teaspoon allspice

1 cup flour

1 teaspoon salt

½ cup ground almonds

12 ounces fresh brown-bread crumbs

1 pound fresh suet, finely shredded

8 ounces dark brown sugar

8 eggs, beaten

1 wineglass brandy (4 ounces)

1 wineglass sherry (4 ounces)

Enough milk to mix (approximately ½ cup)

Chop the candied fruit peel, raisins, currants, and almonds coarsely. Mix them together thoroughly with all the spices.

In a large bowl blend together the fruit mixture with the flour, salt, and ground almonds. Work in the bread crumbs, suet, and sugar (using your hands is easiest) until everything is thoroughly mixed together. Beat the eggs lightly and add them to the mixture. Add the brandy, sherry, and milk, stirring until the pudding is a soft paste.

Let this mixture sit overnight in the refrigerator.

In the morning pour the mixture into a large, well-buttered pudding basin (or pour into two smaller pudding basins—this is an ample recipe), cover with greased paper and cloth (plain muslin), and tie it tightly around the rim of the basin.

Set the basin in a large open roasting pan filled to the sides with boiling water. Steam the pudding in this manner for 8 hours, adding hot water as necessary.

Remove the wet cloths and cover the pudding with fresh greased paper and fresh muslin. Store the pudding in a cool, dark place for 4 weeks. On Christmas Day, steam the pudding an additional 2 hours. Unmold the pudding.

Before serving, add a sprig of holly to the top of the pudding, cover with brandy, and bring it to the table flaming. Serve Christmas pudding with either brandy butter or whipped cream.

Brandy Butter

1 stick sweet butter

1 cup confectioners' sugar

¼ cup brandy

Allow the butter to warm to room temperature. Beat vigorously until creamy. Gradually beat in confectioners' sugar until pale and fluffy, adding the brandy a tablespoon at a time. Brandy butter can be made a few days beforehand; store in the refrigerator.

DECEMBER.

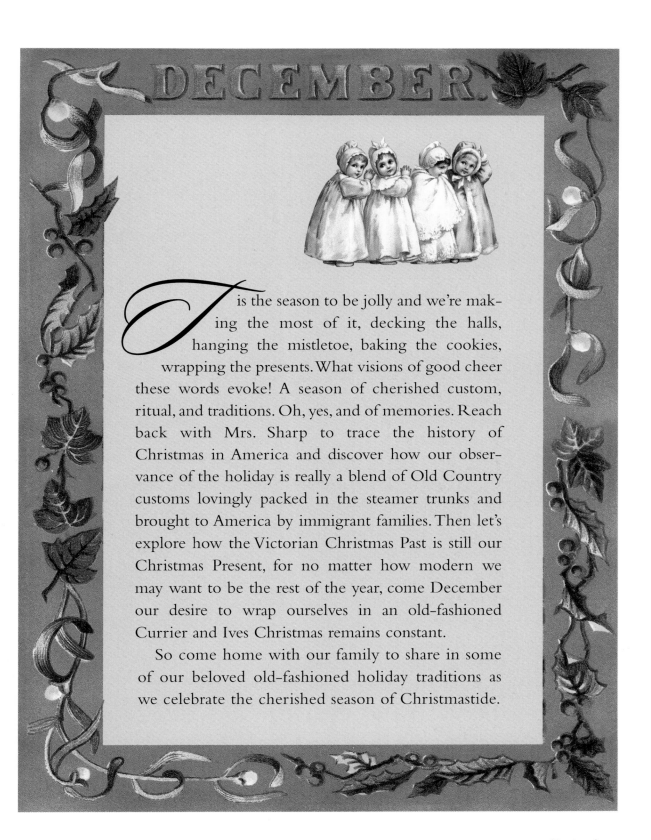

T is the season to be jolly and we're making the most of it, decking the halls, hanging the mistletoe, baking the cookies, wrapping the presents. What visions of good cheer these words evoke! A season of cherished custom, ritual, and traditions. Oh, yes, and of memories. Reach back with Mrs. Sharp to trace the history of Christmas in America and discover how our observance of the holiday is really a blend of Old Country customs lovingly packed in the steamer trunks and brought to America by immigrant families. Then let's explore how the Victorian Christmas Past is still our Christmas Present, for no matter how modern we may want to be the rest of the year, come December our desire to wrap ourselves in an old-fashioned Currier and Ives Christmas remains constant.

So come home with our family to share in some of our beloved old-fashioned holiday traditions as we celebrate the cherished season of Christmastide.

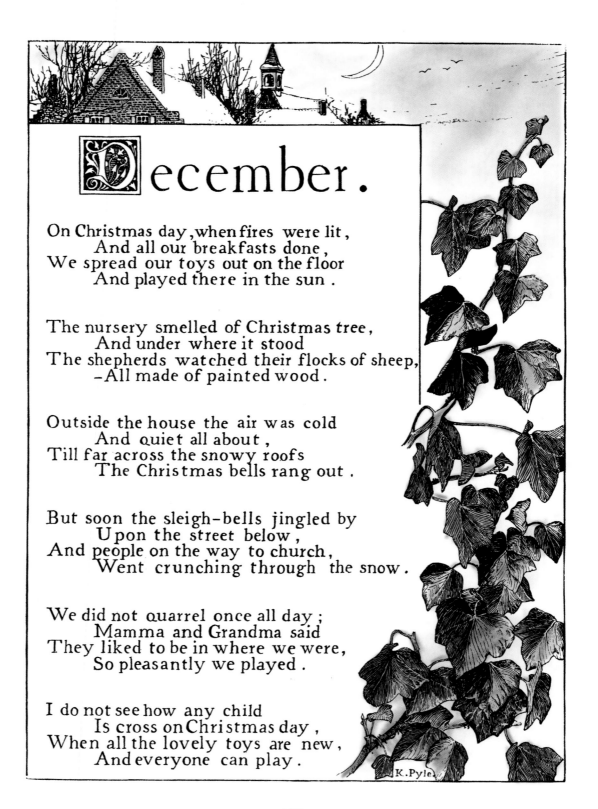

December.

On Christmas day, when fires were lit,
    And all our breakfasts done,
We spread our toys out on the floor
    And played there in the sun.

The nursery smelled of Christmas tree,
    And under where it stood
The shepherds watched their flocks of sheep,
    –All made of painted wood.

Outside the house the air was cold
    And quiet all about,
Till far across the snowy roofs
    The Christmas bells rang out.

But soon the sleigh-bells jingled by
    Upon the street below,
And people on the way to church,
    Went crunching through the snow.

We did not quarrel once all day;
    Mamma and Grandma said
They liked to be in where we were,
    So pleasantly we played.

I do not see how any child
    Is cross on Christmas day,
When all the lovely toys are new,
    And everyone can play.

K. Pyle.

Glancing Back

The Victorians Invent Christmas

The earliest recorded observance of Christmas in the New World was in 1607 at the Virginia colony of John Smith—complete with Yule logs, carols, evergreen-decorated churches, and a sumptuous feast on Christmas Day to which the Indians were invited. Throughout the next few decades in the rest of the colonies, however, it was very different. In Puritan New England, Christmas celebrations were viewed as wanton excesses brought on by the suggestion of Satan, and it would be well into the nineteenth century before New Englanders could feel comfortable enough to begin observing Christmas openly.

In stark contrast to their New England neighbors were New York's Dutch settlers, who not only celebrated Christmas Day but made it a gala finale to an entire month of merrymaking. During December, normal business would grind to a halt except for the confectioners, bakers, and toyshops, and Dutch homemakers cleaned, roasted fowl, and baked for weeks in anticipation of large house parties.

By the mid-1800s, Christmas was being celebrated as a holiday throughout most of America, largely because immigrant settlers brought their favorite holiday customs with them to enjoy in their new home

with their American neighbors. The Dutch brought their beloved gift bringer, Saint Nicholas, who visited good children on December 6; the English, their love of Christmas carols and decorating homes and churches with evergreens, mistletoe, and holly; and the Germans, the Christmas tree.

In the 1830s, German immigrants settling in Pennsylvania introduced the custom of bringing a freshly cut evergreen indoors to celebrate Christmas. They would decorate their tree with brightly colored paper cornucopias filled with nuts, crystallized fruit, and candy; gilded and colored eggshells; and wax candles.

During the 1840s when England's Queen Victoria and her German-born husband, Prince Albert, introduced the Christmas tree as the centerpiece of the royal family's holiday celebration, the scene was immortalized in both the *Illustrated London News* and *Godey's Lady's Book* in America, capturing the fancy of Victorian women. Very rapidly "the pretty German toy," as the Christmas tree was frequently called, passed from interesting folk custom to tradition.

Our modern-day Christmas, with its sentimental visions of an old-fashioned whirl of parties, gifts, and above all a reverence for tradition, was virtually an invention of middle-class Victorians in both England and the United States over just a few decades. By the 1870s, Christmas in America was considered the epoch of each year—"an occasion of literally delirious joy" is how Teddy Roosevelt described it—and the holiday was looked forward to with great anticipation.

The popularization of Christmas probably owes its greatest debt to Charles Dickens's novel *A Christmas Carol,* written in 1843. The story of Ebenezer Scrooge, Bob Cratchit, and Tiny Tim captured perfectly the essence of the Victorian Christmas ideal of high spirits, simple pleasures, good cheer, and generous charity.

Surprisingly, the philosophy of Christmas as a time of "good will towards our fellow man," as put forth by Dickens, was initially given a more enthusiastic reception in America than England. The book was an immediate bestseller, numerous dramatizations of it were produced, and the author toured America giving readings. Dickens made a tremendous impression on his audience, especially in New England, where the Puritan attitude toward Christmas was still hostile. One result of a reading in Boston on Christmas Eve in 1867 was the sudden conversion of a wealthy New England industrialist,

who closed his plant down the next day; the following year, he not only gave his employees Christmas Day off with pay but presented each of them with the gift of a turkey.

In glancing back on the Victorian era from today, we tend to think of Christmas celebrations then as less commercial than today. Mrs. Sharp can assure you, dear Reader, nothing is farther from the truth. Don't let the ghost of Christmas Past fool you. By the 1870s, Christmas was the biggest time of the year for shopkeepers. Our children pored over special catalogs for toys just as yours do today, and there was an onslaught of Christmas advertising in periodicals and newspapers. Even a century ago Santa Claus needed the assistance of parents to make Christmas wishes come true!

However, Mrs. Sharp believes the Victorians' greatest contribution to Christmas was to make it a family affair. For one long, glorious month adults and children spent extra time together sharing seasonal pastimes: the making of special foods, decorating the house, and the preparation of gifts. Mrs. Sharp believes these cherished holiday traditions can unite your family in a season of love, celebration, and joy as well.

THE ADVENT WREATH

Beginning with the first Sunday in Advent, Victorian families would suspend an evergreen wreath with a single red candle over the dining room table. Every day a white or gold paper star with a biblical verse would be added and the candle rekindled. Each successive Sunday in Advent a new candle would be added, lit, and a small celebration of reading verses, singing carols, and the savoring of holiday treats would occur.

Your family will enjoy the ceremony of an Advent wreath, too. To make an Advent wreath, Mrs. Sharp uses a wire hoop with four candleholders or a circular Styrofoam base with four candle holes (available at most craft or florist shops). Place a plain evergreen wreath on top of the base; if using a wire hoop, secure the wreath with thin wire or pin it to the Styrofoam with hairpins. Next insert four red candles.

While the suspended Advent wreath is charming, if there are young children in the house, you might prefer to leave yours lying flat on the table. Each day during Advent have the children take turns adding one large gold-foil paper star to the top of the wreath.

A tradition that European children especially enjoy is creating a tiny Advent garden within the wreath. Legend has it that beginning with the first Sunday of Advent, the natural world—the kingdoms of minerals, plants, and animals—rejoices at the coming of the Christ Child and offers a gift for the Creator's son. Let your children be of assistance: On the first Sunday have the children form a circle of smooth stones and crystals. The second week, add gifts from the plant world: pinecones, holly sprigs, even small red roses. On the third Sunday, the animal world joins the celebration with small toy figures of sheep, donkeys, and other creatures. On the final Sunday before Christmas, the figures of Mary and Joseph are added to the center of the wreath to stay until Christmas Eve.

Finally, at Mrs. Sharp's house, once our Advent wreath is completed on the first Sunday in Advent, the family gathers for a festive tea, featuring a spiced Christmas-wreath cake (use a tube or Bundt-shaped pan and tint the frosting green). We spend the evening cozy by the fire, singing carols and basking in that happy glow of contentment that only the approach of Christmas brings.

The Advent of Christmas

"I can't wait" is an expression parents will hear often in the next few weeks, for indeed, young children think they can't wait for Christmas to come.

Yet waiting patiently is a lesson we all should learn as early as possible, or life can be most disagreeable. There is no reason, however, that developing patience need be unpleasant. Which is why Mrs. Sharp learned a century ago to spread out the joys of Christmas over thirty-seven days, from the first of December until January's Epiphany celebration.

"Thirty-seven days? Sorry, Mrs. Sharp, but I can barely make it through one! Tradition or not, there's no way you're going to get me to celebrate Christmas for thirty-seven days."

But that, dear Reader, is precisely your difficulty. Can you not see it is clear folly to crowd Christmas into twelve very full hours of one day and expect everyone to enjoy themselves? Christmastide is, after all, not just a day but a season. Let us make the most of it. By spreading out the gifts, parties, and special treats over an extended period, parents quiet down the choruses of "I can't wait," as our little ones discover that they can indeed learn to wait—as long as they don't have to wait very long.

There is much to be said for the practical Victorian custom of "keeping Christmas." Our celebration of Yuletide, which embraced both reverently religious and festively secular traditions, was spread out over many weeks and began with Advent, one of the oldest celebrations associated with Christmas. The Advent season—the four weeks preceding Christmas—was the time set aside for prayer and meditation before the nativity of Christ. Celebrating old-fashioned mini-festival days such as St. Nicholas Day (December 6)

and St. Lucia's Day (December 13), which occur during Advent, can also add to your family's appreciation of Christmas as a season of joy.

Remember that for children, Christmas can be the hardest day of the year to live through. Greed, coupled with the stress and strain of "being good" all month, can bring about such tense, nervous excitement in our young ones that they cannot fail to be miserable. By extending the pleasures of the Christmas season, the disappointing letdown that often comes Christmas morning can be diminished.

Try some of Mrs. Sharp's favorite Advent traditions and discover how celebrating Advent can help your very modern family realize an old-fashioned Christmas full of simple pleasures and cherished memories.

Creating an Advent Calendar

During the 1880s, European craftsmen made elaborate Advent calendars, which families used to tell the Christmas story. Each calendar contains twenty-four windows, and beginning on December 1, one little flap is lifted each day to illustrate the story, which is completed Christmas Eve.

While Victorian Advent calendars were almost all religious, today there are a variety of calendars available with holiday themes. To maintain domestic tranquillity, just be sure *every* family member from the youngest to the oldest (including Mama and Papa) has his own Advent calendar. It has been Mrs. Sharp's experience that young children want to open all the windows the first day; by having at least one calendar under an adult's control, you ensure the family will be able to enjoy the tradition of an Advent calendar day by day, all month long.

To make an Advent calendar, sandwich together two sheets of colored posterboard with a piece of gold foil in between and lay them on a flat surface. Now draw and then cut out the shape (on all three pieces) you would like your calendar to be: a square, rectangle, or perhaps even a Christmas tree. Glue the foil shape to the bottom piece of cardboard. On the top piece of cardboard have the children draw a Christmas scene. Now, using a sharp pencil, draw twenty-four small square windows on the top sheet, pressing down hard to make sure you leave an outline of the windows on the gold foil. When you have done this, number the windows (one through twenty-four). Keep the size of all the windows the same (one-inch square works well) except for number twenty-four, which should be the largest and placed in the center of your scene. Now draw on a separate piece of paper the pictures you would like to show through the windows (a Christmas tree, Santa Claus, a star, angel, toys, etc.), ending with a picture of the Christ Child in a crib for Christmas Eve. Cut your pictures out and glue them to the foil-covered bottom sheet.

Now place the top sheet on a cutting board and carefully (this is a job for an adult) cut three sides to each window with a razor or sharp craft knife, leaving the left side of the window intact to act as a hinge. Loop a piece of ribbon in between the cardboard to stick out of the top of your calendar and carefully glue the two pieces of cardboard together around the edges. With a clothespin hold the layers together until the glue is completely dry. Now hang your handcrafted family heirloom with pride.

St. Nicholas Day

For many Victorian families, as well as families today in Holland, Germany, and England, the Christmas season really begins with a visit from Saint Nicholas on his birthday, December 6. This old-fashioned tradition can start setting the mood for a wonderful holiday season for your family.

Nicholas, the Bishop of Myra in Asia Minor, was said to have lived around A.D. 325. He was well loved for his compassion and generosity, mysteriously providing food, warm clothing, and even bags of gold for the needy. Legend has it that Saint Nicholas, riding his white horse down from heaven, pays nocturnal visits to children on the eve of his birthday to prepare their hearts for the coming of the Christ Child.

For parents who feel frustrated by the fact that Santa Claus's visit inevitably overshadows their religious observance of the birth of Christ, a visit from Saint Nicholas can help tremendously. For modern children who no longer believe in Santa Claus (and to Mrs. Sharp's dismay, it seems they get younger with each passing Christmas), a celebration of St. Nicholas Day can satisfy a deep desire in children to believe in a benevolent and generous gift giver who rewards the good.

Before they go to bed, Mrs. Sharp's children place their shoes, filled with hay or a carrot for the saint's horse, beside the fireplace or front door, along with a beverage (traditionally a glass of schnapps) for his servant, Ruprecht, who carries the satchel of sweets and novelties for good children and switches for the bad.

When the children awaken the next morning, they discover delicious seasonal cakes (lebkuchen, a German honey cake, or a piece of iced gingerbread), a small mesh bag of gold-foil-covered chocolate coins, and one longed-for gift from each child's wish list.

Mrs. Sharp's children have been taught that it is Saint Nicholas who inspires us to prepare our Christmas gifts for others, for custom has it that he knows what each family member truly desires and so he puts ideas into our heads.

Saint Nicholas's visit provides our family with just enough foretaste of Christmas to make the waiting pleasurable, and it enables us to look outside ourselves to the holiday needs of others. We can never outgrow the magic of a visit from Saint Nicholas. Invite him into your homes this year and see for yourself.

"A VISIT FROM ST. NICHOLAS"

In the winter of 1822, the Reverend Clement Clarke Moore, a professor at New York's General Theological Seminary, composed a poem to amuse his children on Christmas Eve. The poem began, "'Twas the night before Christmas . . .''

The following autumn Miss Harriet Butler, of Troy, New York, was visiting the Moore family and saw the poem. She was so taken with it that she requested a copy. In December 1823, Miss Butler sent the verse anonymously to the *Troy Sentinel* and the editor printed it. Miss Butler sent Dr. Moore a copy of the newspaper, but he became annoyed that the poem he had written to entertain his own children should be printed publicly, so he never claimed authorship. Very soon the poem, which was now titled "A Visit from St. Nicholas," was being reprinted in newspapers across the country (sometimes with the title "The Night Before Christmas"). In 1837, the poem appeared for the first time in a collection of verse, *The New York Book of Poetry*, but still anonymously. The following year, overwhelmed by the universal delight in the first official account of Saint Nicholas's annual visit, Dr. Moore admitted publicly that he had written the poem. In 1844 he had it published under his own name.

No doubt Reverend Moore, a serious scholar, would have preferred to be remembered for his translations of the Bible from Hebrew rather than as the man who gave the world "Santa Claus." But this is no small legacy. For years after the poem was first printed, artists tried to capture an image of Santa Claus as resonant as Moore's description. They all failed in their attempts. It wasn't until some forty years later when *Harper's Weekly*'s illustrator Thomas Nast, then famous for his caricatures of politicians, began to draw Moore's Saint Nick that the definitive image of Santa as we know him entered into our national consciousness. Thomas Nast also popularized and made official some of Santa's activities, such as manufacturing toys in his North Pole workshop, keeping records of good and naughty children, and answering their mail.

Saint Nicholas, Father Christmas, Kris Kringle, Père Noël—the benevolent Christmas gift giver

What will go into the Christmas Stocking,
While the clock on the mantelpiece is ticking
An orange, a penny, Some sweets, not too many.
A handful of love, Another of fun,
And it's very nearly done.
-Eleanor Farjeon (1891-1965)
"Christmas Stocking"

beloved of children of all ages—evolved into Victorian America's Santa Claus, and by the 1880s he was firmly entrenched as the central character in our secular celebration of Christmas. What would the holidays be without him? The thought is almost too much to bear.

A VISIT FROM ST. NICHOLAS

'Twas the night before Christmas, when all through the house
Not a creature was stirring, not even a mouse;
The stockings were hung by the chimney with care;
In hopes that St. Nicholas soon would be there;
The children were nestled all snug in their beds,
While visions of sugarplums danced in their heads;
And mamma in her kerchief and I in my cap
Had just settled down for a long winter's nap
When out on the lawn there arose such a clatter,
I sprang from my bed to see what was the matter.
Away to the window I flew like a flash,
Tore open the shutters, and threw up the sash;
The moon, on the breast of the new-fallen snow,
Gave a luster of midday to objects below;
When what to my wondering eyes should appear
But a miniature sleigh and eight tiny reindeer,
With a little old driver, so lively and quick,
I knew in a moment, it must be St. Nick.
More rapid than eagles his coursers they came,
And he whistled and shouted and called them by name:
"Now Dasher! now Dancer! now Prancer! now Vixen!
On, Comet! on Cupid! on Donner and Blitzen!
To the top of the porch! To the top of the wall!
Now, dash away, dash away, dash away, all!"
As dry leaves that before the wild hurricane fly,
When they meet with an obstacle, mount to the sky,
So up to the housetop the coursers they flew,
With a sleigh full of toys and St. Nicholas too.

And then in a twinkling, I heard on the roof
The prancing and pawing of each little hoof.
As I drew in my head and was turning around
Down the chimney St. Nicholas came with a bound.
He was dressed all in fur from his head to his foot,
And his clothes were all tarnished from ashes and soot;
A bundle of toys he had flung on his back,
And he looked like a peddler just opening his pack.
His eyes: how they twinkled! his dimples: how merry!
His cheeks were like roses, his nose like a cherry;
His droll little mouth was drawn up like a bow,
And the beard on his chin was as white as the snow.
The stump of a pipe he held tight in his teeth
And the smoke, it encircled his head like a wreath:
He had a broad face, and a little round belly,
That shook, when he laughed, like a bowl full of jelly;
He was chubby and plump, a right jolly old elf;
And I laughed when I saw him, in spite of myself;
A wink of his eye and a twist of his head
Soon gave me to know I had nothing to dread.
He spoke not a word, but went straight to his work
And filled all the stockings; then turned with a jerk,
And laying his finger aside of his nose,
And giving a nod, up the chimney he rose.
He sprang to his sleigh, to his team gave a whistle,
And away they all flew like the down of a thistle;
But I heard him exclaim, ere he drove out of sight,
"Happy Christmas to all, and to all a good night!"

—*The Reverend Clement Clarke Moore, 1822*

A Victorian Sugarplum Tree

id you ever wonder about the Victorian visions of sugarplums dancing around everyone's head in "A Visit from St. Nicholas"? Sugarplums were exotic sweetmeats, a combination of fruit and nuts, traditionally available only during the holidays.

Originally sugarplums were whole eggs, which were transformed into a glacéed fruit by long simmering in a sugar syrup.

Here is Mrs. Sharp's Victorian version. If you would like to create a sugarplum tree, take a cone-shaped form and stick toothpicks all around it; place your sugarplums on each toothpick until the tree is completely covered.

You will need:

1 pound chopped figs
1 pound chopped dates
1 pound chopped raisins
1 pound chopped currants
1 pound blanched almonds, chopped finely
½ pound chopped walnuts
½ pound chopped pecans
1 pound chopped, unsalted, shelled pistachio nuts
½ pound shredded coconut
½ pound crystallized ginger
1 orange (grated rind and juice)
1 lemon (grated rind and juice)
2 tablespoons good sherry
1 ounce orange or peach brandy
Granulated sugar

Chop the dried fruit very finely (a food processor or grinder is a wonderful modern improvement on hand chopping) and set aside. Next chop nuts in food processor. Set aside. Place coconut, ginger, orange, lemon, sherry, and brandy in food processor and process until orange, lemon, and ginger are thoroughly chopped. Combine dried fruit and nuts and add the juice, sherry, and brandy mixture. Mix together thoroughly. Form into small balls and roll in granulated sugar. Store in a covered tin, lined with waxed paper, for one week in the refrigerator to let flavors blend together.

St. Lucia's Day

For centuries the traditional observance of St. Lucia's Day on December 13 marked the start of the Christmas celebration in Scandinavia, as it does today in many Swedish-American homes. Legend has it that once during a great famine in Sweden, Saint Lucia miraculously appeared, her head circled in light, to deliver food.

On this morning, Swedish children awakened early and dressed in long white gowns. The girls wear long red sashes and the boys wear white cone-shaped hats with gold stars. Wearing a wreath of lighted candles on her head, the eldest daughter—as Saint Lucia—leads her brothers and sisters in a procession into their parents' darkened bedroom to deliver a surprise breakfast of such Scandinavian specialties as *saffranbrod* (sweet saffron buns), *pepparkakor* (gingersnaps), and cups of hot, steaming coffee.

Observing St. Lucia's Day is a wonderful way for children to make a contribution to the family's Christmas traditions with this gift of thoughtfulness to their parents.

Although in the beginning (especially with young children) you may need to assist them—such as preparing the breakfast buns ahead of time (or even carrying the tray upstairs and then returning to bed)—it is well worth the effort. If you would like to introduce this charming custom to your family, a lovely story that does so delightfully is *Kirsten's Surprise* from The American Girls Collection.

Now that she has aroused your interest, dear Reader, Mrs. Sharp would like to stress that no daughter of hers ever walked around our house wearing a wreath of lighted candles. Instead, she created crowns of greenery and red ribbons for them to wear at a candlelit breakfast.

Mrs. Sharp has discovered there is no more enriching way to teach children tolerance than by incorporating different ethnic traditions into our family's holiday repertoire. Baking a trip around the world with festive Christmas foods from other countries or serving parents a St. Lucia's Day breakfast can help children understand the true spirit of this season while strengthening bonds and creating memories.

The Gift of Christmas Past

Twas the week before Christmas and all through the land, mothers dragged around a list of "should dos" to rival Jacob Marley's chains.

All mothers—those employed outside the home and those who are full-time homemakers—worry about whether they are giving enough of themselves to their children. At Christmastime, this concern is emotionally heightened and produces great anxiety.

If we have work responsibilities outside our homes, we feel guilty because we are not at home with the children during the days preceding Christmas baking a gingerbread house to rival a magazine cover. So we assuage that guilt by suspending common sense in the department store, until our extravagance for the children's sake is culpable.

If, on the other hand, we are at home with the children full-time, the family is possibly on a tighter budget and so the money question looms over our holidays. However, instead of making the most of being with the children, such as reveling in the fact that we do have the time to bake, we fret over the fact that we can't give them the overpriced trinkets advertised on television.

May Mrs. Sharp make a gentle suggestion? Instead of fretting over the things we cannot do, let us concentrate on the most priceless gift we can give to our families for the holidays. It is the gift you long to give them each year, dear Reader, and feel frustrated when your holiday reality does not live up to your expectations.

It is the gift of yourself.

But you say, "Mrs. Sharp, I give of myself to my family. In fact, that's all I do, which is why I'm dreading the holidays: gift buying, card mailing, present wrapping, present sending, tree buying, tree trimming, cookie baking, holiday entertaining, carol singing, organizing the carol singing. What are you asking of me? To do more?"

No, my dear, Mrs. Sharp is not asking you to do more. In fact, she is asking you to do less, in order that you may give more—to enter fully into this joyous holiday celebration with your children by giving them the gift of Christmas Past. For now, while they are young, you are planting seeds of Christmas memory.

Whether or not you know it, you are creating memories. When your children are grown, the holidays—their Christmas Past—can come to mean memories of gazing out the window at gently falling snow together, the sounds of bells and joyful music, the sweet smells of hot cider, roast turkey, and gingerbread, sipping hot chocolate and reading a holiday story each night at dusk, warm fires crackling on the hearth, bright wrapping paper and ribbons, beautiful cards that arrive each day bringing greetings, the joy of a few choice and desired presents, and the gift of a loving family smiling in the glow of holiday candlelight.

Or their Christmas memories can be of Mother racing around, out of breath, out of energy, out of love, out of patience because she's so exhausted trying to do everything for everybody. It can mean tears and tantrums, screaming and yelling and hustle and bustle, arguing over money, over relations, over holiday humbug.

It's your choice.

You can decide this year to be happy, loving, fulfilled, generous, peaceful, spiritual, joyous, calm, festive, and emotionally connected to the important people in your life from Thanksgiving until the first week in January.

Or you can choose to be a wreck.

The secret is, you can't do everything. You are going to have to make choices, so that you are not so overextended and worn-out that you can't give your precious family the important intangibles that make the real difference in their lives.

But where to begin?

First, let us pause for a moment to consider this fact: Christmas will arrive on December 25 whether we are ready for it or not.

Keeping this in mind, look again at that "to do" list. Now trim it down to the essentials. This is so that during the last few days you can turn your energies toward creating a Christmas worth remembering.

Christmas Eve

One Christmas Eve custom you might wish to adapt is that of the Yule log. The Yule log, which was the largest log of wood we could find, is decorated with a sprig of holly, placed in the fireplace, and lit with much ceremony, where, we hope, it will continue to burn throughout the twelve days of Christmas.

No fireplace, you say? Then try hauling home a festive Christmas cake in the shape of a Yule log (either a *bûche de Noël* or an ice-cream-roll cake will do nicely) and call it your family's Yule log. Remember, it is the essence of the tradition that counts.

Every family has its own beloved customs for Christmas Day, upon which Mrs. Sharp would not presume to intrude, except to suggest that on Christmas Eve while you are assisting Santa Claus, remove four presents from each child's monstrous mountain of gifts. One present the child will receive the day after Christmas (Boxing Day); the other three are to be saved until January 6 (Epiphany).

Boxing Day

December 26 is the Feast of Saint Stephen, the first Christian martyr, and an official holiday in England known as Boxing Day. This was the day that the alms boxes for the poor were distributed, as well as the day that servants took "boxes" of food and gifts from their employer's home to their families.

In Mrs. Sharp's house our children celebrate Boxing Day with a treasure hunt. Each child searches for a specially decorated box in which there is nestled a small gift.

Mrs. Sharp's Boxing Day presents are placed in enchanting, old-fashioned reproduction-Victorian chromolithographed boxes, which are readily available in shops and are delightful presents in themselves. For the little ones, Mrs. Sharp leaves the Boxing Day gift near the fireplace, so that she can exclaim, "Oh, look what must have dropped out of Santa's sack. . . ."

December 27

This is a good day to write holiday thank-you notes, which is done as a family project and made festive with the presentation of new stationery for each member of the family.

December 28

Today is the Feast of the Holy Innocents, the young children killed by King Herod during his search for the infant Messiah. The Victorians called this period Little Christmas, and it was the time that festive juvenile parties were held. Invite your children's friends in for show-and-tell, followed by hot cocoa and Christmas cookies.

December 30

One day during the holiday break, schedule a special entertainment outing (such as *The Nutcracker*), followed by a festive restaurant luncheon or dinner. But, please, no fast-food snack-bar visit. This is a once-a-year grown-up extravaganza for the little set, and they love to live up to the event.

Twelfth Night

On January 6, we celebrate the Feast of Epiphany, or Twelfth Night. This is the day when the Three Kings from the East arrived in Bethlehem with their gifts for the Christ Child.

A Twelfth Night party is a Victorian tradition Mrs. Sharp is sure modern families will enjoy reviving. It provides the family with a simple but festive occasion to look forward to after Christmas and ends our holiday season on a high note.

On this night the children are given three gifts from the Magi (representing one from each king) before a gala dinner. After dinner comes a Twelfth Night cake adorned with figures of the kings (small wooden or plastic ornaments work well) and a silver coin (or foil-wrapped bean) baked into it. The child who finds the coin becomes king or queen of the family and is presented with a gold cardboard crown. A store-bought cake works as well—just make a little slit to insert the coin and then cover with icing. Mrs. Sharp always has some form of frankincense and myrrh incense burning (available at craft and herb-specialty shops and religious stores).

We all have such a marvelous time. The children put on a marionette show. Father performs magic tricks, and Mrs. Sharp organizes parlor games. Coming as it does a few days after the children have returned to school, Twelfth Night, celebrated together as a family, wraps up a beautiful gift of Christmas holiday memories.

Twelfth Night Cake

In many European countries, Twelfth Night is observed as a special event for families. The most famous Twelfth Night cake comes from France and is known as the *galette des rois.* This recipe version comes from the cookbook *A Continual Feast* by Evelyn Birge Vitz.

1 cup finely ground blanched almonds
2½ cups sifted flour
½ teaspoon salt
½ cup sugar
4 egg yolks
8 tablespoons butter, cut into little pieces
6 tablespoons ice-cold water
1 egg yolk, lightly beaten with a little water

Mix the almonds thoroughly with the flour; mix in the salt and the sugar. Add the egg yolks, the butter, and water to make a firm dough. Work this paste gently with your fingertips. Form it into a ball, then let it chill in the refrigerator for 1 hour.

Preheat the oven to 425°. Lightly grease a baking sheet.

On a lightly floured surface, roll the dough out into a *galette* (a circle about ¾ inch thick). Insert a coin or bean into the bottom surface of the *galette.* Cut the edges with a knife or scissors to make a perfect circle with straight sides. With a sharp knife decorate the top with slits. Place the *galette* on the baking sheet. Brush with egg yolk, lightly beaten with a little water. Bake for 25 to 30 minutes, or until the *galette* is golden brown.

Single-Parent Traditions for the Holidays

Many people assume that Christmas is hardest for children who have stopped believing in Santa Claus. But Mrs. Sharp believes the holidays are most difficult for single parents, particularly if this is the first or second holiday season after their separation.

Sometimes Mrs. Sharp's single-parent friends will tell her their holidays are emotionally charged because of their former spouse's behavior (toward them and the children). Certainly it is none of Mrs. Sharp's business how formerly married people behave toward each other. However, she has often thought that before a divorce becomes final, couples should be required to solemnly swear they will not use the children to extract revenge.

If you are a single parent who has experienced a painful divorce, you may still be feeling angry and bitter toward your former spouse. For the sake of your children, please try not to let those feelings be apparent. If the situation is especially difficult because Father is not around or available, don't assume it's best to ignore the situation with the children. Acknowledge it gently and encourage the children to talk about their feelings concerning their relationship with their father. Then see if you can arrange to have the family spend time on Christmas with another special man, such as a grandfather or uncle.

Some single parents who are friends of Mrs. Sharp's admit to feeling uncomfortable at Christmas and convey this discomfort to their children inadvertently. They feel resentful that our contemporary culture—as modern as it acts the rest of the year—wraps itself in old-fashioned family sentiments each December, requiring Mother, Father, and the children to dance around the Christmas tree happily together.

But Mrs. Sharp believes that one of the reasons single parents experience difficulty during Christmastime is because they think holiday traditions should belong only to perfect Currier and Ives families. The first time a single parent has to open up the ornament box alone, she experiences such a great sense of loss that she decides rashly not to engage in customs the family once enjoyed together because the comparison will be too painful.

"What's the point?" she says.

The point is that single parents and their children need the reassuring and powerful message that treasured rituals provide: "We" are a family. A loving, close-knit family shares traditions together. Our family is measured by the love that unites us, not our size or shape.

Just as Victorian traditions can be updated for contemporary family life, so, too, can your family holiday rituals be adapted to fit new circumstances, whatever they may be. Trust Mrs. Sharp. No one parent should have sole custody of family customs. So unpack those beloved family Christmas traditions. They are as resilient as your loving hearts.

Yet single parents should also try to introduce new holiday customs into their family's repertoire. Here are two Victorian Christmas traditions sure to please everyone, ideally suited for single parents to make their own.

The Christmas Stocking

Of course, decorative stockings can still be hung by the chimney with care, but Victorian children who found their Christmas stockings bulging at their bedstead knew true joy. What a thrill it was to reach out for it in the darkness, pull it under the covers, clasp the contents with the imagination running wild, until by dawn's early light it could be emptied out onto the bed and the wrappings furiously pulled off with glee. There is much to recommend the custom of bedpost stockings. For one thing, the youngsters are always wide-awake Christmas morning long before the oldsters. An interestingly filled stocking buys a much-needed forty winks. For another, bedpost stockings can easily be hung at one parent's home, even if Santa officially visits the other.

Victorian parents filled each stocking according to a magic recipe that still works: "Something to eat, something to read, something to play with, and something they need."

Christmas Crackers

Many of our Victorian Christmas customs originated in England, including the Christmas cracker, a festively wrapped cylinder that, when pulled at each end, gives a *bang,* pulling apart to reveal delightful surprises.

No Victorian Christmas dinner table was complete without crackers. They are still delightful novelties and are sure to enhance your Christmas dinner-table merriment as much as they do Mrs. Sharp's and the Queen of England's (from Victoria to Elizabeth II). Their moment of glory arrives at the end of the main course, while waiting for the Christmas pudding. Included in each cracker is usually a paper hat, a motto or fortune, a tiny toy, and a balloon. Today you will find imported English Christmas crackers available in many specialty-gift and department stores.

Finally, one last "tradition" Mrs. Sharp personally draws upon the last week before Christmas, and highly recommends to parents beginning to feel a bit harried from the hustle and bustle of holiday preparations: It is to stop whatever you are doing for a moment, take a deep breath, and gather the children around you.

Next, take a long look at them. See how their eyes sparkle with excitement, how flushed their cheeks are with joyous anticipation. Isn't their happiness contagious? How children love Christmas! If, for whatever reason, you find yourself not enjoying the holidays to the fullest, let a little child lead you.

I have been looking on, this evening, at a merry company of children assembled round that pretty German toy, a Christmas tree. The tree was planted in the middle of a great round table, and lowered high above their heads. It was brilliantly lighted by a multitude of little tapers; and everywhere sparkled and glittered with bright objects. There were rosy-cheeked dolls, hiding behind green leaves; there were real watches (with movable hands, at least, and an endless capacity of being wound up) dangling from innumerable twigs; there were French-polished tables, chairs, bedsteads, wardrobes, eight-day clocks and various other articles of domestic furniture (wonderfully made in tin) perched among the boughs, as if in preparation for some fairy housekeeping; there were jolly broad-faced little men, much more agreeable in appearance than many real men—and no wonder, for their heads came off and showed them to be full of sugarplums; there were trinkets for the elder girls, far brighter than any grown-up gold and jewels; there were baskets and pincushions in all devices; there were guns, swords, and banners; there were witches standing in enchanted rings of paste-board, to tell fortunes; there were teetotums, humming-tops, needle cases, pen wipers, smelling-bottles, conversation-cards, bouquet holders, real fruit made artificially dazzling with gold leaf; imitation apples, pears, walnuts crammed with surprises; in short, as a pretty child, before me, delightedly whispered to another pretty child, her bosom friend, "There was everything, and more."

—"A Christmas Tree" by Charles Dickens

Oh, the wonders of the Christmas trees that delighted Victorian families! Mrs. Sharp knows that your family adores your Christmas tree as much as we do ours. But she thought she might like to share with you two customs that made our trees so wonderful. First, half of the fun on Christmas morning was for the children to search through the evergreen boughs for gifts bearing their names. If your family has never enjoyed the pleasure of a gift-laden tree, why not introduce a small tree just for this purpose?

Another festive and sentimental tree idea is to trim your tree with memories. Victorian families loved to add personal ornaments to the trees. What happened to your family this year? Are there souvenirs from an anniversary, graduation, or class reunion? Turn them into ornaments. One of Mrs. Sharp's favorite ornaments was from the year her eldest son graduated from law school, very shortly after his first child was born. Mrs. Sharp saved his commencement-cake decoration—a young man in cap and gown holding a diploma—and placed a small plastic baby (two inches long) in the young man's other arm. What a joy it is each Christmas when we open up the Christmas tree box and take this memento out and hang it on the tree; invariably we always remember aloud the day in 1912 when we held a family party to celebrate both his graduation from law school and our first grandchild's christening!

You'll recall wonderful memories as well when you add to the tree miniature versions of the children's yearly activities such as ballet shoes, baseball mitts, or footballs. (Just be sure to ink in the year on your ornament.) You can also place your remembrance ornaments on a permanent family wreath to hang on your front door or perhaps over the mantelpiece.

To ensure the family's participation and memories, everyone should come up with an idea for a small token to add each year. If you are using trinkets, such as charms, coat them with clear nail polish to preserve their finish.

Chanukah

In the dark days of December comes a wonderful joyous holiday celebrated in Jewish homes called Chanukah. Originally known as the "Festival of Lights," Chanukah commemorates a miracle that occurred after Judas Maccabaeus and his followers defeated the Greek king of Syria, Antiochus, in 165 B.C. Antiochus had tried to force Jews to abandon their religion and worship Greek gods. By decree they were not permitted to study the Torah, celebrate Jewish holidays, or practice Jewish customs. Many Jews, disobeying the Syrians, were slaughtered for their beliefs. After a three-year struggle, the Maccabees were victorious and reclaimed their temple in Jerusalem. As part of their rededication ceremony (the word *chanukah* means "dedication" in Hebrew), the Maccabees began an eight-day purification rite, only to discover there was barely enough sacred oil to keep the Temple menorah, a candelabrum with eight branches, lit for one day. Miraculously, however, the Temple lamp burned for eight days. Ever since that time the Jewish people have observed Chanukah to remember their struggle for religious freedom and the miracle of restoration as represented by the oil.

In Jewish homes Chanukah is celebrated with the lighting of the menorah on eight nights, the playing of traditional games such as the dreidel (a small spinning top that bears the message in Hebrew "A great miracle happened there"), the eating of special foods, such as potato latkes (pancakes), and the exchanging of gifts.

During the Victorian era, Chanukah was not the major gift-giving occasion that it has become today. While the holiday was celebrated in the home with the lighting of the menorah and a special dinner, it was the custom to give children only gelt (the Yiddish word for "money"), either a few real coins or chocolate-candy coins wrapped in gold foil.

It is only in recent years that Chanukah has been elevated to the status of a major annual holiday—with an emphasis on gifts—as many Jewish families discover they are unintentionally offering their children a Jewish substitute for Christmas, which occurs around the same time. As Jewish parents increase the importance of celebrating Chanukah with lavish gift giving over eight days "for the children's sake," the real meaning of the festival and its celebration of being Jewish becomes diminished.

Still, it is difficult for many families, particularly those with young children, to resist the powerful lure of Christmas customs when approaching the celebration of Chanukah. For parents who find themselves not wanting to imitate Christmas in their Chanukah celebrations yet searching for a way to make the holiday more meaningful and joyful to their children, one solution is to begin to reclaim the holiday's distinct Jewish character.

A marvelous resource that can help is *The Complete Family Guide to Jewish Holidays* by Dalia Hardof Renberg. Here is a book that celebrates all the Jewish holidays throughout the year with recipes, arts-and-craft projects, songs, prayers, and historical background that enhances a family's understanding of each holiday.

Another idea is to make at least one of the gifts something that celebrates Jewish life, such as Jewish calendars, books and magazines of Jewish interest, tickets to a Jewish cultural event, or arts-and-craft kits to make a Jewish object, such as a wooden dreidel or clay menorah.

Finally, remember that at the heart of Jewish holidays are treasured home-centered customs that speak eloquently to people of all faiths. Hosting a Chanukah party one night during the holidays and letting the children invite their Christian friends to come to your home to share in your Jewish holiday traditions (such as delicious potato latkes!) can radiate the joy of this festive family celebration beyond the boundaries of your own hearth. In this season of goodwill, there can be no more precious gift.

New Year's Eve Good Riddance Party

There are several warm and comforting homemade year's-end customs the family can enjoy for a festive New Year's celebration. Begin with Mrs. Sharp's tradition of an annual New Year's Eve Good Riddance Party.

In the late afternoon on New Year's Eve, everyone gathers together for a festive and substantial tea party (which stands in for supper), and our family celebration begins, complete with paper hats, horns, streamers, and confetti. Does it matter that we are celebrating seven hours early? No, dear Reader, it makes eminent sense. No Victorian mother ever voluntarily chose to be awake with her children at the midnight hour. Nor should you.

However, before we can welcome in the New Year, we ought to put the old year's unfinished business—mistakes, regrets, shortcomings, and disappointments—behind us. Here's how: Have each family member write down whatever it is he or she wishes to forget, then place the small slips of paper in a shoebox. While it is not required to reveal what is written down, this is the perfect opportunity for past hurts to be forgiven and hearts to be mended. Often it is difficult for us to share our feelings of regret, or to ask forgiveness of family members. This New Year's Eve tradition gently provides the way to do so.

Next, with ceremony, we wrap the box with black paper, sealing in the sorrow and bad luck. While we hold hands and say, "Good riddance," the box is placed into the fireplace to burn away the past. Everyone can then begin the New Year with joyous anticipation and a clean slate.

This restorative tradition grew out of a need to demonstrate to the children in a tangible way that we can put the past behind us and go forward with renewed hopes. If you do not have a fireplace, why not simply "bury" the past in the backyard, or just throw the box away? Trust Mrs. Sharp; this is a New Year's tradition that will please all family members. A ceremony of renewal, it provides much solace as well as positive memories.

Now it is time to celebrate. Surely the past year was not just filled with disappointment, but much good. How to show the family? Mrs. Sharp goes to her Bible and takes out our prayer list, written last New Year's Eve. Look how many of our prayers were answered! We have truly been blessed. Keeping an annual prayer list is a marvelous way to demonstrate to children the power of faith and the miracle of answered prayer. Our prayer requests are then sealed in an envelope and placed in the family Bible until next New Year's Eve.

Bibliography

The following is a selected bibliography of the works mentioned in *Sarah Ban Breathnach's Mrs. Sharp's Traditions*, intended to be used as a starting resource for readers interested in further exploring the works I mention herein. Unfortunately, many deserving Victorian-era books have not been reprinted in the past century and so are not listed here. Any books that have been issued in a modern edition, whether in or out of print, are listed below. The editions listed here represent in many cases currently available reprints, and not the original publication, although every effort has been made to give complete and accurate information.

—SBB

Alcott, Louisa May. *Little Women*. Aladdin, 2000.

Ayers Company Publishers, ed. *Eureka Entertainments*. Ayers Company Publishers, 1969.

Beard, Daniel Carter. *The American Boy's Handy Book*. David R. Godine, 1998.

Beecher, Catharine, and Harriet Beecher Stowe. *The American Woman's Home*. Harriet Beecher Stowe Center, 1996.

Beeton, Mrs. Isabella. *Mrs. Beeton's Book of Household Management* (abridged). Oxford University Press, 2000.

Brokaw, Meredith, and Annie Gilbar. *The Penny Whistle Party Planner*. Fireside, 1991.

Burnett, Frances Hodgson. *Little Lord Fauntleroy*. Puffin, 1996.

———. *The Little Princess*. HarperTrophy, 1987.

———. *The Secret Garden*. Aladdin, 1999.

Carey, Diana, and Judy Large. *Festivals, Family and Food*. Anthroposophic Press, 1996.

Cooper, Stephanie. *The Children's Year*. Bell Bond Books, 1986.

Dawe, Karen. *The Beach Book and Bucket*. Workman Publishing, 1988.

de la Mare, Walter. *Rhymes and Verses*. Henry Holt, 1988.

Eastman, Philip D. *The Best Nest*. Random House, 1968.

Giblin, James Cross. *Fireworks, Picnics and Flags*. Houghton Mifflin, 1983.

Grahame, Kenneth. *The Wind in the Willows*. Aladdin, 1989.

Green, Harvey. *The Light of the Home: An Intimate View of the Lives of Women in Victorian America*. Pantheon Books, 1983.

Hall, Donald, ed. *The Oxford Book of Children's Verse in America*. Oxford University Press, 1985.

Hart, Cynthia, John Grossman, and Priscilla Dunhill. *A Victorian Scrapbook*. Workman Publishing, 1989.

Jordan, Dorothy, and Marjorie Adoff Cohen. *Great Vacations with Your Kids*. World Leisure, 2000.

Kander, Mrs. Simon. *The Settlement Cook Book*. Applewood Books, 1996.

Levy, Esther. *The Jewish Cookery Book*. Applewood Books, 1988.

Nathan, Joan. *The Jewish Holiday Kitchen*. Schocken, 1998.

Renberg, Dalia Hardof. *The Complete Family Guide to Jewish Holidays*. Adama Books, 1985.

Stevenson, Robert Louis. *A Child's Garden of Verses*. Simon & Schuster, 1999.

Thompson, Flora. *Lark Rise to Candleford*. Viking, 1983.

Tudor, Tasha. *All for Love*. Simon & Schuster, 2000.

———. *The Jenny Wren Book of Valentines*. The Jenny Wren Press, 1989.

Wasserman, Selma. *The Long-Distance Grandmother*. Hartley & Marks, 1996.

Weintraub, Stanley. *Victoria: An Intimate Biography*. Plume, 1992.

Withers, Carl. *A Rocket in My Pocket*. Henry Holt, 1988.

Wood, Mrs. Henry. *East Lynne*. Broadview Press, 2000.

Other Books Worth Noting

Victorian Splendor: Recreating America's 19th Century Interiors by Allison Kyle Leopold. Stewart, Tabori & Chang, 1986. Lovely to peruse, informative, and well researched, a primer on the Victorian decorative arts.

Private Woman, Public Stage: Literary Domesticity in Nineteenth-Century America by Mary Kelley. Oxford University Press, 1984. An illuminating study of Victorian women writers. (In this book Mary Kelley coins the expression "literary domestics" to refer to a school of nineteenth-century female fiction writers. I have expanded the concept of literary domestics to include any Victorian woman writing on home-related subjects.)

Permissions

Text and Illustration Credits

"Night-time Stars" and "Now the Harvest Is In" from *Follow the Year, A Family Celebration of Christian Holidays* by Mala Powers and illustrated by Frances Livens. Text copyright © 1985 by Mala Powers. Illustrations copyright © 1985 by Frances Livens. Reprinted by permission of HarperCollins Publishers, Inc. and McIntosh & Otis, Inc.

Recipe from "Twelfth Night Cake" from *A Continual Feast* by Evelyn Birge Vitz. San Francisco: Ignatius Press, 1991. Reprinted by permission of the author.

"This Is Hallowe'en" by Dorothy Brown Thompson originally appeared in *Subject to Change,* BkMk Press, 1973. It is reprinted here with permission of the University of Missouri-Kansas City, University Libraries.

Excerpt from *Lark Rise to Candleford* by Flora Thompson. Copyright 1945, Oxford University Press, reprinted by permission.

Page 5 Francis Coates Jones, *Mother and Child,* c. 1885; oil on canvas; Terra Foundation for the Arts, Daniel J. Terra Collection, 1999.80. Photography courtesy of Terra Foundation for the Arts, Chicago.

Page 32 The portrait of Mrs. Beeton used by courtesy of the National Portrait Gallery, London.

Page 33 *Portrait Group of Queen Victoria with Her Children.* The *Forbes* Magazine Collection, New York. All rights reserved.

Page 51 *Baby's Birthday,* 1867 by Frederick Daniel Hardy (1826–1911), WAG5304, Wolverhampton Art Gallery, West Midlands, UK/Bridgeman Art Library.

Pages 66, 107, 113, 123, 127, 214 copyright © 1989 Lisa Mathias.

Page 92, "Crocus" from *Flower Fairies of the Spring* copyright © 1985 The Estate of Cicely Mary Barker. By kind permission of Blackie & Sons Ltd.

Pages 148, 179 courtesy Historic Takoma, Inc., Takoma Park, Maryland.

Pages 36, 38, 41, 42, 44, 46, 102, 106, 109, 122, 136, 141 photographs from the Collections of the Library of Congress, Washington, D.C.

Pages 49, 52, 115, 153, 158, 168, 176, 181 used by permission of the Smithsonian: National Museum of American History. Copyright © 2001 Smithsonian Institution.

All other art from the Mrs. Sharp's Collection of Historical Images.

My Heart's Dearest

With Fondest Love.

With Thanks and Appreciation

Blessed are those who can give without remembering,
And take without forgetting.
        —*Elizabeth Bibesco*

"I must frankly own, that if I had known, beforehand, that this book would have cost me the labor which it has, I should never have been courageous enough to commence it," Isabella Beeton confessed about her *Book of Household Management* in 1861. Nearly a century and a half later, I feebly echo my spiritual mentor's sentiments. Thank God I didn't know how complicated the making of this or any book was, for I would have abandoned all hope before undertaking it.

But gratefully, I didn't have to do it alone. Warm hands, brilliant minds, magnanimous hearts, and generous souls were there to assist me. So many kindred spirits were part of the mystical chain of chance that led to the publication of *Mrs. Sharp's Traditions,* both the original edition in 1990 and this revised and redesigned edition. They may have given without remembering, but I haven't forgotten, which is why it gives me enormous pleasure to echo the thanks extended in that first edition.

Once more with feeling: Ed Sharp, Caroline A. Herter, Carole Lalli, Laura Yorke, Barbara Marks, Dona Cooper, Bill Dickinson, Jan Harrod, Barbara Mathias-Riegle, Cathryn Wolf, Carolyn Starks, Joan Almon, Colleen Taliaferro, Fran Goldfinger, Susan Abbott, Lisa Mathais, Julia Moed, and Lorene Mayo— your contribution is appreciated even more today than yesterday.

With hindsight, I'd also like to thank Jack Voelker, director of special studies at the Chautauqua Institution, Chautauqua, New York, for inviting me to teach *Mrs. Sharp's Traditions* and then, *Simple Abundance,* in workshop settings. And to the wonderful, enthusiastic, delightful women who first found me at Chautauqua, I haven't forgotten any of your smiles.

My dear friends, Dawne and Tom Winter, loved Mrs. Sharp from the moment they met her. A decade ago, Dawne tested recipes and fretted when I'd show up at a bookstore and no one else would be there. Today she helps me answer all the correspondence I receive (and during the past four years that's been over forty thousand letters). This is an enormous task, but Dawne does it with grace, good humor, and generosity of spirit.

One of those letters was from Debbie Kelly, who was so passionate and persuasive in her plea that I reconsider *Mrs. Sharp* that I pulled the book off the shelf for the first time in many years and had a wonderful time making peace with my past. Over the years, countless other readers have written, called, and posted so many wonderful comments on Amazon.com that I began to feel like a cult figure. To everyone who nagged me senseless, my endless thanks.

To my new colleagues at Scribner and The Simple Abundance Press, thank you for the gifts of your most precious natural resources: time, creative energy, and emotion. From the first production meeting to the last, it was always apparent how much everyone loved this book, and the result, as you can see, is the embodiment of the Victorian philosopher John Ruskin's belief that "when love and skill work together, expect a masterpiece."

One of the most amazing and delightful truths that I rediscover every day is how adaptable the six Simple Abundance principles are in any setting, but particularly with book publishing. Gratitudes go to Scribner publisher Susan Moldow, editor in chief Nan Graham, and associate publisher Roz Lippel for answering all my questions with attention, consideration, and thoroughness. But most of all I'm grateful for your buoyant enthusiasm and the kind of commitment to my work that most authors only dream about.

The Byzantine maze of publishing becomes "simplicity itself" once it is explained by Jake Morrissey, The Simple Abundance Press's editorial director. No matter how harried we might be, Jake's civility, empathy, wicked sense of humor, and wry appreciation of the absurd makes him a delight to be around. Ethan Friedman, our editorial assistant, adroitly renders the complex chaos that frequently engulfs our projects into *compte rendu,* with an equilibrium that is enviable, and both men make it look easy. Perhaps that's why "Call Jake—ask Ethan" have become four of my favorite words. But here are two more: "Bless you," especially because making it look easy is the hardest thing in the world to accomplish.

To the Scribner production team, I hope each of you realizes that I know how much a single suggestion of mine impacts on the order of your entire day and how very much I appreciate your efforts upon my behalf. The cover of this book may only have my name on it, but thank you Laura Petermann, Alexandra Fox, Mia Crowley-Hald, Angella Baker, and Olga Leonardo for giving me a book that I'm very proud of to send out into the world. Design director Erich Hobbing and former Scribner art director John Fontana blurred boundaries so that the inside and outside of the book were in harmony and reflected my sensibilities. Angela Skouras and Michael Curry of Skouras Design, this edition of the book is more beautiful than I ever dreamed it could be. The first layouts took my breath away and the finished book is a thrill.

Book promotion becomes a joy when it's orchestrated by Scribner's vice president of publicity Pat Eisemann and her talented team, including Erin Cox and Martin Barabas. Kudos to all for deftly managing to promote my work while protecting my precious private time. After a decade Pat's and my paths crossed again when we were searching for a home for The Simple Abundance Press. Her fond remembrance of Mrs. Sharp and genuine appreciation for my home-grown philosophy touched me deeply then and now. Pat, I hope you know I'm one of your biggest fans.

And Roger Williams, I know I'm not the only S&S author you hand sell, but thanks for making me feel that way.

Karen Woodard, Joslyn King, Jennifer Page, Ana Anadrae, and Patti Roberts demonstrate every day that there is nothing, nothing, nothing on earth that women working together cannot accomplish by noon, which is why I always have more than five names on my gratitude list every day.

My business manager and best friend, Chris Tomasino, and I began our amazing romp in 1988 after another literary agent told me my work was "not commercial enough" to be worth her time. Ten books, eight bestsellers, and one publishing imprint later, Chris and I may have disagreed once or twice, but we've laughed a thousandfold, which proves again that I am the most blessed writer on this planet. Every book I've ever written is inscribed with your absolutely fabulous name as spiritual and creative collaborator.

But my greatest debt of gratitude is expressed in my dedication: Katherine Éireann Crean Sharp, my inspiration. Remembering and honoring some of my life's happiest memories during the revision of this book has awakened within me the secret ache that the Irish poet W. B. Yeats confessed when he wrote about his daughter: "I sigh as I kiss you, for I must own, how much I shall miss you, when, dear, you have grown." This book was conceived when you were a little girl. Your secret joys—from fairy cakes to Magi visits— revealed how magical and mystical the journey is supposed to be. Thank you for letting me share them with the rest of the world. Now that you are grown, Katie, I hope that someday these pages will keep alive some cherished memories for you as well. My prayer is that you will realize as you read between the lines of *Mrs. Sharp's Traditions* that truly, madly, and deeply, we gave birth to each other.

Although lightness of being is not the first thing most people associate with the nineteenth-century Russian author Fyodor Dostoyevsky, he was aware that "only the heart knows what is precious" is really life's big secret. So, as he put it, "Forgive us our happiness."

The past asks only to be remembered.

Sarah Ban Breathnach
May 2001

Index

About the Author

*S*arah Ban Breathnach's (pronounced "Bon Brannock") work celebrates quiet joys, simple pleasures, and everyday epiphanies.

What began as a personal safari to unearth her authentic self transformed into her No. 1 *New York Times* bestsellers *Simple Abundance: A Daybook of Comfort and Joy,* and *Something More: Excavating Your Authentic Self.* These were followed by her bestselling *Simple Abundance: Journal of Gratitude, The Illustrated Discovery Journal, The Simple Abundance Companion,* and *A Man's Journey to Simple Abundance. Simple Abundance* has been translated into twenty-eight languages around the world.

Sarah is also the founder of the Simple Abundance Charitable Fund, a nonprofit bridge group between charitable causes and the public, dedicated to increasing awareness that "doing good" and "living the good life" are soul mates. Since 1995, the Simple Abundance Charitable Fund has supported the vision of more than one hundred nonprofit organizations by awarding more than $1 million in financial support. The Simple Abundance Charitable Fund is underwritten with proceeds from Sarah's speaking engagements, royalties, and products.

Sarah Ban Breathnach is the publisher of The Simple Abundance Press, a groundbreaking joint venture with Scribner, as well as president and CEO of Simple Abundance, Inc., a consulting firm specializing in publishing and multimedia projects.

She divides her time between Maryland and New York.

Sarah Ban Breathnach would like to hear from you. Please write to:

Simple Abundance
P.O. Box 5870
Takoma Park, MD 20913–5870

Or visit her Web site at:

www.simpleabundance.com

To find out about forthcoming books from The Simple Abundance Press, and to register for The Simple Abundance Press e-mail update, please visit its Web site at:

www.simpleabundancepress.com

Happy Memories